D0341025

Last Call at Elaine's

Also by Brian McDonald

My Father's Gun: One Family, Three Badges,
One Hundred Years in the NYPD

Indian Summer: The Tragic Story of Louis Francis Sockalexis,
the First Native American in Major League Baseball

Safe Harbor: A Murder in Nantucket

Last Call at

Elaine's

A Journey from One Side
of the Bar to the Other

BRIAN McDONALD

St. Martin's Press
New York

Author's Note: What I've written in this book expresses my opinion and experience and not those of any organization or fellowship.

www.stmartins.com

Design by rlf design

ISBN-13: 978-0-312-34754-3
ISBN-10: 0-312-34754-5

First Edition: April 2008

10 9 8 7 6 5 4 3 2 1

In memory of Francis E. Waters

Acknowledgments

This is a comeback story, and no one makes a comeback alone. There are far too many people who've played important roles in my recovery to list here, and anyway, most of them wouldn't want their names in print. You all know who you are, and I am forever grateful to each and every one of you. As far as the less anonymous who have had a hand in this project and have my gratitude, there's Diane Higgins, who first bought my idea but then moved on, my editor, Nichole Argyres, and her capable assistant, Kylah McNeill. Once again, Joe Orso lent an invaluable eye. As always, I heap enormous gratitude on Jane Dystel, my agent. And, finally, I would like to thank Elaine Kaufman and her cast and crew, who, in my thoughts and elsewhere, continue to grow in importance.

It's a long time between drinks.
  —Anonymous

Last Call at Elaine's

Chapter One

I**T WAS TWO O'CLOCK** in the morning one night in early
October 1986 when I looked into my tip cup and saw six
crumpled dollar bills. There hadn't been a customer since
midnight, and I was seriously wondering if I'd made a mistake
taking this job. Then, just as I was thinking that at least I would be
going home at a reasonable hour, the front door swung open and
in he walked with a cigar the size of a Louisville Slugger in his
mouth, his young wife, blond and giggly, trailing behind along
with another couple.

"Elaine! I'm starving!" he screamed. He had a voice like a
blender on chop.

There was, I'll admit, a childhood flashback when I saw that it
was Ben Gazzara. I remembered the mid-sixties TV show *Run for
Your Life,* where he played a lawyer with two years to live. But at
two o'clock in the morning, having spent a good part of my first
night behind Elaine's bar, the famous Elaine's bar, polishing the
same glass over and over, with Elaine sitting for most of the time
alone at her big round table, number 4, right in front of the bar,

and looking at me not once the whole night, the sight of Ben Gazzara didn't exactly make me go weak in the knees.

"Sit down, Benny," Elaine cooed. Her girlish pose, the back of her wrist demurely placed against her side, was somehow sexy, even considering her abundant girth. She swiveled her head in my direction.

"You see?" she said in way that really needed a tongue sticking out. She made me feel as if I'd doubted Gazzara's arrival all my life.

Meanwhile, in the back, Carlo the waiter was staring off into space. Carlo looks remarkably like Henry Kissinger. He's Italian, from Lake Como, but has a Cockney lilt to his voice from years of living in London and a stint in the British navy. By his own frequent admission, his life has been a series of near misses and might-have-beens. He is the Italian Willy Loman. After World War II, he worked as a waiter in London's Savoy hotel, where he waited on Winston Churchill, a fact that he would often, usually apropos of nothing, remind anyone who would listen. " 'E had the same thing every night," he would say with the appropriate Cockney delivery. "Scottish prime ribs of beef, Yorkshire pudding. Napoleon brandy and a Havana cigar for dessert."

One night in Elaine's, Carlo was waiting on Jackie Safra and Jean Doumanian, who had ordered a bottle of Petrus, a Bordeaux that, even back in the eighties, went for about four hundred bucks. After the couple left, when Carlo began to bus the table, he discovered there was still a swallow or two in the bottle. He put it under his arm and headed around the corner to the waiters' station.

Never one to miss an opportunity for a practical joke, Brian, who worked alongside me when I first started at Elaine's, bolted from behind the bar and peeked around the corner to the waiters' station, which is opposite the bathrooms and just before the door to the kitchen. As Brian expected, Carlo looked left, then right, then lifted the Petrus bottle to his lips and slugged its contents back like it was Gatorade and he'd just run a 10K. Brian made his way back to the bar and was standing nonchalantly behind it when Carlo came up to drop off a dupe. "Elaine wants what's left of the Petrus," Brian said, the line delivered so expertly, so offhandedly, that for a moment it hovered somewhere over the waiter's head.

Desperation gave way to an emergency plan. "Glass of red," said Carlo, his voice atremble. Brian poured the wine and again followed. Peeking around the corner, he watched as Carlo rooted through the garbage, flinging those of lesser vintage back into the trash. When he finally found the bottle, he poured the house red into it with a shaky hand, as if he were working with nitroglycerin. Wiping away beads of sweat from his forehead and several strands of spaghetti Bolognese stuck to the bottle, but missing the clump of broccoli rabe that hung from the bottle's bottom, Carlo put on a brave face and headed to table 4, where he placed the phony Petrus right in front of Elaine.

"What the fuck is that?" she said.

Back at Gazzara's table, Elaine's eyes searched for her wayward waiter. "Carlo! Stop jerking off!" Her bellow reverberated through the hollow restaurant.

At the sound of Elaine's holler, Carlo snapped to, slapping a napkin over his shoulder like a self-flagellating Shiite, and bounded over to the boss.

"Yes, Elaine?" he asked, conspiratorially leaning his head close to her.

"In case you were wondering," she said, indicating Gazzara with a tilt of her head, "that's a customer."

Carlo looked at Gazzara's table as if it had magically appeared. Gazzara broke the spell by barking at Carlo to bring a bottle of wine. "Chianti," he said, to which Elaine quickly added, "Reserva," adding a few bucks to the check with the premium brand. Carlo returned with the bottle, opened it with a motion that was honed and beautiful in its dexterity, and poured Gazzara just a sip to taste. The actor threw it back in a gulp and motioned in a circle with the hand holding the cigar for Carlo to fill the glasses. A ring of thick white cigar smoke drifted to the ceiling.

Elaine sat on the armless chair with her legs spread, each foot planted firmly on the floor. Her dress, black with neon-colored polka dots, draped from her like a parachute. Full and black, her hair was tucked back behind her ears. She wore black-framed glasses. She had one hand propped on her thigh as she leaned into Gazzara's conversation, as if he was saying something very important.

"Make Benny something to eat," Elaine said to Carlo, her tone changing one hundred and eighty degrees. She was almost sweet. But then again, she knew that her kitchen was closed and her staff was already headed to the Bronx on the 4 train. Copping the old *Honeymooners* line, Carlo turned to me and announced, "Chef of the future!" Then he disappeared into the kitchen. In no time, the waiter returned wearing an apron and holding four plates of roasted red peppers, prosciutto, and buffalo mozzarella. Bottles of extra-virgin olive oil and balsamic vinegar were squeezed under one arm. Gazzara tucked a napkin in his shirt, like Stanley Kowalski. Carlo held a two-foot-long pepper mill over the plate of peppers and cheese. The actor waved a finger back and forth to indicate he didn't want any. Carlo cracked the peppercorns with a twist of his wrist.

The appetizers soon were followed by steaming plates of spaghetti with tomato and basil, piles of spinach sautéed with garlic and oil, then finally cheesecake and espressos. Carlo had learned his craft the old European way, starting as a pot washer and then working every station in the kitchen before getting a chance on the floor. Back in the day, when Elaine was often a guest on television morning talk shows, she'd bring Carlo along to prepare a dish on the air.

It was well after four in the morning when Carlo collected the empty plates. Gazzara lit up another cigar. A wineglass with an inch of Marie Brizard anisette sat in front of him. The actor's speech was slurred, his eyes half closed. At the service end of the bar, Elaine added up the check for Benny. I stood behind the bar, not two feet from her and uncomfortable in the silence between us.

In the dining room, Carlo shuffled around pulling the cloths off tables. He used his chin to hold and fold them. He looked like a mother at a backyard clothesline. One of Carlo's favorite stories was about waiting on Robert Taylor in the Savoy hotel. One night Carlo complimented the movie star on his hat, and Taylor gave it to him as a tip. In those fancy-free times, Carlo would wear the hat out in London's West End, where it never missed, he often insisted, as a conversation starter with the birds he was chatting up. But Elaine was no profligate Robert Taylor: She was a "saver," Carlo would say often, the tone of his voice a mixture of reverence and jealousy.

Sometime around five A.M., Gazzara and his party stumbled into the still darkness of Second Avenue. A moment later Elaine followed them out the door escorted to the sidewalk by Carlo. On the street, a yellow taxi waited for Elaine. The same cabbie came every night to drive her home.

Alone then in the restaurant, I sat at table 8, which I knew was Woody Allen's table. Large and round, the table sits right past the archway that leads to the bathrooms, kitchen, and Siberia, the mirrored back room. From Woody's vantage, you see most of the restaurant, including the alcove in the back where Elaine and Lucille Ball had often played backgammon for big cash. My pal

Brian told me that Elaine routinely cleaned Lucy's clock. He remembered one night when Lucy's face was as red as her hair as she stomped out of the restaurant. There is also a clear view of the front tables, the ones opposite the bar. It was at one of these that Rudolf Nureyev sat, his bags piled on a chair next to him, the Ballets Russes's jet back to Moscow still sitting on the runway, the Soviet officials slowly losing hope of their star's return. Nureyev toasted his newfound freedom with champagne Elaine sent to his table. From table 8, you can also see the main part of the dining room. At one of those tables, with the *Harper's* editor Willie Morris, a youthful Bill Clinton sat the night before he left to study at Oxford. Morris had asked the Rhodes scholar where he would like to spend his one night in New York City. "I want to see Elaine's," he'd answered in his Arkansas drawl.

I stood and took one more look at the book jackets on the walls. There were scores of them, and though I knew some of the names—Gay Talese, Terry Southern, Joan Didion, and Phillip Roth—I hadn't read any of them. The metal gates screeched like a subway train as Carlo pulled them down over the front windows. Carlo was in the doorway now, calling for me to come. But there was something comfortable about the brick-colored Spanish tile floor, the mural on the wall that was never finished, and the book jackets and photos that held my stare.

At the time, I was thirty-two years old and hadn't had a drink of alcohol for five years. I'd been tending bar for fourteen years and, frankly, most of the fun of the job disappeared when I stopped drinking. By definition, bartending is a closed-end affair, a stopgap or last resort, a profession filled with those who have run away from life or marriage, who want to stay under the IRS's radar, or who have just never fulfilled a potential. There are exceptions, bartenders who carve out nice livings, play a lot of golf, and die early. But I didn't want to be one of those. When I walked behind Elaine's bar for the first time, I was half an actor, taking a couple of classes and performing in plays so far off Broadway you couldn't get there by subway. I thought I'd just shop some head shots around to the showbiz big shots who frequented Elaine's and be on my way to stardom. That was my plan.

Chapter Two

O VER THE COURSE OF MY TIME at Elaine's, I would assemble the backstory for Elaine Kaufman and her restaurant from a variety of sources. Some of this information comes from bartenders and waiters like Carlo who worked for many years at Elaine's. Some of it comes from newspaper, magazine, and book sources. And plenty of what I know about Elaine's comes from Elaine herself.

My boss began her restaurant career as a waitress in East Harlem. An Italian enclave in an otherwise solid Hispanic neighborhood, that part of Harlem was home to the famous Rao's restaurant, a place called Patsy's, which served pizza pies for a couple of generations, and the Genovese crime family. But Elaine only worked in Harlem for a short time. She told me once that when the people who owned the Italian restaurant in which she worked found out that she was Jewish and not Italian, they fired her.

Undaunted, Elaine hopped on the IRT subway and headed to Greenwich Village. Years before it was the punk fashion, Elaine died her hair in neon colors. One day she walked into a restaurant called Portofino. The owner, a man named Alfredo Viazzi, hired her as a waitress.

Right off Elaine was good for Alfredo's business—her stiletto wit and shocking hair color fit right in with the Village counter-culture. One of the first writers Elaine befriended was Terry Southern, a sixties icon who would go on to help write the screenplay for *Dr. Strangelove*, among many other works. Southern once held the ceremonious title, bestowed on him by *Rolling Stone* magazine, of the "hippest" person on the planet. Southern called Elaine "El." He would be just one of her Village following.

It was while at Portofino that Elaine fell in love with the restaurant business. The money was good, and the people exciting. This was the early 1960s, and the Village was an epoch of self-expression, home to the likes of Bob Dylan and Allen Ginsberg. It was while at Portofino that Elaine also fell in love.

According to Carlo, who worked alongside Elaine in the Village restaurant, Elaine didn't have much romantic experience when Alfredo thrust himself into her life. " 'E was the first one she 'ad," Carlo once told me. Alfredo made Elaine promises of marriage and a future together. They were to run the restaurant as a couple. But then one day Alfredo went alone on vacation to his hometown in Italy, the same town Carlo came from. He left Elaine to watch the store, which she did happily. He was supposed to be gone two weeks but stayed four. Carlo was working in the restaurant the day Alfredo retuned with a woman, an Italian. Without explanation, Alfredo sat at a table and told Elaine to bring some soup. Elaine dutifully fetched the dish. It was then that Alfredo finally introduced his companion as his new wife. For a moment Elaine stood there, too shocked to move. But the shock wore off quickly. "She dumped the soup right on his lap," Carlo said. "And she walked out the door for good."

In 1963, with Portofino and Alfredo a simmering memory, Elaine came uptown looking to buy a restaurant. She had a partner named Donald Ward, whom they called Red, who had also worked with her at Portofino. Elaine and Red found an old Austro-Hungarian cider stube in Yorkville, the then-hardscrabble, German-immigrant section of the Upper East Side. Ruppert's Brewery, once a major employer in the neighborhood, was just a few blocks away. Restaurants in Yorkville had names like the Heidelberg and Hauf Brau. On Eighty-sixth Street oompah bands played in the Loreeli. There men dressed in lederhosen, women in long skirts with aprons. Bund meetings were held in the Jager House on Lexington Avenue before World War II and, some say, for years after. There was Karl Ehmer's butcher shop, Kramer's bakery, and the Berlin Bar. It was seemingly no place for a young Jewish girl.

The store cost them fifteen grand, half coming from Elaine's hard-earned tips, the other half from Red's wife, who was a Lardner, a descendant of Ring Lardner, the preeminent sports and short-story writer of the Jazz Age. They flipped a coin to see whose name would go on the window.

Elaine would tell me about the moment she knew they had started something special. Because of the perilous nature of the neighborhood then, Elaine had a buzzer system installed on the front door that was operated by the bartender. On a late, bitter-cold January night in 1964, my boss was sitting at the front table with a playwright named Jack Richardson when the bartender called over to her to ask if he should buzz in Mrs. Kennedy. At first Elaine thought it was a joke, but then she looked out the window and saw the First Lady out on the sidewalk with a group that included the songwriters Adolph Green and Betty Comden, the writers George Plimpton and Susan Sontag, and Leonard Bernstein. Elaine's memory of Mrs. Kennedy is vivid. She was dressed in a Chanel suit and wore a starburst brooch. Elaine waved to the bartender to buzz open the front door.

Once they were inside, someone from the entourage put dimes in the jukebox. Betty Comden led the sing-along to Elvis and Roy Orbison songs. Elaine believed that it was Mrs. Kennedy's first night out after the assassination of the president. Much of the country was still deeply wounded by that day two months before in Dallas. But with "Blue Suede Shoes" as the soundtrack, the healing might have begun that night in Elaine's. It was a phenomenon that would repeat itself over and over again on the corner of Eighty-eighth Street and Second Avenue. Things just seemed to happen at Elaine's a moment before they happened anywhere else.

Another replicating phenomenon would occur the following day. A small item about Jackie Kennedy and friends at an outpost of an uptown restaurant called Elaine's ran in Dorothy Killgallen's column, "The Voice of Broadway." Killgallen's item was just a pebble tumbling down a hill. But it began what would become an avalanche of free publicity for the restaurant. It was the Stork Club and El Morocco that owned the society and gossip columns of the forties, and Toots Shor who dominated newsprint in the fifties. But Elaine's newsworthiness would usurp them all.

One day I found myself in the clip morgue of the *New York Post*. I'll tell you more about how I got there later. But in that room, in a wooden file cabinet, was a drawer that was as long as my arm given only to newspaper and magazine clippings about Elaine's. From gossip items to full profiles, there were hundreds of stories, scores of "Page Six" items alone. On one quiet evening after I'd been at the restaurant for a while, Elaine told me about the night she was crowned the champ of the columns. Late one afternoon, several years into her run on Second Avenue, she wandered into P.J. Clarke's with some friends. There, standing at the bar, was an older man, thick around the middle with thinning hair.

He wore a sports coat with a pocket square. By that time, Toots Shor's neon had dimmed considerably. His pal Jackie Gleason had already moved his shop to Miami, and *The Honeymooners* had slipped into TV lore. Joe DiMaggio was long gone from center-field. Even Mickey Mantle was limping into the twilight at Yankee Stadium. Though he would last in the business another ten years, Shor himself had started to break down. The rough Philadelphia neighborhood of his youth, the rumbles as a speakeasy doorman in New York, and the thousands of gallons of booze he'd poured down his gullet had all taken their toll. In many ways, that moment at Clarke's was a poignant one: the aged heavyweight champ passing the belt to the brash, glistening youngster. The old nightclub fighter slowly walked over to Elaine and, in typical Toots fashion, summed the scene up in a sentence: "I hear you're the new me," he said.

When Elaine's started to become successful, when writers made the tiny Yorkville storefront their home away from home, when her own table 4 became the most celebrated literary gathering spot since the Algonquin's Round Table, when the joint began to appear almost daily in Kilgallen's and Earl Wilson's newspaper columns, Elaine saw no reason to be anywhere but at her restaurant. Red, her partner, thought differently. Enjoying his newfound celebrity, he spent weekends in the Hamptons or jetting to the Caribbean, and weeknights out on the town. Often Red would have Elaine wire him money so his traveling party could continue. One day Red came back from the beach and Elaine told him they had a new landlord and the rent was going way up. Furious, Elaine's partner demanded to see this new landlord. "You're looking at her," Elaine said. She had bought the building without her partner's knowledge and was buying him out.

Elaine's big, masculine personality proved to be a magnet that attracted, over the years, tough-guy writers like Norman Mailer,

Jim Harrison, and Pete Hamill. Along with the tough guys came a living literary pantheon: Philip Roth, Frank Conroy, A. E. Hotchner, Kurt Vonnegut, William Kennedy, William Styron, George Plimpton, Jerzy Kosinski, Carl Bernstein, Dan Jenkins, Bruce Jay Friedman, Paddy Chayefsky, E. L. Doctorow, Irwin Shaw, and Joseph Heller. They came, one following the other, because they had heard tales of a woman who didn't care how much they acted like children, a motherly saloonkeeper who made them eat and made them laugh at themselves. They came because there were other writers there to talk to.

They came, too, simply because Elaine gave them credit. A playwright named Larry King once said that in Elaine's he could act like a rich Arab even though Con Ed had turned off the electricity. One night, early on in the restaurant's history, a tall, gangly man with a loping gait approached Elaine and asked to cash a check. The fellow, whom Elaine didn't know, said he was a friend of Warren Hinckle, the eye-patch-wearing editor of *Ramparts Magazine*. At the time a vouch by Hinckle wasn't exactly a letter of credit from Chase Bank. Still, Elaine cashed the check for the fellow, who introduced himself as Hunter Thompson.

Carlo used to tell about how Elaine let Willie Nelson float a tab for months. At the time the country musician's career was in free fall. His partying and divorcing had left him flat broke. Then he recorded a cover called "Blue Eyes Crying in the Rain" and followed up the number-one hit by collaborating with Waylon Jennings and Jessi Colter on an album titled *Wanted! The Outlaws,* which would go on to be one of the biggest-selling country records of all time. "We all wondered where he went after that," Carlo remembered. Willie seemed to have forgotten about Elaine's. Then one night, months after his resurgence, the country star walked into the restaurant with an envelope stuffed with several thousand dollars in cash and handed it to Carlo. "That's for all the nights I stiffed you," he said. He straightened his account with the restaurant, too. Dozens of writers had house accounts at Elaine's, and in all my time working there, I don't remember my boss getting stuck once for a tab. I doubt whether their publishers could say the same. The writers loved that Elaine trusted them, and they'd pay her back before they'd pay rent.

Throughout the 1970s, Elaine's notoriety streaked upward. Partly this assent was as a result of movie stars and Hollywood moguls who sought to cash in on the cache of the restaurant. With these luminaries came their attending publicity, and Elaine's went from a local to a national story. In 1979, Hollywood, by way of a New York filmmaker, paid the ultimate tribute to its East Coast headquarters.

Right after the crescendo of Gershwin's *Rhapsody in Blue,* and after the loving black-and-white homage to New York City, right after the fireworks fall on the East River in front of the United Nations, and as Isaac's voiceover concludes, the front window of the famous restaurant with *Elaine's* emblazoned in black, freestyle script fills the screen. The reel blinks, and the camera zooms into a front dining room jammed with customers engaged in witty banter and then match-cuts to a back table where, in real life, the star and director sat nearly every night. With the release of Woody Allen's *Manhattan,* Elaine's was the most famous restaurant in the world.

But, by the time I sat at Woody's table that first night, Elaine's glory years had seemingly passed. What was once the hippest of restaurants was now cobwebbed and as waxy as Madam Tussaud's. The last chapter of Elaine's fabled existence, however, had not yet been written. And I would be an eyewitness for most of that part of the story.

Chapter Three

I N ONE SENSE, my circuitous journey to behind Elaine's bar began on Christmas Eve 1980, in a detoxification unit in Pomona, New York. I will get into some details a little later of what led me to detox, but for now, suffice it to say I was there because I'd used up all other options. I was out of work, practically unemployable given my propensity for binging on alcohol, and owed money to a variety of institutions and individuals, including the IRS and a gentleman whose collection practices lay outside federal standards. I was also emotionally and spiritually bankrupt. I was twenty-six years old.

The detox shared the cafeteria with patients from an adjoining unit, people with emotional problems other than addictions. After lunch, someone wheeled in a piano. An attendant dressed in conventional white pants and shirt rounded up the patients from the psych unit and led them in impromptu Christmas caroling. Dressed in an open-backed hospital gown and paper slippers, I shuffled over to a window and sat alone. Outside, the sky was brushed gray. As if on some kind of cruel cue, it began to snow.

With falling flakes like a miniature parachute drop, the ground was covered in no time. Serenaded by the sing-along behind me, I began to cry.

One might think that such an episode would have propelled me into some kind of long-term recovery program. But, in what can only be described as delusional reasoning, I rallied from the emotional bottom I'd experienced in that locked ward and upon my release made the decision simply not to drink and drive anymore. The sober thought of just not drinking didn't dawn on me.

It's a theory of mine that plenty of alcoholics find their way to Manhattan for precisely the same reason I did: public transportation. For me, having wrecked a half dozen cars drunk, it was simply a matter of survival. I took a job in a small Greenwich Village restaurant named Bert McPhillips. Actually, there was no Bert McPhillips associated with the place, and though I know there is a story to how the name came about, for the life of me I can't remember it. Anyhow, I had yet again moved into my parents' house in suburban Rockland County. The last bus from Manhattan to Pearl River, my hometown, left at 1:15 A.M. But Bert's closed early—we were usually all cleaned up and counted out by midnight at the latest, plenty of time for me to hop a subway or taxi up to the Port Authority Bus Terminal and get out of Dodge.

Rarely, however, did I make that bus. Although I didn't drink much behind the bar (at least when the boss was there), I'd have a couple of quick after-work cocktails after I'd put the lock on the front door.

Looking back, I can't really blame myself for not rushing to make the bus. Why would I be in a hurry to go home? Like my friend and future bartending partner Tommy would always say: "I already know everybody there." And although the Village of 1980 had lost a bit of the bohemian expressiveness it had in Elaine's youth, it still held fast to some wonderful peculiarities. One day, a guy came into the bar dressed only in cellophane; one of the regular customers had a pet llama. One Halloween, after the Village parade, I was followed down a dark block by a sequined Lone Ranger. Also, like any good drunk, I had a fallback plan for how to get home, a plan that centered on Elaine's restaurant.

Brian and I had known each other in high school. Though never at the same time, we'd worked behind three of the same bars, including that of a restaurant in Rockland County where we both worked with a Liverpool Englishman named Tommy. It would be sometime in the mid-seventies when Tommy would be the first of our gang to take a job behind Elaine's bar. A few years later, Brian joined him. With Brian, who also lived in Pearl River, working five nights a week at Elaine's, I was almost assured of a ride home from my nights of debauchery in Manhattan.

Brian's shifts usually ended at four in the morning. I'd stagger into Elaine's sometime around three and drink on the house while I waited for him to finish. Tall and craggy-faced with a bushy mustache, Brian had a marvelous sense of humor and was great fun to be around. One night, on impulse, we drove to LaGuardia Airport, where we caught a flight to Miami. Carefree and single, I had little to worry about. But Brian had then been married for only a few weeks. We stayed in the hotel where he'd spent his honeymoon and received numerous double takes from the staff. Though our impromptu trip would relegate Brian to the couch in his own home for about three weeks, every time the subject of our Miami weekend came up, he would giggle at the memory.

But even with his affable personality, Brian quickly tired of his role as my late-night chauffeur. And he certainly didn't appreciate me coming into Elaine's totally pulverized. One night, while wobbly drunk, I put on a lady's mink coat that was hung on a hook near the bar and started to walk out the door. Brian

literally jumped over the bar to stop me. Another night, I saun-
tered over to George Steinbrenner's table and pointedly shared
my thoughts on the Boss as a baseball team owner and a person.
Almost every time I was there, I'd drop quarter after quarter into
the jukebox, play Billy Joel's "Big Shot," and, at the top of my
lungs, sing along with his line *"and the people that you knew at
Elaine's . . ."* In my foggy memory of those nights, Elaine is
somewhere in the background. I remember seeing her in the
restaurant, but to my knowledge we never said a word to each
other. Later, when I was working for her, I would find out that
my boss ceded much of the control of the bar to her bartenders.
"I have enough to handle out on the floor," she once told me.
Those drunken nights at Elaine's, however, had little to do with
my future employment there. That connection would occur in a
more sober light.

After only a couple of months, I lost my job at Bert McPhillips.
I had been out on a bender and missed several shifts in a row. I
never even found out if I was fired, I just didn't go back. I saw no
reason to stop my run. Having spent at least forty-eight hours
rolling around Manhattan in and out of an alcoholic blackout, I
awoke one morning—I guess Brian had driven me home—in my
own bedroom with a hangover of gargantuan proportions. Guilt
and dread overwhelmed me. Out of focus snapshots of the nights
before appeared like photos in developing solution. My body
flinched with the remembrance of each embarrassing action, each
inappropriately uttered sentence. Worse, though, was the ugly, dark
void of what I couldn't remember. Once, a few years earlier, my
father had shaken me awake after a drunken night and asked
where my car was. I lay there dumbfounded, blinking my eyes,
dozens of horrible scenarios unfolding. The car was in a parking
lot outside a nearby bar. A friend had driven me home. But until I
knew, the photophobia was pure torture.

That morning after my drunken Manhattan run, I was lying on my bed wearing a navy blue shirt that said *Texaco* on the pocket and *Bud* in script over the heart. I still have no idea where I got the shirt. The only things I wasn't wearing were my shoes, which were side by side under my bed. That I couldn't remember most of the week before, or how I got home, somehow didn't bother me as much as the neat placement of my shoes. It was a wonder that anything could command my attention—that my brain could function at all. To try to explain the pain of a hangover is an exercise in self-pity. But the physical agony of my hangovers, as bad as it was, was a distant second to the emotional anguish. My hangover pain was a hopeless pain, one that no amount of aspirin or ibuprofen could alleviate, and it seemed like it would last forever.

At some point I managed to check my pockets for any cash that I might have forgotten to spend. In one of my back pockets was something that felt like a travel brochure. I wrestled it out, and had to read it twice to make sure the title really said what I thought it said.

All active alcoholics live in some level of denial. Even ones who drunkenly boast about their alcoholism are really just trying to talk their way out of it—at least that's been my experience. And though denial can be as thick as a block wall, it is also fundamentally flawed and can easily crumble. When the wall of denial does come down, it leaves you most vulnerable. Staring at the ceiling of my bedroom, my head throbbing in pain, I went through a series of emotions. First I was repulsed. I held the pamphlet like one would a dead mouse by the tail. Then I became indignant: How dare it make such an accusation? Finally, curiosity won through. How the hell did a pamphlet titled "Are You an Alcoholic?" find its way into my back pocket? Even though the simplest thought was painful, a plausible scenario began to form in my mind. The blurry image of Frank, the cashier at Elaine's, came into focus.

In those years, just before the dawn of the answering machine, there was no way of knowing what danger lurked at the other end of a ringing phone line. Throughout my early twenties, I gave great import to things like pinkie rings and rubber bands around wads of cash. There were all sorts of unsavory characters in my life, like loan sharks, racetrack touts, and degenerate gamblers, all of whom I would end up owing money. Most times my mom would serve as my gatekeeper; she even started answering the phone with a phony Irish brogue so she could pretend not to understand my creditors' demands. Still, so as not to take any chances, I would issue codes to a select group of people that included anyone to whom I didn't owe cash or an apology. I would even, after an agent from the IRS somehow broke the code, change my routine weekly. Ring once. Hang up. Call back, ring twice. Hang up. Ring once, hang up, call back, and so on.

One day, the phone rang twice, then stopped, which was the code of the day. When the phone rang again, seconds later, I picked up the receiver. The voice on the line was not one I'd expected. It was an older voice with a New York City accent. The intonations sounded very much like the ones I knew from my childhood. My father was a detective squad commander in the Forty-first Precinct in the Bronx, and often I would answer the phone when one of his detectives called him at home. As it would turn out, my assessment wasn't that far off.

I don't remember much about that conversation, but whatever Frank said, it must have been persuasive. I thought I had my out when he asked if I'd like to go to a meeting with him. I'd make a date a couple of weeks down the road, then freeze him out with my phone defense. So when I found myself driving south toward

New York City on the Palisades Parkway that very afternoon, I was more than a bit surprised.

Frank lived in a top-floor apartment in an old wooden building on Lexington Avenue at Ninety-first Street, about four blocks from Elaine's. I rang his bell, and a window three floors above the sidewalk opened. "Move back a little," said the head sticking out. I followed the order. Then something—at first I thought it was a pair of boxer shorts—was thrown from the window. It turned out to be a parachute, on which hung the key to the front door. Frank's buzzer was on the fritz (and would stay on the fritz for as long as he lived there), and this was his entry system.

The staircase was crooked; the whole building felt like it was about to tip over. The door to the modified railroad flat opened into a middle room, which separated the kitchen and bedroom from the living room. Bookshelves lined the walls, a desk was strewn with papers and open reference books, and an old-style Royal typewriter sat on a metal table. I thought I had wandered into Mickey Spillane's writing hideaway.

Though the middle room had a 1930s detective look, the rest of Frank's apartment took its inspiration from Robinson Crusoe. In addition to the parachute key delivery system, he had a series of strings and pulleys to turn on and off lights and appliances. Some months later, Frank would tell me he was planning a footbridge to run from his apartment over Lexington Avenue to the roof of the bookbinder's building across the street. He was only half kidding. He once told me that, during his drinking years, he would decorate his homes by walking into a furniture store and ordering the display living room: couch, rugs, end tables, lamps, the whole lot, right down to the plastic fruit in the dishes. But now that he was in sobriety, Frank's apartment took on his potent personality—part tough-guy hideaway, part tree house, with leather chairs, heavy wooden tables, a globe, and a telescope.

Frank himself looked a bit like my mental image of Spillane: middle fifties, stocky with a face that could've said either "You're under arrest" or "Give me your money" with equal result. He invited me in and made, in two glasses the size of flowerpots, concoctions that consisted of diet chocolate soda and skim milk. He said he drank the mixture by the gallon.

The meeting was seven or eight blocks from Frank's apartment. It was mid-March, and the late-winter city had the gray look of a black-and-white movie. We walked down Park Avenue. Doormen in front of the swanky buildings wore heavy overcoats like World War II German officers. Ghostly white breath came out of their mouths in puffs. I felt as if I was being marched.

The church on Park Avenue, St. Ignatius Loyola, is like a cathedral to the rich and famous Catholics of the Upper East Side of Manhattan. It was Jacqueline Bouvier's parish. The organ in the place weighs forty tons and cost $1.25 million. But the rarefied air existed only upstairs, where the smooth oaken pews were filled with the Catholic swells. Frank was taking me in the other direction, down a staircase that led to a basement room lined with lunch tables and bench seats. The place was jammed with clusters of people in animated conversation. Everyone seemed to wear a sweet, knowing smile, like the nuns in the convent scenes in *The Sound of Music*. Frank led me through the mass of recoverers and a miasma of cigarette smoke, introducing me along the way to people with names like Staircase Charlie, Harry the Hat, Teddy Coffee. We wound our way to the far corner and through a doorway that was at least fifteen feet high, then through a catacomb-like hallway lined with dark mahogany, then through another doorway and into a room like no other I'd ever seen.

It was an undercroft with vaulted ceilings that were thirty feet high, held up by stone, capital-topped columns. Like the hallways, the walls were deep mahogany. The lighting was poor at best, and the huge stained-glass window, under street level, offered little help. There was a marble altar at the front of the room with a reredos of stone carved with cherubs and angels that crawled to the ceiling. A separate chancel was to one side, with stone railings. The cold marble floor squeaked beneath my sneakers. In little grade-school desks, the ones with the armrests to write on, were seated at least a hundred people. It seemed that all of them wore the same smiles as the folks in the cafeteria. I folded my six-foot-three length into one of the seats. The room had a chill, but sweat leaked from my pores. I wrestled myself out of a golf jacket with an ink-stained pocket, closed my eyes, and shivered.

Only in hindsight can I see the fundamental change that happened to me that afternoon. A young, rather pretty woman sat behind a desk in front of the altar and told a story of her drinking and drugging that would make a biker blush. And the worse things got for her, the more people laughed. There are only two real defining moments in any alcoholic's life. Two, that is, if they're lucky. The night, way back in my early teens, when I had my first taste of alcohol was the first of mine. An inexorable journey that would eventually fill with misery began in that moment. The second for me happened in the basement of St. Ignatius Loyola on Park Avenue.

I started going into the city every evening to meetings. Frank bought me a yellow-covered book with the title *Living Sober.* When I first saw it, I was repulsed in the same way I had been by the pamphlet I'd found in my pocket that morning. The word *sober* was embarrassing to me, like it was the worst kind of character weakness. Or maybe it was a condition I wasn't too familiar with. Frank also bought me a big blue book that was called, with little imagination, "the Big Book." He told me that if I was embarrassed to carry it, I could turn the paper book cover inside out, which I immediately did. But if I was embarrassed by "program literature," as they called it, I began to be swept along by the program itself. With each church basement I entered, I experienced great relief, a feeling like the worst was over.

There is a sense of safety that comes from being surrounded by people who share the same problem and struggle you do. But maybe the most powerful sensation one feels there is far less tangible. Many of the meetings I attended were held in church basements. Above me were the trappings of the faith of my youth: stained glass, somber statues, and flickering shadows. But down in the rooms where the meetings were held, there was light and laughter. There is a saying in the program that captures its core: Religion is for people who are afraid of going to hell; spirituality is for those who've already been there. In the rooms, it felt like my hell was already behind me.

After the third or fourth day in a row of meetings, and not drinking, I cleared up enough to hear someone say something about a sponsor. After the meeting I asked Frank what a sponsor was. "Me," he replied.

Most of the time, Frank dressed in jeans and polo shirts. Around his neck, he wore a chain with a small gold crucifix, which he fingered all the time. He talked in riddles, parables, and metaphors. Over and over he told me the importance of making ninety meetings in ninety days, the program's tryout period. "It's like a pitcher with a no-hitter," he'd say in earnestness. "You got to keep the streak going." I did keep it going and with each day felt a little better, a little more hopeful. Though, after a month or so, I developed second thoughts. "If you're wondering whether or not you're an alcoholic, why don't you also give up asparagus for the next sixty days?" Frank suggested. "At the end of that time, if life has gotten better, if you're starting to get some hope, if the future looks a bit brighter, slowly, carefully go back to eating asparagus. Then, if your life doesn't fall apart, you can be pretty sure the problem lies with your drinking."

Though Frank could be almost Zen-like with his spirituality, he reminded me of one of those crocodiles you see on nature shows, the ones that look so serene just before they swallow the pelicans. He had had a storied career in law enforcement. Before he worked for Elaine, he'd been a federal agent and was involved in the investigation of one of the most famous heroin-smuggling cases ever. The French Connection case, of course, inspired both a best-selling book and an Academy Award–winning movie. In neither did Frank get nearly the credit that he deserved—I knew this not from Frank but from other cops and feds from his era.

About two weeks into my sobriety, I had my first real crisis. A few months before, when my life had come completely unhinged, I'd borrowed a thousand dollars from a Rockland County loan shark. With all the good feelings I was experiencing in my early sobriety, I almost forgot about Tony Lips. Tony, however, had not forgotten about me. He began to call my house with disturbing frequency. His tone with my mother-gatekeeper became scary. I didn't know what to do. I wasn't working at the time, and a grand might as well have been a million. With great anxiety, I told Frank my tale at a coffee shop after a meeting. As I did, Frank stared out the window. His eyes were squinted and hard. Finally, after what seemed like forever in silence, he took a deep breath, let it out, and began to speak in a low, scary tone. "Okay," he said. "This is what you do. Call this Tony up and tell him you'll meet him out there in Jersey." I nodded my head. "Pick some parking lot off the beaten track. Someplace not too busy," he continued. I stopped nodding. "We'll take two cars. When we get to the parking lot, lure Tony out of his car." He started to sound like a Robert De Niro character. "I'll come up behind him, and I'll shoot him in the back of the head."

He let his words hang in the air like gun smoke.

"Or," he said finally, his voice a parish priest's, his smile as soft, "you can call him up, tell him you're trying to get sober, and you'll pay him as much as you can every week."

I think I left a vapor trail running to the pay phone to call Tony.

At about the six-month mark of my sobriety, I moved into the city. I took a one-room studio above a Greek diner on Sixty-first Street and First Avenue. Frank got me a job in a ladies-who-lunch restaurant on Madison Avenue. It was the least alcoholic bar job I'd ever had.

One day Elaine came into the restaurant alone for lunch. She sat at small table in the crowded dining room. The waitress was confused by Elaine's order and brought out two whole entrees. Several nearby tables watched and whispered as the large amount of food was placed before the heavyset woman. Elaine was red-faced. After sending the unwanted order back to the kitchen, she hurriedly ate her lunch and quickly walked out the door.

Although she didn't acknowledge me, by that time she had an idea who I was. Often I'd go up to Elaine's and sit in the back room with Frank on his dinner break. Frank would have Carlo make me a plate of spaghetti, and when they were in season, we would eat casaba melons for dessert. Most of the time I'd sneak in and out the kitchen door so Elaine wouldn't see me. But several times, when I was there so late the gates were pulled down; I'd have to walk right past Elaine and out the front door. Though she never said anything, she knew I wasn't a paying customer, and she'd gimlet-eye me as I slunk by.

At the Madison Avenue restaurant, I worked mostly day shifts, and most of my customers drank Perrier or hot tea. In the evenings, I'd go to meetings all over town. Some of them were filled with hardscrabble neighborhood guys who made me feel like I was in a longshoremen's union hall. One meeting I regularly attended, with its attendees' neon-colored hair and Mohawks, had the look of a punk rock concert. There were meetings where I'd see movie stars sitting next to homeless people. A meeting at the Church of the Heavenly Rest seemed like opening night at the opera. There the men dressed in blue blazers with crests, and all the women wore pearls. Some of the meeting rooms seemed as big as Madison Square Garden (for some reason, remembrances in early sobriety are out of proportion, like the memories of childhood snowstorms). Still, some of the rooms in my memory are small and intimate. All of them contained stories—one after the other, told with astonishing honesty and even more amazing humor. But it was meeting Frank after the meetings that was the most fun.

Frank was the first person I heard call the program "the program." His terminology made it all so deliciously mysterious. "We're a secret society, Brian," he'd say. "All we're missing is the handshake." In this vein, he'd leave cryptic messages on my newfangled answering machine or on a slip of paper I'd find behind the bar in the Madison Avenue restaurant. The message would read or say only "the Greeks. 5 pm." I knew Frank had a favorite restaurant near his apartment that was owned by a Greek man. I'd walk into what I thought was an empty dining room, and a potted palm would part, revealing Frank's smiling face.

In the nice weather, Frank and I and several other program people would spend hours sitting outside Eric's, a bar-restaurant with sidewalk café that was right across the street from Elaine's. Frank was actually working most of time we'd have these get-togethers, but he'd take dinner breaks that would last half his shift. The wide leeway Frank received from Elaine was a result of her self-admitted separation anxiety. She would rather suffer the situation than see him leave. It was that and the fact that Frank and Elaine had been through plenty together. Frank was working as the cashier early one morning when a stickup team burst into the restaurant. Frank had seen more than his share of bad guys in his law enforcement career, and the demeanor of the armed men told him to comply. Elaine, Frank, and the bartender were all herded into one of the bathrooms. Although Frank had trouble believing it, he kept quiet as stone as Elaine shrugged when the stickup man demanded any money she was carrying. Having already given Elaine the take for the night, Frank knew that there was at least a grand held tight by the strap of his boss's brassiere. The robbers emptied what was left of the cash draw, change for the next day's business, and unhappily departed. The following week, the same team stuck up a liquor store where they shot and killed an employee.

Frank worked for Elaine for ten years. He was a bartender when he started at the restaurant but moved to the cashier's job a few years later, the same progression I would take. And he had the perfect personality for the place. He didn't care who you were and cared less who you thought you were. One night when Steve Rubell was zipping around the restaurant in high-altitude spin, Frank told the Studio 54 impresario to "sit down and shut up." Rubell meekly complied.

But Frank never really enjoyed working at Elaine's, and his job was only a vehicle—the money was good, and there was no pressure. By the time I met him, Frank was working his way through a master's in social work at nearby Marymount Manhattan College. As soon as he graduated, Elaine's would be history. With Frank, on warm summer nights, I'd watch the procession of limousines pull up in front of the famous restaurant across the street. My sponsor would tell story after story of the craziness of his place of employment and his boss. Part of me wondered why he wanted to leave; it sounded all so exciting.

As the years went by, I settled into a comfortable routine. Being sober was fun. I had plenty of friends and even a lover. The only part of my life that felt uncomfortable was the way I made my living. Though the money I made tending bar wasn't bad, it was a pocket fortune. I'd spent my formative educational years in saloons. Although that lifestyle did teach me a thing or two, it wasn't the type of education that translated into a more traditional career, with a future.

Four years into my sobriety, I decided to stop tending bar. Several sober friends had gently suggested that I get out of saloons for good. Even though I wasn't drinking booze, just being around it, they said, was detrimental to my mental well-being. A friend from the program had an apartment-painting business and for about two weeks I worked for him. Since that time, I've often said that if there is such a thing as a personal hell, mine would include a paintbrush and a roller.

By 1985, Frank had left Elaine's and begun to work as a therapist in the field of addiction. In his new role, my sponsor was an instant success, as I knew, from all of his asparagus analogies, he would be. After Frank quit the restaurant, my pal Brian moved into the vacated cashier's position, which created an opening behind Elaine's bar. It was then that Brian gave me a call.

Chapter Four

IN SOME WAYS, Elaine's and the program are very similar. Both are inhabited by drunks and dreamers, the lost and lonely, and both have their share of nuts. But the famous bar and the church basements were also the direct opposites of each other. Whereas the program is filled with light and hope, the Elaine's of the mid-eighties was a dark and dreary place with Edward Albee–like cynicism and negativity. This feeling flowed from the top down. Elaine's dour disposition was mainly a result of the dearth of business, but she also had a kind of celebrity leave-me-alone crust accumulated from years of people wanting her time and attention. I found out pretty quickly that people who knew Elaine the best—her staff—took two tacks in trying to communicate with her: Half tried to flatter and appease, half joined in with her misery. And then there was Tommy, my bartending partner.

At one hundred and twenty pounds and five foot eight on his tiptoes, Tommy Carney was a Liverpool wharf rat. He'd left home when he was just sixteen to work as a waiter on the Cunard lines.

He was never handed anything in his life, and he didn't take crap from anyone. Nothing annoyed Tommy more than cheap customers, especially customers who obviously didn't need to be cheap.

There's a famous Elaine's tale about a waiter named Dominick, a sweet older man who had worked for Elaine from the restaurant's beginning. One night Dominick was waiting on Mick Jagger. When it came time to pay, Jagger gave Dominick a hundred-dollar bill for an eighty-dollar check. In making the change, Tommy gave Dominick a twenty-dollar bill. A few moments later, Dominick was back at the bar. "Mr. Jagger wants change to leave a tip," he said innocently. Behind the waiter stood the rock icon. Tommy snatched the twenty-dollar bill from Dominick's hand and stuffed it in the waiter's top pocket, all the time glaring at the Rolling Stone. "Mr. Jagger doesn't need change, Dominick," Tommy said. Jagger turned meekly away.

Tommy's irreverence made him a bartending legend on the East Side of Manhattan. One of the first nights we worked together, my bartending partner took an order from a couple dressed for a night on the town. After extended deliberation, the woman asked for a brandy Alexander. Tommy stuck his hand in the register and pulled out a ten. "Here," he said, handing the bill to the stunned lady. "Go across the street, they make that crap over there." On another night, three guys in suits came to the service end of the bar, where Tommy was working. They ordered a round of drinks—a couple of scotches and a vodka on the rocks. Tommy served them and started a check. At Elaine's, the bartenders either folded the check and put it in front of the customer or, for a regular, kept the check behind the bar, usually slipped between bottles of booze. Because he didn't know these guys, Tommy tented the check and dropped it in front of them.

After a while, the men had another round, and Tommy took care of them.

The bar started to get busy, and soon Tommy was up to his elbows with waiters ordering for the tables. While he was working the service bar, he noticed the three guys in suits getting ready to leave but also noticed that one of the guys looked at the check, then threw some money on the bar. When Tommy had a moment, he collected the check and the money. It was then he realized the man in the suit had left the exact amount—back then I think it was about thirty dollars. Tommy's expression didn't change one bit. I don't even remember him mentioning the guy stiffing us. But Tommy had filed the information.

About two weeks later, the same guy came into the joint, this time by himself. He put a twenty-dollar bill on the bar, and before he even ordered his drink, Tommy took the twenty, made change, then put one ten in his tip cup, the other ten back on the bar.

"What are you going to have?" Tommy asked, as if nothing had happened.

"What did you do with my ten dollars?" asked the customer.

"That's my ten dollars. You didn't leave a tip when you were in two weeks ago," Tommy replied. The fellow in the suit, who happened to be a producer for Rush Limbaugh's radio show, was Tommy's steady customer from that moment on.

Tommy's relationship with Elaine was even more interesting than his relationships with the customers. He and his boss would have an argument and not talk for months. One time, before I worked at the restaurant, Elaine bought a glass washer for behind the bar. Because of the incredible volume of drinks the bartenders made, back when the place was busy, the glasses were washed in the kitchen. But the headwaiter, then a chesty Italian they called Joe, came up with the bright idea to let Tommy wash his own glasses. Tommy came into work that night and walked behind the bar. Elaine was at the end, doing the checks. Tommy didn't say a word when he saw the glass washer; he just unplugged it, pulled it out of the sink, and threw it in the garbage pail. Elaine watched the scene unfold from her barstool. She didn't say a thing to Tommy. Instead, she yelled across the dining room: "Joe, get me my money back for that machine!"

But working with Tommy was the easy part; I'd known him for years and knew what I was getting into. Working with my new boss was another story. When Elaine was "doing the checks," as we called the cashier's job at the restaurant, she looked like a loupe-less jeweler searching for a flaw. Nearsighted, she'd push her glasses up on her forehead, close one eye, and hold the slips just an inch or two from the open one. With her barstool blocking my only exit (except for jumping the bar, which I did often), I felt like Jesus in the tomb.

Elaine stayed with a system of figuring a dinner check that was almost as old as the abacus. Waiters would write your order on a "dupe" pad, the top two white sheets separated by black carbon paper. The duplicate copy would be taken to the kitchen. The top copy would go to the cashier, who would tran-scribe the chits onto green dinner checks. Carlo, who had worked for Elaine from the restaurant's beginning, would some-times, half hidden by the pay phone, wait countless minutes un-til his boss's attention was diverted to slip a dupe onto the pile. He would then tiptoe away like a cartoon cat burglar. One of the reasons Carlo was so fearful was that he mangled the written English language. One of his more egregious mistakes would occur when soft-shell crabs, a dish that would appear on his dupes as "social crabs," were in season. No matter how bad Elaine's mood, she always got a giggle out of that one. Sooner or later, however, every waiter would get a "cigar," as those of us who worked for her called our boss's wrath. With a new waiter, the cigar usually came sooner.

"What are the specials tonight, Sergio?" Elaine growled one night without looking up from the checks. Sergio's career at the restaurant had spanned all of two weeks. His hands shook as he took the dupe pad out of his top pocket and read from the back of it. "We have cheeckeen Sorreenntinnnooo, Miss Elaine, we havva veeeell saltonbuuuuccooo, we havva tooona steak and broil scrad."

Elaine half-turned her back to him and jabbed her number 2 pencil in the sharpener. "What was that?" she grunted, above the high-pitched whine of the electric gadget.

"Excussaa me, Miss Elaine?" The sentence came with a squeak in the middle.

"The specials," she snapped, as she gave him a sideways glance.

The new waiter's eyes, as dark as a Sicilian night, darted back and forth like those of a guilty man on the witness stand.

"We havva cheeckeen Sorreenntinnnoo . . . ," Sergio began, his bravado beginning to weaken.

"The last one you said!"

"You meanna broil scrad?" He was truly confused.

"Yes, broil scrad. What the hell is broil scrad?"

"Isa feesh, Miss Elaine."

With that, Elaine dropped her pencil on the pile of green checks. After several heaves, she managed to move around on the stool to face him.

"There is no fish named scrad," she announced loudly enough for most of the front of the restaurant to hear.

"Oh yes," said the innocent Sergio. "Isa fluffy white feesh—"

"It's not called scrad, goddamn it! No wonder you never sell any of the specials. Nobody knows what the hell you're talking about."

By this time, the repartee had gained the attention of several tables of diners and most of the bar patrons. Drinks and forks were frozen in midlift.

"Now say it right," Elaine demanded.

Sergio was done. With his pronounced Italian accent, his chance of a correct pronunciation of *scrod* was one in a million. Elaine sat there waiting, her fists propped on her hips, an incredulous look on her wide, chubby face.

"Srood?" he uttered meekly, his head bowed like that of a schoolboy who hadn't done his lesson.

"No," came the reply.

"Schred?"

"No."

"Scrud?"

"No,"

In unison, the eyes of the onlookers followed the volleys back and forth as though they were watching a tennis match on a short court.

"Schrood?"

"No."

It might have gone on all night like that had not Ann Downey, a socialite and friend of Elaine's, walked in the front door with a party of eight. Elaine slid off the stool, stuck her tongue out, and issued a short Bronx cheer in Sergio's general direction. Pulling up her panty hose, as if to accentuate her disdain, she then duck-toddled off to greet the customers. As the curtain fell on the act, the audience resumed their own dinner and over-drinks conversations as if nothing had happened. Still mouthing pronunciations, Sergio slunk to the back room.

Elaine was no easier on the customers. I quickly figured out where customers stood just by watching the way she let them kiss her. If you weren't that close, or you hadn't "been in," as Elaine referred to regulars' appearances, she'd bow her head at

the very last moment and instead of your lips landing somewhere on her fleshy cheek, you'd end up with a mouthful of
hair. This was also an indication of the table you received. Hair
kissers had little or no chance of sitting at one of the optimum
tables in the A line. More likely, they were given a table in the
back alcove or, worse than worse, table 21, which sat right in the
middle of the dining room. Twenty-one served as a kind of
celebrity-on-display table to appease the gawking out-of-
towners. It was a table that Regis Philbin would be given, or one
at which Donald Trump might have ended up. If Elaine gave up
some skin to your kiss—that is, if your lips found cheek or side
of face—you had *been in* enough, but it didn't necessarily mean
she was thrilled you were there. The cheek was given to longtime customers, stodgy old men and crinkled, bony women,
who, under Elaine's absolute scorn, would order main-course
salads and drink Perrier water. But if you got her lips, baby, in
Elaine's world, you had it made. Lips were saved for the every-
night crew of manly guys, or those who had earned their places
in Elaine's by years and years of patronage.

When Elaine wasn't doing the checks, she served as hostess. She
would go from table to table, make small talk, and smoke cigarettes (you could back then). But mostly, I'd notice, she'd watch
the other tables. Elaine could count the house better than any boss
I'd worked for, and she knew exactly what someone ordered, or
didn't order, all the way across the restaurant. I remember once
when the Broadway star Elaine Stritch, who'd actually worked for
Elaine in the early days of the restaurant, was in for dinner. When
the waiter took the table's order, Stritch wanted only a lettuce
salad.

Elaine yelled over to her: "What are you, a wise guy? Order
something to eat!"

"I have to watch my figure!" Stritch replied.

"You're the only one who does," Elaine shot back.

Not only was Elaine as fast with a rejoinder as anybody I'd ever known, she wasn't afraid to openly use language usually reserved for the back of the house. I was working at the restaurant only a couple of weeks when one early evening a table of four, two couples in their sixties, sat up front near the bar. Park Avenue types, the men wore blazers with pocket squares, the women were rake-thin and wore pearl necklaces. Elaine was doing the checks, and the waiter dropped off a dupe with only three entrees listed. When Elaine asked the waiter why only three dinners, he shrugged and mumbled something about one woman having already eaten.

"What did you come in for?" Elaine yelled over to the woman who didn't order.

"I'm just tagging along," the woman replied brightly, thinking Elaine was joking.

Elaine wasn't. "There's a cunt in every crowd," she yelled. The woman's face was frozen in an amazed expression, her mouth forming a perfect O. I bent down behind the bar and pretended to be rearranging some stock so the people couldn't see that I was bursting with laughter. I couldn't look at the table for the rest of the time they were there. I don't know why they stayed, but they did, and ate in a kind of flabbergasted silence.

How Elaine did business was just as inventive as her language. One night when he was working as cashier, Frank left his station at the end of bar for a few minutes to sit with friend who was in for dinner. When Frank returned, a waiter named Peter asked for Woody Allen's check. The filmmaker was at his usual table, with Mia Farrow and several other people. Just as Frank finished totaling the check, he realized that Elaine had been there and had added twenty-five cents to the price of two fifteen-dollar chicken specials Woody and Mia had had. Frank was about to erase the check and retotal it when Peter stopped him. "Don't bother," the waiter said. "Woody never looks at the check." But this night, for some reason, Woody's eyes were drawn to the line that read: "2 chicken specials—$30.25."

"Not for nothing, Peter," Woody said, in his Brooklyn–Ocean Parkway dialect. "How does two go into thirty twenty-five?"

"She's running a special," Peter said, without a change in expression. "You buy one chicken for thirty bucks, you get the second for a quarter."

Yet at Christmas, Elaine would lavish gifts and bonuses on her employees. For years, she shopped at a very expensive men's store called Andre Oliver's on Fifty-seventh Street. There she'd buy five-hundred-dollar sweaters for all twenty of the waiters and bartenders. In a business not known for Christmas bonuses, Elaine would stuff envelopes with cash for all of her staff, right down to the pot washer.

And there were moments when Elaine was truly endearing, when, after a Polish vodka or two, she would show me the side of her that was an engaging raconteur. One of my favorite of her stories was about the drunk who staggered into the restaurant one afternoon. Before he made it to the bar, Elaine was up and in his face, shooing him. "Go on, get out of here," she yelled. The drunk shrugged, turned, and walked unsteadily out the door. Five minutes later he was back again. Undoubtedly, the man had gotten turned around on the sidewalk. "What did I tell you?" Elaine yelled. The drunk squinted at her unsteadily and replied, "What do you own the whole block?"

It didn't take me long to figure out that the restaurant took its erratic personality from the woman whose name was on the window. One night early on in my time at Elaine's, a waiter on his first shift walked out on a full station, taking all the dinner checks with him. A soft-spoken Italian, he had put up with being yelled at by Elaine, the chef, the other waiters, and customers who weren't even seated in his section. One table, in another waiter's station, had placed empty bread baskets on their heads in protest of the lack of service. But the breaking straw came when the new waiter went to the kitchen to pick up a dinner order. Carlo had already picked up the order, four entrees, and served it to the wrong table. When the customers at the wrong table tried to explain that they hadn't ordered those dishes, Carlo told them he wasn't their waiter.

As those first months went by, I gave my boss as wide a berth as I could. Her anxiety would fill the whole restaurant. She'd sit on a stool at the end of the bar and fold her arms tightly around her large bosom. She hated when the place was empty, which happened a lot in my early years, and would wantonly assign blame for that situation.

My first Super Bowl Sunday behind her bar, she came in early to watch the game. Though Elaine's drew its share of sports personalities, it wasn't the best place to watch a game. There is only one, smallish TV, which, if you're at the bar, you have to turn completely around to see. I had two customers the whole day, a French couple who didn't look at the TV once. First thing Elaine said to me as she sat down was "Nice following. What do I need you for?" For most of the four-plus hours the game was on, she sat at the end of the bar wearing an expression, directed at me, of utter contempt.

I'd worked in every imaginable type of tavern and restaurant, from a college rathskeller to an English chophouse, from seventies discos to an Irish steam-table joint. I worked for a couple of gay guys, a Jewish garmento, and a hotheaded Irishman, and I got along with every one of them, even during the worst of my drinking. The owner of one place, called the Talk of the Town in

Hillsdale, New Jersey, fired me three times. I was like Billy Martin to his George Steinbrenner. He fired me once when I got drunk and fell asleep in the fireplace of the restaurant. When he fired me the last time, he told me it broke his heart to do so. But it seemed as though Elaine could barely stand me.

Chapter Five

PERHAPS IF HER RESTAURANT had been busy in my early years, Elaine and I would have gotten along fine. But night after night, empty tables and waiters with nothing to do surrounded us. Partly the reason her restaurant fell out of favor during this time was that Elaine's hard-edged personality didn't play well with the "me" generation of the eighties. By the mid-eighties, the bulls on Wall Street stampeded to the sushi restaurants and Nuevo Italian joints that littered Manhattan. Neighborhoods like the Flatiron District and Union Square were hot. There was a place on Twentieth Street called America that was as big as a canyon and served alligator sausage and ostrich burgers. There was the new Union Square Cafe, where the clientele was incredibly pretty, and the food even prettier. Positano, with its star-studded customers, was a new and improved Elaine's on Twentieth Street. There was a restaurant called Canastels that was so popular they laughed when you tried to make reservations. This was the age of Jay McInerney's *Bright Lights, Big City,* the era of the hip and trendy. Elaine's was old and dusty, the place where movie stars went to die.

One night, through the front door walked a woman who looked vaguely familiar. She had her hair piled high, à la Audrey Hepburn, and wore oversize sunglasses. I turned to Tommy and said, "Look at this one, dressed up like a sixties movie star." Elaine was writing the checks and overheard me. Over her glasses, she glanced at woman and then turned her stare on me. "That's Gina Lollobrigida," she said, as if only a buffoon wouldn't know.

For the first two decades of the restaurant's existence, my boss's biggest problem was too many customers. Nights back then were dedicated to turning the tables over, getting people out of the joint. According to Elaine's lore, one packed night in the early 1970s, she told the chef to turn off the exhaust fans over the broilers. Smoke tumbled from the kitchen into the dining room. Elaine then stood on a chair and calmly announced that everyone should pay their checks and leave immediately, the kitchen was on fire. Once the restaurant was cleared, she flipped on the exhaust and opened the door for a new round of business.

But there were no such shenanigans in my early years at Elaine's. We had to go and pull the customers in off the street— literally. Elaine had a menu with the daily specials posted outside next to the front door. If she saw people looking at it, she'd send one of the waiters out after them. "Go get 'em," she'd say. If the waiter came back empty-handed, she'd shake her head in disgust.

Some of her old famous customers remained faithful but did so more out of guilt than anything else. Among the ones who stuck by Elaine were Christo, the conceptual artist who draped Central Park in Home Depot orange, James Nederlander, of the Broadway theater Nederlanders, and James Brady, the inaugural editor of the *New York Post*'s "Page Six." Some of her writers—Plimpton, Talese, Hotchner, and Styron among them—continued to make obligatory visits. A few of the power couples, like Helen Gurley Brown and her husband, the producer David Brown, made appearances.

But when her old customers did come in, Elaine would park herself at their tables and make them stay for hours. For the regulars, coming to Elaine's must have been about as much fun as paying a shivah call.

Though back then these moments were few and far between, Elaine's star-drawing power could still surprise you. One of her regulars was Ahmet Ertegun, the founder of Atlantic Records and the man responsible for groups such as the Coasters and the Drifters, Led Zeppelin and Ray Charles. One night, Ertegun came in with Eric Clapton. After dinner, the record producer felt like hearing some jazz. If you're Ahmet Ertegun and you want to hear some jazz, you have it delivered. He made one phone call, and twenty minutes later a trio was unpacking their equipment from a cab in front of Elaine's. The trio played all night to a crowd of, counting Eric Clapton, about eight people.

For a few months, Elaine lent the back room out to Libby Titus, the songwriter girlfriend of Donald Fagen of Steely Dan. Each Sunday night she would put on what essentially was a rock-and-roll cabaret. Among those who performed were Dr. John and Phoebe Snow, and, of course, Fagen, who played keyboards every week. Despite the big names, the cabaret night was never that popular. I don't think Fagen's girlfriend was very good at promotion. Still, the staff got to hear some terrific music. One night, to an audience that consisted of Elaine, the waiters, and myself, a band that included Dr. John, Donald Fagen, and James Taylor performed at least two sets.

About a year into my time at the restaurant, a brand-new upright piano was delivered, a gift to Elaine from the film director Sydney Pollack. For six months or so, the piano sat in the back room with a tablecloth draped over it. Someone, I don't remember who it was, talked Elaine into putting the piano to use. My boss hired a piano player named Loren, who was very funny and talented in a honky-tonk style. Loren livened the place up, although Elaine wasn't all that thrilled with his following—they weren't the biggest of spenders. Still, Loren provided some memorable duets, including a Motown set with Donna Summer, one with Christopher Plummer singing "Edelweiss," and the Broadway star Patti LuPone, who one Tuesday night drank a ton of bourbon and Cokes, incessantly smoked Marlboro Reds, and sang Beatles songs with Loren until four in the morning. At some point during the night I realized that she had two shows of *Anything Goes* to do the following day.

In spite of Loren and the odd busy night, for the most part, my early years at Elaine's marked the lowest point of my boss's run on Second Avenue. Just about all of Elaine's "faithful" customers ate down the street at restaurant called Elio's. Just the mention of Elio's name made Elaine's face turn crimson in anger.

Tall, dark, and nearly princely, Elio had for years worked for Elaine. From what I understand, my boss was very fond of him. It was crime enough that he left her to open his own restaurant (the first one he opened was called Parma on Third Avenue), but to open one exactly four blocks south on Second Avenue? This was a sin of cataclysmic proportions. And any customer of hers who patronized Elio's was a traitor of the worst sort. Still, those who did dare to dine at Elio's were treated to some of the best Italian food on the East Side of Manhattan. Several times I found myself walking past Elio's on my night off and saw A. E. Hotchner, Gay Talese, William Styron, or some other Elaine's writer sitting at a window table. On seeing me, they'd lift a finger to their lips, their expressions imploring my silence. A few nights later, they'd slink in Elaine's door, overcome with guilt, like schoolchildren who'd gotten away with playing hooky.

Although eating at Elio's was a capital crime, there were plenty of other felonies in Elaine's penal code. In fact, it was a punishable offense to eat dinner at any other restaurant, and Elaine acted as judge, jury, and executioner. One night the movie producer Robert Evans walked in the door with his arms draped around the shoulders of two willowy blondes. The encounter started out as one of those magical Elaine's moments. Elaine slid off her barstool and met the producer just in front of the bar. The blondes parted as Elaine threw her arms around Evans's waist and grabbed a handful of his ass.

"Bobby, baby," she purred.

"Elaine, sweetheart," he growled back as the bar crowd and the front tables froze in awe. Even Jack, the hard-to-impress headwaiter, stood there with a tight smile creasing his face. But his smile flatlined when Evans made the biggest of mistakes.

"Sweetheart, we were just at Le Cirque for dinner, and we thought to come here for dessert," said the film legend.

It was as though all the air was sucked out of the restaurant. Elaine took a step back, her welcoming expression puckering into one of disgust. Evans's expression, too, changed. All of a sudden he didn't seem so tan. He knew he had said something wrong, but, for the life of him, he couldn't figure out what it was. The seconds struggled to pass like somebody was holding their tail.

"What do you think I am? An ice-cream parlor?" Elaine said finally, and with a contempt that dripped and pooled on the floor. "You had dinner at Le Cirque, you should have had fucking dessert there."

The blondes simultaneously looked down at their high heels. Customers pushed broccoli and veal scaloppine around on their plates. Jack slowly shook his head, his smile not even a memory. Elaine stood there, defiantly, hands on her hips, daring Evans to try an excuse. Any excuse.

Later I made it a point to walk past Evans's table. The three full meals he had ordered sat untouched. After what she deemed suffi-cient penance, Elaine had gone over and sat with him. Evans was telling an off-color story, and Elaine was giggling away. They looked like two old drinking buddies. The blondes stared absently out over the dining room.

Though the dinner landscape of Manhattan had changed by the mid-eighties, and the "me" generation had come to the fore, perhaps the main reason Elaine's wasn't doing business was the state of the food. For a decade or two, Elaine's was impervious to bad reviews. Year after year, a slam from Zagat would ensure a full house for weeks. One food critic, I think it was James Beard, wrote early on in the restaurant's history that the fare at Elaine's was "wholesome." Elaine would repeat that one positive word over and over when people asked her to rate her restaurant's food. And, in one sense, the food was truly wholesome. Elaine never cut corners— this I knew right from the beginning of my time work-ing for her. Her veal came from the butcher next door at consid-erably more than what she would have paid a wholesaler; she bought mostly organic vegetables from a Long Island hippie veg-etable farmer years before organic farms were in vogue. She paid top price for everything. While I was setting up the bar in the af-ternoon, I'd watch as Elaine would settle up with the purveyors, pulling a wad of cash out of her big black handbag. Unfortunately for Elaine, a kitchen is rated not by the quality of the provisions going in but by how the prepared food comes out.

Despite her decades in business, Elaine's knowledge of restau-rant kitchens was suspect. In the eleven-plus years I worked at her restaurant, I remember actually seeing my boss in the kitchen maybe a dozen times. There could be a psychological footing to her reluctance. When Elaine was a little girl, she had rickets, a dis-ease that can result in bowleg, which she developed. Elaine once told me her mother was tremendously guilty over her malady.

Rare, rickets is caused by a deficiency of vitamin D and sunlight. Elaine's mother thought that the cause of rickets was malnutrition, and that she had somehow deprived her daughter of an adequate amount of food. Although I never heard Elaine complain about this, I knew her father had lost a business during the Depression, and for years afterward the Kaufman family had struggled just to put food on the table. To make up for what she perceived was her mistake, Mother Kaufman practically force-fed Elaine. For my boss, the inviting warmth of a family kitchen was replaced with an atmosphere of medical urgency.

But there was another reason for Elaine's unwillingness to enter the kitchen. For the first five or six years I worked for Elaine, her chef was an Argentinian man with a broiler-hot temper. I never met Alfredo Viazzi, Elaine's ex-beau, but it would be my guess that there were similarities between the two chefs in Elaine's life. Both at least had old-world attitudes in common when it came to running a kitchen. The South American ran his like a despot and would never admit to a mistake. More than once I saw waiters refuse customers who wanted to send back their orders for a variety of reasons. And they had plenty of reasons to send the orders back. One afternoon, I saw the chef slicing a roast beef into half-inch slabs, pounding and breading them, then passing them off as veal cutlets Parmesan. A customer who ordered one called a waiter over and asked if veal cutlet was supposed to bleed so much.

It was puzzling to me why my boss let her chef get away with what he did. In a business dominated by men, Elaine had been unbelievably successful—for years she ran what might have been the most famous restaurant on the planet. If there was a cop in her dining room, it was Elaine and not any of the waiters or male customers. She once told a police beat reporter for the *New York Post,* a guy whose hard-edged reputation was his currency, that he didn't have any balls. I personally saw her throw a dozen drunks

out all by herself. One night, with a few one-liners, she reduced
the comedian Alan King to the demeanor of a six-year-old who'd
just had his lunch swiped. Police escorted her out of the restaurant twice because of altercations with male customers. One arrest
landed her on the front page of the *Post*. But there was also a part
of Elaine, a part that every so often you'd see flash in her eyes,
that was a lonely little girl who was both scared of men and
wanted them. In my opinion, the two men in Elaine's life who
exploited that part the most happened to be chefs: Alfredo and the
Argentinian.

So when, night after night, the dinner specials would go un-
ordered, instead of blaming the chef, Elaine would fault the waiters for not talking the specials up. There was one story my pal
Brian told about a waiter they called Pio. On this night, Elaine
animatedly chastised Pio for not selling a special called "bollito
misto," a gray and soggy assembly of boiled meat and potatoes. As
Pio's luck would have it, right after Elaine's tirade, in came a table
of Swedes. Though the tourists spoke little English, they were
able to communicate to Pio that they would leave the ordering to
him. With Elaine within earshot at the bar, Pio began to shout a
most flattering description of the horrid boiled dish. The Swedes
had no idea what he was saying, or why he was talking so loudly,
but they smiled and nodded politely. Pio then delivered eleven
bollito mistos to the table, easily an Elaine's record. Later, after the
dishwasher had dumped most of the intact entrees into the
garbage can, the tourists frantically waved off Pio's suggestion of
coffee and dessert and implored him for the check, which they
paid hurriedly and in full.

Though Elaine could turn a blind eye, she was not by a long
shot naive. She knew her chef was killing her business. But it took
years, into the late eighties, and countless hours on the psychia-
trist's couch, for her to summon the courage to fire him. In the

meantime, the restaurant had become a sad caricature of its former self. The black-and-white photos of Elaine's heady, hip nights that hung on the walls mocked the empty tables below them. I remember one night looking at Elaine seated alone at table 4 surrounded by a customerless vacuum, and, despite the unfriendly relationship we had, felt enormous sympathy for her. In that moment I knew the restaurant was everything to her. It was her family, her love, her life.

Chapter Six

As TIME WENT BY for me at Elaine's, my boss stayed distant at best with me and at moments was downright surly. One night she admonished me for wearing my tie loosely around my collar. On another occasion, when I walked into work with a then-fashionable *Miami Vice* five o'clock shadow, I was met with such a snide remark about my grooming habits, it left a razor burn. Obviously, she was the boss, and if she wanted me buttoned up with a close shave, that was her prerogative. It was her delivery, however, just this side of utter disdain, that bothered me the most. I guess there was a part of me that was just a glutton for punishment—a bottom-rung low self-esteem that alcoholics learn to live with. But there was something behind Elaine's remarks—a kind of quiver in her voice, a way that her eyes glanced away when I looked into them—that made me begin to believe she didn't dislike me at all. She just didn't know how to tell me that.

I didn't have enough insight then, but now I know that her tough act was a way of cloaking her vulnerability around men. I remember one night Elaine was sitting at the bar with Chris Noth. That same night the Abbey Theatre was having a party in the back room, and Elaine pointed out the Irish actor Milo O'Shea to the *Law & Order* star. Noth didn't know who O'Shea was. "You wouldn't know a real actor if you fell over one," Elaine said to him. But my boss also told me about the time Marlon Brando came into the restaurant and all she could manage to say to him was a timid "hi." She had seen him on Broadway in *A Streetcar Named Desire* six times. That it took me a while to figure out how to get on Elaine's good side now baffles me. You certainly didn't have to be a psychologist to know where her allegiance lay.

Mario Puzo once told a magazine, I think it was *Vanity Fair,* that if Elaine had her way, "there wouldn't be any women in there." If you discount the short time in which Elaine Stritch was behind the bar, there have been, to my knowledge, only three women who have worked for Elaine in the forty-plus-year history of the restaurant.

One was a neighborhood girl named Katie O'Donnell. In the early seventies, Elaine hired Katie first as a day waitress and, when Katie became pregnant a little while later, for the cashier's job because it came with a chair. Pretty, with curly strawberry blond hair and bright green eyes, Katie was a prime target (before she was pregnant and after she gave birth) for the male heat-seeking missiles that frequented Elaine's bar throughout the seventies. But Katie had a fiery personality and was as tough as or even tougher than the boss—a trait that endeared her to Elaine. One night, a bar-rail Romeo made the mistake of putting his hand on Katie's bottom. The next thing the guy knew, he was looking up from the floor. A few nights later a regular customer came in with a pair of boxing gloves, which he presented to Katie to commemorate the right hand she'd hit the guy with. Those gloves hung behind the bar at Elaine's the whole time I worked there and probably still do.

The other two women were Mary, who worked as the daytime bartender before my time in the restaurant, and Diane, who would become Elaine's longtime manager.

Though Elaine surrounded herself with men, she didn't have any luck with them when it came to affairs of the heart. Despite her heft, she had her share of suitors. I remember one hopeful paramour who came in night after night and sat at the bar waiting for a chance to chat with Elaine. As I recall, he was a widower and worked as a waiter. He brought flowers and candy. But Elaine wouldn't give him the time, maybe because he was a waiter, or maybe because she was too frightened. You couldn't blame her for being scared of intimacy. It seemed any time she allowed a man to get close, she'd end up being hurt.

The whole affair began innocently enough. My bartending partner introduced Elaine to one of his old mates at the bar. Henry had once worked with Tommy as a waiter on the Cunard lines and was then employed as a manager of a restaurant at the Helmsley Palace Hotel. Elaine and Henry sat together that night in the bar area, on the bench that covered the radiator under the front window. After only a short conversation, they were engaged in a full and extended make-out session. Even Tommy, about as unflappable as a man could be, was a bit nonplussed by the rapid developments on the window seat. And things didn't slow down.

After only a couple of weeks of dating, on Christmas Eve of 1980, Henry asked Elaine to marry him. Elaine said yes and was determined to proceed with the ceremony right away. They took a cab that very afternoon, wending their way through the holiday traffic snarled by the snow, to City Hall. By four P.M., according to the newspapers, they had had their requisite blood tests but were told that law required them to wait twenty-four hours for the marriage license. Elaine wasn't about to wait. According to a story in *The New*

York Times, she called Peggy Cooper Davis, a regular customer of her restaurant and a criminal court judge. Mrs. Davis then called her husband, the city parks commissioner Gordon Davis, whose secretary called a friend in the city clerk's office. The woman in the city clerk's office called a political public relations woman she knew, who then tracked down a state supreme court justice by the name of Hortense Gabel, who happened to be in a beauty parlor getting her hair done for the holiday. Justice Gabel hurried home to sign a waiver, and the married-couple-to-be picked it up and rushed to the apartment of China Machado, a Eurasian model and fashion editor, where the ceremony was performed in front of what Elaine called "family and old friends—fifty or seventy-five or whatever."

One newspaper article called Elaine's husband "a wine connoisseur." Heavyset and balding, Henry resembled Robin Leach from *Lifestyles of the Rich and Famous.* He also embodied a television star's self-importance. It didn't take him long to start acting as if his marriage partnership with Elaine included free reign at his wife's restaurant. According to Tommy and Brian, each night Henry would park himself at table 4, wetting the end of his cigar in Louis XIII Grande, then gulping the cognac down. He also developed a penchant for sending very expensive bottles of wine to celebrities around the restaurant. He'd introduce himself by saying his name and adding Elaine's address: "Henry Ball, eleven fifty-five Park," said with as much pomposity as he could muster.

The bartenders and waiters couldn't believe the marriage lasted as long as it did, which was only a few months. But each bottle of wine the Englishman would send, each expensive cognac he'd guzzle, brought the union one step closer to dissolution. Henry's motives were made clear during the divorce proceedings. Although I don't know the terms of the settlement, I do know that whatever price Elaine had to pay (some say it was hefty), she was glad to be rid of him. At one point Elaine's attorney deposed all the employees. When it came Tommy's turn, the attorney couldn't believe that the bartender still worked at the restaurant, considering he was the person who'd set the whole debacle in motion.

I met Henry several times at meetings when he was still married to Elaine. She'd demanded that he go. But Henry couldn't seem to grasp the program's tenant of admitting powerlessness over alcohol, and from what I heard, he struggled with addiction for the rest of his life, a period of time that wasn't all that long. I don't know how Henry's failure to get sober affected Elaine's view of the program. I do know that the odds against any alcoholic getting and staying sober, in the program or not, are very long. I remember the night, years later, when a customer delivered the news to Elaine that Henry had died of a heart attack. Elaine told me to open a bottle of Cristal and pour for the bar, which I did. But her act was transparent. She was quiet most of that night and went home unusually early.

Though Elaine let her guard down with Henry, it went up again afterward. The Elaine I knew surrounded herself with tough guys; writers like Jim Harrison, a fullback of a man with a glass eye and an appetite for straight booze and red meat, and the sports novelist Dan Jenkins, a Texan with the same blistering sense of humor in person that he brought to the pages of *North Dallas Forty,* were among her favorites. One of the regulars who sat at Elaine's table all the time was a retired first-grade New York City detective named Wally Millard, who talked out of the side of his mouth and seemed as though he sprang from the imagination of Raymond Chandler. Another of her favorites was a news photographer named Mickey Brennan. Rough-edged, maudlin, but with an arid sense of humor, Brennan had all the attributes Elaine admired in a man. Though I didn't see him in a fight at Elaine's, his reputation was one of never backing down from a row. And sometimes he got more than he gave. Once, I remember, he had his arm in a sling after some altercation; on another occasion he came in sporting a black eye. Elaine always mothered him. She would pat his cheek, sit him at table 4, and make sure he had something to eat.

It was watching the attention my boss lavished on Micky that gave me the insight on how to gain Elaine's favor. But before I get to that, let me give you a bit of context:

With those who have never been there, there still exists a misconception about Elaine's restaurant that it is a modern-day Stork Club, where the men wear dinner jackets and silk scarves and the women wear cocktail dresses. I'll admit, there was a modicum of high tone to the place, a few dilettantes and a Park Avenue dowager or two who frequented the restaurant. There were also plenty of people with plenty of money who were regular customers. One of the odder Vanderbilts would often wander into the restaurant wearing a raincoat, dress shirt, and boxer shorts (to this day I believe the absence of his pants was due to an oversight and not some sexual inclination). But for the most part, Elaine's is a not a salon but a saloon.

For many years, until it yellowed and bowed, Elaine's front window was made out of plastic. Elaine had the Plexiglas installed after one disgruntled patron threw a garbage can through its glass predecessor—twice. I don't want you to get the wrong idea—Elaine's wasn't exactly a bucket of blood. But it had its rumbling moments, and the characters involved in the tussles gave the joint its own take on the age-old rite of barroom brawling. One night, I watched Al Pacino go after Elliott Kastner, a movie producer and onetime business partner with Marlon Brando. I don't know what started it, but Kastner had a reputation for not having the quickest checkbook in Hollywood, which could have been the cause of Pacino's ire. Elaine, quick as a jungle cat, jumped between the two before any punches were exchanged.

Maybe the oddest fight I witnessed at Elaine's was also punchless. Nevertheless, the scrum has a secure place in Elaine's lore. With tinted eyeglasses held up by an elfish nose, platform shoes, and a six-ties British Invasion hairpiece, the Wall of Sound music producer Phil Spector looked to me like a combination of Austin Powers and a ferret. Usually he'd have a couple of vodkas and cranberry juice, but never more than two. Given the reserved amount of booze he ingested, I have no idea what elevated him to the elliptical orbit he always seemed to be in. At least one newspaper article reported that Spector was diabetic, and that even small amounts of alcohol had a severe effect on him. Some nights he'd wander in all alone, but most times he came with a makeshift entourage. For a few weeks he was friendly with Jack Maple. At the time, Maple was a lieutenant in the transit police department, but he would go on to be something of a legendary crime fighter. With an appearance more like that of a boulevardier than that of a transit cop, Maple wore a homburg hat and spats and drank champagne. Another of Spector's provisional acolytes was Charles Kipps, a onetime songwriter and record pro-ducer who collaborated on Van McCoy's "The Hustle," perhaps the only song ever written in which the words of the title consti-tuted all of the lyrics.

When he was in New York City, Spector lived in an apartment in the Waldorf Towers. Kipps told me he'd call his secretary in Los Angeles to have her call room service at the Waldorf for him. Some nights, Spector would slide behind the piano at Elaine's and, be-cause of his mysterious inebriation, barely be able to play "I Want to Hold Your Hand" or some other old Beatles tune. Other times he'd tinkle "God Bless America" and sing along decidedly off-key. As far as the bartenders and waiters were concerned, Spector could be as weird as he wanted. I'd hand him his bar tab, sometimes as lit-tle as twenty bucks, he'd pay with a platinum American Express card and usually leave a tip of five hundred dollars or more. When Spector walked in the door, your night was made.

In the other corner this night was the newspaper columnist

Steve Dunleavy, a saloon legend. Tommy often told the story about a drunken Dunleavy sliding into a slowly moving Second Avenue bus in front of Elaine's one snowy night. Thinking someone had sucker punched him, the scribe wheeled and punched the trolley right in the movie advertisement. Elaine's was usually one of the final stops on the Dunleavy nightly tour. I served the guy countless early morning drinks, yet each time he'd come in, he would reintroduce himself, having no recollection of me or the night before: "Steve Dunleavy, mate," he'd say in an Aussie bark.

On the night of the altercation, Spector was sitting at a back table with Kipps, Maple, and Shannah Goldner, a producer for *A Current Affair,* a television tabloid news show. A well-oiled Dunleavy decided to stop to say hello to Ms. Goldner, with whom he had worked on the show. Actually, according to his own account, later published in one of his columns, Dunleavy was trying borrow a couple of bucks from Shannah to pay for his bar tab or, more likely, to hang the tab and use the money for a taxi to the next saloon. As Dunleavy pulled out a chair, Spector yelled: "Off!" The command took him by surprise, and uncharacteristically, given his Aussie cheekiness, Dunleavy slunk away. But when Spector left the table to use the washroom, Dunleavy again sidled up to Shannah. He later wrote that, when Spector returned to the table, he told the newsman he had a gun, knew karate, and would "kick his ass."

By his own admission, Dunleavy would sink many levels in order to acquire a loan. But now it was his manhood being questioned. The Aussie jumped unsteadily to his feet and assumed a Marquis of Queensberry pose, with his fists curled upward. Turning to Maple, Spector said, "Take care of this guy." Maple chuckled, took a sip from his champagne flute, then leaned back on his chair with his hands behind his head. Left to fend for himself, Spector brought out his best Bruce Lee stance and began to circle Dunleavy. The circling actually took up most of the altercation.

There were a couple of flails, most of which took place over the head of a short waiter who tried to play peacemaker. It was hard to say who ran out of gas first. But Maple ended up deciding the fight by throwing his napkin onto the floor, declaring a draw.

The denouement came two weeks later, when, at about nine o'clock on a slow evening, the front door, like that in a cowboy saloon, flew open and Spector appeared, flanked by two African-American fellows the size of linebackers. "Where's Dunleavy?" he bellowed.

"You're about six hours early," I replied.

There were also plenty of fights with a lot more substance. One that comes to mind involved a pepper mill that was swung like a baseball bat. But I certainly didn't feel uncomfortable being in a volatile environment. I grew up with three older brothers, each a volcano in temperament. My mother would hang pictures, images of the Blessed Virgin her favorite, over the punch holes in the walls of our house. So perhaps the way I first started to curry my boss's favor was not odd at all.

It wasn't as though I had a grudge against all Wall Streeters. In general, they're a funny and generous group. Partly, Tommy bought his big house in New Jersey because of their largesse. Still, there is a specific type of financier, usually young and flush with success, who is among the most obnoxious of human beings. One night I remember one of these types sneering to one of his buddies that he made more in two weeks than his father, a cop, made in a year. Later that night, Tommy had him by the tie, trying to pull him over the bar after the guy stiffed us on a hundred-dollar tab. On another night, in 1987, after the stock market had crashed, a couple of young brokers were at the bar crying in their beers. One of them, no older than twenty-five, said to me: "Life as you know it will never be the same." Yeah, I'm going to go home and lock myself in, I said to myself as I marked a couple of extra drinks on his check for good measure. But the night of my induction into Elaine's fight club, no amount of padding the check was going to defuse my anger.

He was already drunk when I came to work that night. I didn't even get the chance to hang my house keys on the side of the register when he started yelling at me: "Hey, hey. I need a drink here." Out of all the ways to have gotten me to make you a drink, that might have been the worst. I noticed that the bar in front of him was a wreck; there were wet cigarette butts and piles of ashes. He saw me looking and swiped the whole mess to the side with the back of his hand, then said, "You gonna clean this up, bub, or what?" The bar was packed, and the waiters were lined up around the corner. My roommate Randy happened to be in that night on a first date. I walked down to the service end of the bar in a slow burn.

Even still, going from a slow burn behind the bar to a fight on the sidewalk in front of the restaurant is quite a jump. And as angry as I was back then, for me to get physical was out of character. But as the guy spat out a couple more orders at me, the last one ending with the word *asshole,* something within me snapped. I dropped the drink I was making into the garbage can and flew out from behind the bar. "Let's go," I said, with a quick tilt of my head as I barreled passed him toward the door. To be honest, I was a little surprised when he jumped quickly off his stool to follow.

Lest you think me some kind of scar-faced street fighter, allow me a short highlight reel of my fight career: In grammar school a neighborhood bully by the name of Mike Ross shook me down for my lunch money for years. In high school I was beaten to an unrecognizable pulp in a local saloon by a guy who was six inches shorter than I was. And in my early twenties, I was carted out of a saloon fight on a stretcher after coming to the defense of the reputation of a girl I barely knew.

But this particular night, I was as angry as I've ever been. There was absolutely no chance of me backing out. Plus, unlike in the saloon fight, I was sober, which, I came to find, was a distinct advantage. He swung first, wildly, and missed. He was still off balance when I delivered a straight right hand that landed directly on his nose. The punch was so good it almost made up for all those encounters with Mike Ross. My Wall Streeter went down like a bowling pin.

Inside, Randy threw a twenty on the bar and guided his girl out the door. But as he passed, he gave me a quick thumbs-up. All of a sudden, out of nowhere it seemed, an ambulance appeared, lights flashing. I don't know who called, but I do know that the Wall Streeter was cognizant enough to ask the EMS workers to radio the police. Next thing you know, I was marched out of the restaurant in handcuffs. He had pressed charges. I ended up spending most of my shift in the holding pen of the Nineteenth Precinct.

Now, in most establishments, my actions would have resulted in termination. Not so in Elaine's. In fact, when I was released later that night and returned to the bar, I received a round of applause. Although I don't remember whether Elaine was applauding, I do remember the slightest smile on her face.

Though my fight outside the restaurant was partly a way of showing Elaine my tough guy within, it was also an indication of the mounting frustration I was feeling in my job and in my life. Most of my time at Elaine's is documented in journals written in tired script in the quiet early-morning hours after my shifts. Individually, the entries tell nutty stories of Elaine's, and the travails over the love du jour of my life. But read together, they form a sad, frustrated tableau—months and months of feeling miserable and trapped. I don't mean to sound whiny. I was truly grateful to be sober and healthy. It's just that, perhaps because I was sober, I could feel the years slipping by.

The quandary was, my participation in the program did nothing to alter my career path. In my new sobriety, I quickly found myself back behind the bar but now miserable in the task. For me then, working the bar was a tug-of-war I couldn't win. Though the sober, healthy part of me was repulsed by what alcohol did to the alcoholics who crowded in for drinks, there always was a little voice urging me jump over to their side and join what the voice called "the fun."

And I felt like I deserved more than a job as a bartender. At meetings, I often heard people with years of sobriety say how their lives were better than their wildest dreams. I knew this was true. I saw friends who were street junkies get better, find and hold jobs, gain promotions, and then get married. I had a friend who got sober, then had to go to jail for a pending drug charge. He managed to stay clean for two long years in a place that wasn't, by any stretch, a country club. When he came out, he started up again in a career as a sports television cameraman. He went to meetings, shared the ups and downs of his life, stayed sober even through his son's suicide, and eventually things began to break his way. A few years removed from a drug addiction and jail term, my pal was now a sports TV producer. He also found love in the meetings. I'd see him step out of the back of a limousine in front of Elaine's. Surrounded by his big-shot TV buddies, sportswriters, and baseball stars, he'd sit at a table just across from the bar smoking a cigar.

I never resented my pal. I liked him a great deal and truly believed he deserved everything he achieved. But I couldn't help thinking: *What about me?* I'd put in the effort. I went to meetings just about every day. Like Frank did for me, I sponsored newcomers, including a twenty-year-old trust-fund kid who had a drinking and drugging story that would make your hair stand on end. I made amends to friends and family. I repaid most of my debts.

Though my feelings about the Catholic Church have always been conflicted—thanks, no doubt, to my experience in a Catholic school run by old, frustrated, and angry nuns—I gave my childhood faith the benefit of the doubt by going back to Mass regularly. But all of this piety came with expectations. I wanted a payoff. I wanted my dreams to come true.

In the program there was a collective mind-set that allowed for, even encouraged, dream chasing—no matter how long the odds against the dream being chased. In my early years of sobriety, I chased a bunch of them, and each seemed to run out of air quicker than a day-old birthday balloon. I took a stand-up comedy class at the New School taught by a very funny man who was a chain smoker and suffering from not-so-funny emphysema. You could hear him wheezing and whistling through his nose all the way down the hall. The course's final consisted of performing an eight-minute routine at an open-mike night in a Greenwich Village comedy club. Those eight minutes were longest of my life. It was the first time I was ever under a spotlight. I couldn't see. At one point, I was sure the audience had left. The only sound was an occasional clink of ice in a glass. It must not have been the most popular of venues for comics, because the emcee asked me back for the following week. Not at gunpoint, I told him.

Next, I took a beginners' class at HB Studio, a well-known acting school that, although it counted Al Pacino and Robert De Niro among its graduates, was a low-priced factory that turned out hundreds and hundreds of "actors" a year—a workforce that kept New York City's restaurants fully staffed. I had headshots taken and fudged a résumé. Just before I took the job at Elaine's, I worked for a short time as a chauffeur. My boss was friendly with a real-estate lawyer named Jay Weiss and his then-wife, Kathleen Turner. On a few occasions I drove the movie star to the Long Wharf Theatre in New Haven, Connecticut, where she starred in *Camille*. One day I was driving her to a lunch appointment at Cipriani's in the Sherry-Netherland Hotel on Fifty-ninth Street. Madison Avenue was jammed with traffic, and we were running late. Ms. Turner decided to hop out around Fifty-eighth Street, right in front of the construction of a new building. It was lunchtime; the girders of the building were lined with hard hats, their lunch boxes at their sides. One of them recognized the star and whistled, which prompted a cascade of wolf whistles from the legion of workmen. Instead of being embarrassed or angry, Ms. Turner turned it on, swinging her hips like Jessica Rabbit. The construction guys gave her a standing ovation from the girders.

At that time, I was living in an apartment over a drugstore on the corner of Eighty-sixth Street and Lexington Avenue with my roommate Randy. (Randy and I worked behind a couple of the same bars. One was a country-and-western-themed chicken and rib joint, and the other was the Lone Star Café, a pretty well-known country and rock club.) Randy's mom was a successful Broadway actress. She hooked me up with her agent, who arranged an audition for the soap *All My Children*. The character I was to play was a New York City detective. Perfect. I'd just pretend to be dear old Dad. When I arrived for my meeting with the casting director, her office was empty. I sat down to wait. I began to rise when the casting director entered the room, but she waved me down. I read from the sheet of dialogue called, in the business, "sides." She told me I was fine, to go to wardrobe to be fitted. As I stood up, her eyes followed my six-foot-three height. She slowly shook her head. The scene I was to be in was with the star of the soap, the petite Susan Lucci. "Your head wouldn't even be in the frame," the casting director said. My acting career spanned all of two years and included roles in two plays that were held in a theater so broken down the seats would collapse under the weight of the audience members.

Though my actual acting experience was limited, for the first time in my life I fell in love with the written word. I read dozens and dozens of plays and knew by heart scenes and speeches from Eugene O'Neill, Arthur Miller, and David Mamet. O'Neill's Jamie Tyrone spoke to my very soul. After about six months, I left HB and enrolled in an acting class held in a studio above Carnegie Hall. Soon I began to write little scenes and monologues that I would perform in class. Most of the time I tried to write humor, and several times I even got a laugh from my fellow acting students. But with the disappointments piling up, I wouldn't dare let myself dream of becoming a writer.

I started to believe that I had boxed myself into a corner. Except for a short stint when I sold accident and health insurance to poor people in the Bronx, a policy that had coverage so limited the joke was you had to get gored by a bull in Times Square at midnight to collect, I'd been a bartender for as long as I could remember, so long that a future without bartending seemed impossible to me.

In the program there is saying: "Don't quit five minutes before the miracle happens." The slogan is both a childish way to keep addicts occupied until they're well enough to want to get better and something of a self-fulfilling prophecy. If you do stay clean and sober, the miracle has already happened. For me, the miracle had happened. Considering my car accidents alone, it really was a miracle that I survived my early drinking life. I should have been more grateful.

Chapter Seven

VERY SOON AFTER I STARTED at Elaine's, I tended bar for the wedding reception of Pete Hamill and his wife, the writer Fukiko Aoki, which was held in the back room of the restaurant. I remember being very excited about working the party because Pete Hamill was then my favorite writer. Actually, to say he was *my favorite writer* is a little misleading because it implies that I read a lot, which, back then, I did not, and that I read a lot of Pete's books, which I also did not, at least not right away. The reason I knew about Pete's writing was that he wrote a newspaper column, which I did read because it was not too far from the sports section and the horse page. But, in retrospect, I think it was more what Pete represented than what he wrote that made him my favorite. Years before I read *A Drinking Life,* I saw Pete as something of a hard-drinking New York City hero.

There's a black-and-white photo of him in the restaurant that captured that sentiment. In the picture, Pete, with glass in hand and loosened tie, leans through his cigarette smoke into the conversation. He also seems oblivious of whoever took the picture.

That image of Pete was what I drank to become. "Drinking was part of being a man," he wrote in *A Drinking Life*. "Drinking was an integral part of sexuality, easing entrance to its dark and mysterious treasure chambers. Drinking was the sacramental binder of friendships. Drinking was the reward for work, the fuel of celebration, the consolidation for death or defeat. Drinking gave me strength, confidence, ease, laughter."

That was all I asked of my drinking.

My drinking, however, would end up disappointing me on just about every count.

In 1969, I was a freshman in high school in Pearl River, a town only twenty-five miles but a universe away from Second Avenue and Elaine's, where Pete Hamill and Shirley MacLaine then sat at a back table. Already six foot one and a hundred and fifteen pounds after a full breakfast, I was a mop handle. What's more, I had carrot-red hair, freckles, and a pair of ears better suited for the Serengeti Plain. My father compared them to an image a bit closer to home. He said I looked like a taxicab with its doors open.

As the youngest of four boys, I was attached to my mother for longer than I imagine I should have been. Although I don't remember being paraded in sailor suits and tiny blue blazers, the photos of me in those outfits poked fun from the mantel in the living room. I do remember being with Mom as she hunted through the racks at Alexander's in the mall a few weeks before my freshman year started. With some residual emotional pain, I also distinctly remember wearing a pair of red plaid slacks to school. Mom dressed me like a couch.

But the social apartness I felt and the discomfort I experienced had little to do with what I wore. I don't know whether my insecurity was more than the average teenage anxiety. Though, as my brother Tommy is fond of saying, my family was not Bill Cosby and the Huxtables. For the most part, I would say, my childhood was a happy one. My parents, especially my mom, gave me plenty of love, and although my dad wasn't around all that much because of his job, he was reliable if emotionally reserved.

I was less of an athlete than my brothers; maybe that had something to do with my feeling less than. Frankie and Tommy (no slight here against Eugene—as the oldest, he was just off my radar screen) were legendary high school athletes. Okay. Maybe *legendary* is a bit of an exaggeration. But they were good. And I, with a see-through build, was just okay. When my freshman football coach first saw my bird legs sticking out from a pair of shorts, I remember him remarking that I possessed no visible means of support.

I could probably go on at length guessing about how my insecurities formed, but what is far more important is how they went away.

When two of the best players on my freshman basketball team asked me to hang out with them, my immediate thoughts were that they were going to tie me to a telephone pole, pull my pants down, and run away. But even that humiliation would have been an improvement to my social standing. One of the guys was Joe Caso, the other, John Sisler. Those aren't really their names, and to be truthful, they're not even clever disguises, but they serve the purpose of keeping unwarranted blame away from them. Joe Caso was my age, fourteen, but looked like he was twenty-nine. He had a five o'clock shadow at lunch. He was tall, broad-shouldered, and from one of those families that have towns in Italy named after them. Of average build, with tousled blond hair, John was a wise-cracker, a clever mimic, and he had my nasal speech down perfectly. I remember specifically once saying the word *novelty* to John, but it came something like "na-*VULT*-ee." When I saw him from then on, he barraged me with "na-*VULT*-ee," sounding—I risk showing my age here—much like the old television comic

Georgie Jessel. Most of the time, I kept my mouth shut around John for fear of giving him more ammunition.

That night, the three of us walked together to Williams Street, a side street in downtown Pearl River. My hometown included all of four traffic lights. The main drag, called Central Avenue, was lined with sidewalks and quaint shops and an inordinate number of saloons, one of which I will tell you about in a bit. Joe and John wore navy peacoats, their collars up against the chill. I wore a corduroy coat with a hood that zipped open flat against my back that my father bought at Mel's Army & Navy store. Triangles of light from streetlights illuminated Williams Street. There was a red glow in the middle of the block from a neon sign. I didn't ask where we were headed, afraid Joe and John would suddenly realize they had invited me and change their minds. Standing across from the neon, we pooled about eight bucks in singles and change. Joe stuffed the money in his jeans, crossed the street, and entered Peckman's liquor store.

There were a few anxious minutes, during which John and I shuffled in our Chuck Taylor sneakers, not the good ones we wore on the basketball court but older ones that had cracks in the circle where Chuck's name was in script. Finally, Joe emerged with a plain brown paper bag containing three pints of an orange substance called "Tango," premixed vodka and Tang, with water. Much later, when telling this tale, which I have done often in front of rooms filled with recovering alcoholics, I would joke that NASA came up with the concoction in case Dean Martin was ever sent into space. Off we went to a secluded spot near Burns Glass, which was housed in a red-painted shed with an alley on one side, and twisted open the hooch.

Although the stuff smelled like a combination of rotten oranges and formaldehyde, the offensive odor did not dissuade me from lifting the small, flat glass bottle to my lips and tipping it back. Something tremendous happened in the milliseconds it took for the syrupy liquid to travel from mouth to stomach—something truly miraculous. Incredibly, I didn't feel so skinny anymore. And I didn't hear the ocean in my oversize ears when the wind blew. But perhaps the most amazing realization was yet to come.

Emboldened by the Tango, we bought three tickets to *Midnight Cowboy*, an X-rated film playing in the Central Theater. Actually, Joe bought the "18 and over" tickets and received not so much as a second look from the cashier. Although I squirmed in my seat a couple of times during the film, especially in the flashback scenes where the grandmother of Joe Buck (Jon Voight) dressed him up in cowboy suits (this brought back memories of shopping trips to Alexander's with Mom), the seminal moment for me came after the film was over. Right there, in front of the Central Theater in downtown Pearl River, in front of the two best and most popular players on the Pearl River Pirates freshman basketball team, and bolstered by the Tango, I did a perfect imitation of Enrico Salvatore "Ratzo" Rizzo. It was as if someone had snuck into my body, ripped out my personality, and, for a moment, replaced it with Robin Williams's or, more appropriate to the era, Rich Little's.

After a moment of silent shock at my outburst, my new friends howled. I remember, for a second, being taken by surprise by both what had come forth from my mouth and their reaction. Like a new imitation-leather jacket, my budding personality was still stiff and uncomfortable, but I loved the way it looked on me. We walked home that night talking about sex with girls and sports. I would never be the same. I had found the magic.

Now, about that saloon: One night, a couple of years into my time at Elaine's, the actor Bryan Brown was having a drink when I asked him if he'd like to join me behind the bar. It was just a few months after the release of *Cocktail,* the bartender movie in which he played Tom Cruise's mentor. In trying to re-create his bottle-throwing, fruit-juggling character, Brown broke at least two glasses and would've crashed a bottle of Absolut into the ice if I hadn't snagged it out of midair. But a crowd did gather at the service end to watch his act. So as not to disappoint, I did a couple of my basic moves: throwing ice behind my back into the glass and bouncing the mixing glass off my bicep. When I started to juggle three rocks glasses, even Brown was impressed. "How'd you learn that?" he asked.

From the moment I walked into the Commodore Bar & Grill, all the way back in my sophomore year in high school, I'd wanted to be a bartender. That first evening in a barroom is still imprinted in my memory. With my friend Gerard, I concocted a plan to bluff my way into the twilit darkness of the Commodore, which sat in the middle of Pearl River's neon-light section. The success of the elaborate scheme mostly depended on my speaking in a deep voice. I nervously climbed onto the wooden captain's chair barstool. I remember vividly the pageant before me: the muted sound of Bobby Darin wafting from the jukebox, the gay clink of glasses and ice, the witty banter of the patrons, the backlit amber liquors splayed in a wondrous array behind the bar, the gumdrop maraschino cherries in stemmed cocktail glasses held at jaunty angles by manicured fingers. To tell you the truth, it was more like a couple of fat guys staring up at a game show on a TV, and what I remember most was the sour smell of stale beer. Still, as I watched the man in the butcher's apron orchestrate the festivities from behind the bar, something within me stirred. The feeling was powerful. Intoxicating.

Just over two years later, right after I graduated from high school, I took my first bartending job, at a place called Chuck's Pub in a strip mall in Pearl River. Mom and Dad weren't overly pleased with my vocational choice. My mom held fast to a fantasy that I would go to Notre Dame or, at the very least, Fordham University, the Bronx version of Notre Dame. Her faith in me was both undying and unrealistic given the fact that I had graduated from Pearl River High School with a straight-C average.

My father had started looking in the other direction when it came to my decisions. Maybe he was worn out by the antics of my three older brothers. He did have his hands full with them. More likely my father's reluctance had to do with the job he'd just retired from. For years he had run a detective squad in what was then the busiest police precinct in the world, a job that nearly killed him. It wasn't a bullet that almost got him, though. It was an ulcerated esophagus and additional stress-related maladies from seeing others with bullet holes and knife wounds. Now and then he would weigh in on my life, using one of his well-worn phrases: "You're spinning your wheels," he'd say about my bartending. When I started to come home at five or six in the morning, he gave me a few not under my roofs, but he knew—and I certainly knew—there was nothing he could do to stop me.

When I first moved out of my parents' house and in with a high school pal to a garden apartment a few towns away, my mother stood crying on the front steps while my dad sat in the living room reading the paper. He was right in not getting overly emotional about my move. Two months later I was back in my old bedroom, the one still adorned with baseball pennants, with fresh bed linen that my mother had changed regularly when I was away.

There is an obvious incongruity in being a bartender at eighteen. As with a teenage prostitute, the lifestyle just doesn't fit the face. While working at Chuck's, I bought a lime green leisure suit, which I accessorized with a pair of pearl-colored loafers. Years ago, the comedian Red Buttons did a television commercial for a retirement community just outside of Boca Raton wearing a similar outfit. While most of the college-age customers were listening to "It's Only Rock 'n' Roll" by the Rolling Stones, or "Everyday People" by Sly & the Family Stone, I knew by heart the words to Sinatra's "In the Wee Small Hours" and "From This Moment On." One of my first cars was a 1965 Lincoln Continental, with "suicide doors" that opened like those to a cabinet. The Lincoln was about as long as a cruise ship.

My customers at Chuck's were a stay-at-home lot, guys and girls who, mostly for financial reasons, didn't go away to college like a legion of suburban kids did. And most of them had already signed contracts with their futures. The guys worked in local gas stations, for building contractors and roofers, or as landscapers. They would find their way into the bar dressed in greasy overalls, or crummy jeans, with dirty fingernails like black half-moons, a job-related consequence that would persist for the rest of their lives. Whatever extra money they had was poured into the cream of the golden era of Detroit. Any given night in Chuck's thin parking lot there was an array of Corvette Sting Rays of late 1960s vintage, 1964–65 Ford Mustangs, and '69 Oldsmobile Cutlass Supremes. There were '68 GTOs, or "goats" as they were inexplicably called in greaser lingo, 1970 Ford Torinos, and one 1966 Chevy Nova, a car that, when it rolled off the assembly line, was a nondescript box on wheels but when muscled up and tricked out drew the envy of the most jaded greaser. Unfortunately, like many of the others, this particular Nova ended up wrapped around a telephone pole.

In the sixties, more kids died on the roads across America in drunk driving accidents than died in the war in Vietnam. Route 303 was a four-lane highway that ran from New Jersey to New York State. Teens from Jersey who were too young for that state's twenty-one-to-drink laws would pile in their cars and head north on 303. It would be on the trip back that their cars would wander across the medianless highway into the oncoming traffic. It seemed every week there was a late-night head-on collision, and plenty of times the Jaws of Life were anything but.

It was a spring night in 1973 on that road, and behind the wheel, that I experienced my first alcoholic blackout. What I didn't know then was that an alcohol-induced blackout is an indication of alcoholism. Only alcoholics have them. That night should have been a sign the size of a billboard indicating I was heading down a dangerous highway. Instead, I gave it about as much thought as a flat tire.

The Lincoln had died of natural causes, and I was driving a Volkswagen. Ownership of the VW Beetle was actually a partnership between my mom and me. Mom was a sport. She didn't even mind when I switched the little round knob on the gearshift with a Budweiser tap. I was off from Chuck's that night and at a house party thrown by some kids who went to nearby Dominican College. Most of the crowd was from the city, Catholic guys and girls from the Bronx and Upper Manhattan. The party featured something called "bash." A midnight playground concoction, bash was mixed in one of those twenty-gallon plastic garbage cans (a new one, I'm hoping). The recipe called for three quarts of gin, three quarts of vodka, three quarts of rum, and a bottle of tequila. To that lethal combination were added ten cans of Hi-C fruit drink, ice, and sliced peaches, pears, and lemon and orange wedges. I don't know how many plastic cups of this crap I drank, but I do remember thinking that the brew didn't have a big enough kick.

That was the last thing I remembered. When I came out of the blackout, I was behind the wheel of the VW on Route 303 in the midst of a three-hundred-sixty-degree spin. At one point, the Bug was pointed in the right direction, in the correct lane, but traveling backward. Car horns wailed, then faded, like in a dream. Headlights flashed at odd angles. Back in the land of consciousness, it took me a few moments to realize what was happening. By some miracle, I was able to get the car under control. I pulled over to the side of the road and lit up a cigarette. A guy came running up and knocked on my window. "You okay?" he asked, having witnessed my whole fortunate ballet. Fine, I said in a tone that made it perfectly clear he should mind his own business.

From that moment on, the price of my alcohol consumption increased dramatically. From that night on, I never knew when my drinking would cause a blackout. There were nights when I poured incredible amounts down my throat and stayed semiconscious. On other nights just a six-pack had me in a black hole.

Still, I was willing to pay that price to keep alive my romance with drinking and saloons. After closing time, I would sit at the bar alone with Sinatra on the jukebox. In the bar mirror, I'd admire my pose—glass of scotch and a cigarette in the same hand, smoke curling to the ceiling. Sometimes, after my shift, I'd visit a bartender I knew who worked down the block from Chuck's. We'd sit and drink until five or six in the morning. I can still conjure the pain in my eyes that the morning sun would cause when I'd walk out of the joint. Nothing I've since experienced is like that feeling. The closest thing I can liken it to is when you open your eyes inside a tanning bed. I liked the darkness better. The movie of my life was backlit by neon signs.

On the way home in those early hours, I'd drive past bus stops filled with commuters, or see freshly scrubbed faces behind the steering wheels of cars, and think, What a bunch of stooges. There they were, rushing off to work, while I was headed home for a nap, a pocket filled with tip money, the last Marlboro of the some two packs I'd smoked that night dangling from my lower lip. In the driveway of my parents' house, I'd stab the butt out in the ashtray of the car and then stagger inside. There my father would be sitting at the kitchen table, his tie folded into his shirt, a bowl of cornflakes in front of him. He never said a word, but his disappointment was loud and clear.

Back then, I didn't care what he thought. I was having too much fun to care.

Obviously, in my early saloon years, I wasn't giving my future a whole lot of thought—a primary reason why I ended up working at Elaine's in my early-thirties. Back in those nearsighted days, I spent my afternoons at Aqueduct or Belmont Park, or just sleeping off the late night before. What with the leisure suits, my scotch on the rocks, and my days at the track, I was eighteen going on forty-five. The truth was, I was a scared little kid in white shoes. If somebody had said "Boo," I would have jumped right out of them. Nowhere was my extended adolescence more evident than in my relationships. I stayed a virgin until I was nineteen—no easy feat, considering I was working behind a bar and it was the early 1970s, an era when even the guys in the high school audiovisual clubs got laid.

Opportunities were ample, though. One that I distinctly remember had almost jet-black hair and a body like that of a high school baton twirler. I took her out once for drinks and then, a week later, for dinner. We had a make-out session in her car after the meal. I worked my hand down her back and fumbled with the clasp of her bra. She put her hand right on my zipper, and I almost jumped out the car window. The next day she called me at Chuck's to tell me that she didn't want to go out with me anymore. She didn't say why, but a few days later she came into the bar with a girlfriend. I overheard them talking about me. "He's too slow," said my ex-date.

Perhaps the most embarrassing moment on my road to sexual conquest was a trip to New York City with some pals to pick up a hooker. The ringleader of our gang was a savvy hooker frequenter named Dave Walcott. A steady customer at Chuck's, Walcott had bug eyes and fiery red hair that stuck up as though some unseen hand was pulling it from his scalp. He drank screwdrivers in one gulp, ice and all, and followed them up with a shout: "I get my orange juice in the morning! How 'bout some vodka the next time?" I can't remember which of his cars we used—he had an array. I do remember Walcott had it floored all the way down the Palisades Parkway, over the George Washington Bridge, and down the West Side Highway into the bowels of forbidden Gotham.

The neighborhood around the Port Authority Bus Terminal was, in the early 1970s, one of the highest-crime-rate areas in Manhattan. I knew this for a fact because at the time my brother worked there as an undercover New York City policeman. Crime was so rampant, he and his anticrime unit pals played a game called "pick the perp," where they would guess which of the square's denizens would commit the next crime. Robberies, stabbings, drug deals, even murders were commonplace. When I offered this information up from the backseat of the car, Walcott shouted my words down as if I were some kind of alarmist.

Walcott pulled the car up right in front of an-about-to-be-condemned hotel on Eighth Avenue, directly across from the bus terminal. Next to the hotel was a saloon with a buzzing neon sign that read TE MINAL BAR. It certainly was. Inside, there were a couple of skinny, toothless old guys with bony hands wrapped around those old-fashioned-style straight highball glasses. Cigarette smoke curled to the ceiling. The bartender had a black patch over one eye. Walcott asked for a screwdriver "in a clean glass." The bartender did not, out of his one eye, see the humor. He dropped one large cube of ice in the jelly glass and about a finger of vodka. I ordered a bottle of beer, since it came in its own glass. Before I was halfway through my beer, Walcott had drained his cocktail and without comment dragged me out the door. The rest of our pals were outside, doing the sidewalk shuffle: hands in the pockets of their jeans and casting furtive glances at the surrounding sights.

With Walcott leading the way, we entered the hotel and climbed the crooked stairs. On the third or fourth landing, as I remember, we were met by the management: a large black man with a wide, flat face. Walcott, our spokesman, stated our intentions. "Two at a time," we were told, which by quick calculation meant, with five in our party, that someone would have to go third, and alone—that would be me.

The surroundings of the waiting room were less than genteel. There was a ratty old couch, which, no doubt, had accommodated all manner of ass and circumstance, and a few folding chairs. Although it was probably just a few minutes, the wait seemed interminable. Walcott was first back, fixing his belt as he walked in, his lips pursed in a satisfied smile. Finally, I was led down a hall and through a doorway with a stained white sheet for a door. Inside was a huge black woman, dressed only in a brassiere and pair of panties so big you could have jumped safely out of an airplane with them. She told me to strip down to my underpants. I had about the same level of excitement that I'd had at my first school physical. She swiped off my Fruit of the Looms. I was so skinny and so white, the veins in my legs were visible; my apparatus looked like it belonged to an eight-year-old.

Her touch was like new sandpaper, her expression was dreamy, but not in a sexual way. Instead she looked like someone trying to figure out what she was going to have for dinner. From out on the street, I could hear the noises of the city: sirens speeding by, the blast of a horn, the shout of an angry drunk. It didn't take long for my courtesan to lose heart. She put me on an imaginary clock almost immediately: "Somethin' best start happenin' soon," she said in her version of pillow talk. I didn't have a chance.

Happy to be dressed and through the unfulfilled ordeal, I stumbled down the crooked staircase wearing a crooked smile to mask any trace of failure on my face. As I stepped out of the hotel doorway and into the night, parked right in front of me was a dark green and white NYPD cruiser with the bubble gum machine lights flashing. The cop on the passenger side, his eyes shining in merriment, started the chant. Maybe it was just a guess on his part, or maybe he saw through my façade. Either way, his partner caught on and joined in and added two sets of two short beeps of the horn after each line. Then several street guys, maybe muggers on a break, added their voices to the conga chorus. By the time I climbed into the backseat of the car, it sounded like the whole of Times Square was singing along: "He couldn't get a hard-on, beep, beep. Beep, beep. He couldn't get a hard-on, beep, beep. Beep, beep . . ."

My embarrassment lasted only as long as it took us to drive back to Chuck's and for me to get to the bar. Alcohol erased all my uncomfortable feelings, and much of the painful memory. After just a beer or two, I was laughing about the road trip and rearranging the details. But the truth was, I was an absolute mess when it came to sex and sexuality. It was no wonder when you consider I learned the birds and the bees from a Catholic priest in St. Margaret's grammar school who explained the sex act in nautical terms. By the time I was in high school, I was frightened by what were undoubtedly normal attractions to both girls and boys. Then I took a swig of Tango, followed by a beer truck filled with Budweiser. My just postpubescent alcohol intake erected an emotional detour. And I was never confident in my sexuality again. What a lovely excuse to drink.

After about a year, I was fired from Chuck's for giving away the store. All you had to do was be nice to me, or leave a dollar tip, and I would let you drink for free. The reason I lasted a year, I guess, was that Chuck liked me. My enthusiasm for my job made it hard not to like me. That is, until Chuck's accountant had a word with him. In no uncertain terms, the accountant told my boss to fire me as soon as possible.

I wasn't out of work for long. I found a job just down the block from Chuck's, in a place called the Black Bull Pub, which was filled with long hair, unemployment checks, and hippie girls, one of whom especially drew my attention.

Chris thought everything was funny. She had one of those laughs that made you laugh, a belly-shaking giggle that belonged to an old fat guy and not a slim twenty-year-old with long chestnut hair. Though her sense of humor beckoned me, it was her butt, accentuated by the tight hip-huggers she wore, that made me pant.

I took her to Monticello racetrack in upstate New York, where we won a couple hundred, and then went out to a restaurant where we told everyone within earshot that we had just been married so they would send us drinks. They did, and we both got wobbly drunk. A couple nights later, we met at the pub, got drunk, and, at some point, engaged in a sloppy make-out session but eventually parted ways in a two-pronged stagger. The following week Chris called and invited me over. She said she wasn't feeling well, she wanted to stay in. I walked across town to her house.

She answered the door dressed in pajamas with little angels on them. Her hair was pulled back in a ponytail. She didn't look very sick. The whole house smelled of burnt popcorn. She had made Jiffy Pop but had forgotten to shake it. We sat close to each other on her couch. She told me her parents weren't home, information that made me nervously excited. I realize now that she had orchestrated things so we could be together without drinking. It was the first time up to that point that I had been in such a situation sober. We ended up in the sack, in her bedroom. I don't really remember how that transpired, what happened between the couch and the bed, but I do remember laughing a lot. The act itself was fast but sweet. We held each other for a few minutes, until she pulled her knees up and playfully kicked me out onto the floor. On the way home, I took a shortcut through a field and howled there like a backyard dog at the moon.

As my drinking continued, I seemed to have less and less control of my destiny. I made several attempts at a college career, first at a nearby community college, then at St. Thomas Aquinas, a four-year Catholic school. At the former, I took police science classes in a halfhearted attempt to follow family tradition. But I missed more classes than I attended, frittering away my time in the cafeteria playing hearts or spades. By the time I enrolled in St. Thomas, my hangovers made morning classes out of the question. I had trouble showing up even in the afternoon, and when I did, the nuns who taught had dispositions far too sunny for my sour stomach and pounding head. I didn't know it then, but what I thought was my own decision to tend bar for a living was a fate dictated by my alcoholism.

I was fired from the Black Bull Pub for coming in on my night off drunk and disrupting a dominoes game that was being played for a considerable amount of money. I'm not really sure what happened to my relationship with Chris—she became just another shrug in an alcoholic's life. I also shrugged off my second bar job termination, and moved on to what I thought was a better situation. A real restaurant—decorated with fake coats of arms, fake suits of armor, and a fake fireplace, but owned by a couple of genuine Englishmen. It was here that I first met Liverpool Tommy, who back then worked not as a bartender but as the restaurant's manager.

The Tommy I remember from those days contrasted starkly with the dissident with whom I would work behind Elaine's bar. In tailor-made suits replete with pocket hankies, Tommy then seemed to me elegant and worldly. Often, near the end of the night, clusters of customers would gather around him as, wineglass in one hand, a cigarette in the other, he would regale them with tales of the Cunard lines. Tommy had a network of English scallywags who had worked alongside him on the high seas (one was Richard Dawson, who went on to have a television acting career and later was the host of *Family Feud*), and each story he told of them was more audacious than the last. But though Tommy would be the first link in the chain of events that would ultimately lead me to Elaine's, the relationship at the English pub that had the most impact on me was with my fellow bartender.

With the exception of a bent nose, which actually furthered the look, Joe was smooth and pretty in a fifties-movie-gangster kind of way. He wore his bottle-black hair slicked back on the sides and had a wisecracking style that, like his candy-apple-red Coupe de Ville convertible, was somehow both obnoxious and very, very cool.

The bar crowd at the English pub was mostly Rockland County mommies and daddies playing weekend hipsters, and on Friday and Saturday nights, with a five-piece band performing, the place hummed. It was on those nights that I honed my craft. Joe called himself "Mr. Speed," and he was a pretty fast bar mechanic. But I was just as fast a study and in no time made Mr. Speed looked like he was in reverse. Along with the regular bar and restaurant business, the pub had a very busy catering room. I worked scores and scores of weddings, bar mitzvahs, and anniversary parties. Most of them were package deals that included open bars. I could easily handle a party of two hundred by myself. Though I had an awkward appearance, so tall I had to duck under the overhanging glasses above the bar, I found I had terrific hand-eye coordination. In no time, I was juggling four oranges, lemons, even small rocks glasses. When Joe and I worked together behind the main bar, I would take care of the service station by myself.

On busy nights, both the dining room and the catering hall would be filled. Sometimes there'd be as many as a dozen waitresses lined up for drinks. I would get into a zone: a blur of hands, bottles, glasses, and ice. Customers were often awed by my act. I had this little routine with the shaker, where I'd put the ice, mixer, and booze in and slap the metal cup over the mixing glass. With one hand, I'd shake it next to my ear. Then I'd pretend that I'd lost my grip and let it slide down my back. I'd catch it with my other, hidden hand. When there was a break in the action, I'd light a cigarette, lean against the backbar, and, as I looked out over a restaurant filled with people holding my drinks, feel like Alexander surveying his kingdom. I had so much enthusiasm for tending bar then, a keenness that was all but lost by the time I stepped behind Elaine's bar.

Though, for sure, speed and dexterity are important attributes in the art of attending the bar, they are by far not the only assets a good barman should possess. At the English pub, I'd find that I still had lots to learn and that Joe was the perfect Fagin. All the basic moves he knew, of course: what everybody drank, the repertoire of jokes and stories, even handshakes. He created nicknames for customers, and the customers loved it even when Joe was about as far off the mark as you could get. One fellow, who talked with an Alabama drawl, Joe christened "the Best in the West." At the end of the night, our tip cup would overflow.

One of the ways Joe made us money was by being very lenient when it came to buying back drinks for customers. Years later at Elaine's, Tommy's approach was the exact opposite. In an era when it seemed everyone paid with a credit card, Tommy ran up the check as high as he could and worked the percentages. Though the rule varies widely with buybacks, a house rule in a local establishment might be every third or fourth round is on the house. With Joe, however, if you were a good tipper, the ratio was almost reversed. With my dismissal from Chuck's still fresh in my thoughts, one night I asked Joe how he got away with giving away so many drinks. The trick, he said, was to keep the house's liquor costs down. That very night, he showed me how to do just that.

In the after-hours quiet of the restaurant, the cheap whiskey flowing though the funnel sounded as loud as an old sink emptying. Joe tiptoed around, a Parliament cigarette clenched in his teeth—like a cross between the Grinch Who Stole Christmas and FDR. He had this ritual of renaming the brands: Seagram's 7 became Seagram's 6, Johnnie Walker Red became Johnnie Walker Pink, Old Grand-Dad became Old Grand-Ma, and so on. We kept two bottles of Dewar's White Label real, for us, the bar staff. But sometimes mistakes were made. Perhaps I just couldn't stop myself. The name of the bar scotch was Crawford's, and several times Joe came into work the next day with a ferocious hangover and accused me of "Crawfordtizing" him. Perhaps I did. For Joe had opened a door to a dark side in me I never knew existed.

One thing I didn't learn from Joe was how to drink, and I drank way too much behind the bar, first trying to keep up with my mentor, then setting my own standard. We had a kind of silent pact that we wouldn't start until midnight. Still, a four A.M. closing time left plenty of room to get plastered. The ritual would begin with Joe suggesting "a pop." I would pack two highball glasses with ice, then pour the *real* Dewar's over it until the scotch almost filled the glasses. My nights at the English pub marked a dramatic change in my drinking. No longer was I interested in kids' stuff like draft beer and garbage can bashes; along with working in a grown-up place, I was drinking in a grown-up way. It was during this time I realized that, once I picked up the first drink, I never wanted the night to end.

Though I didn't have a good handle on my limit, I certainly knew when Joe had had too much. I'd be talking to him and his eyes would start to flutter, fixing on a point over my head. One night, after we had drunk well over a bottle of scotch behind the bar, Joe drove his Caddy off Route 303 going home. He missed work for a couple of nights. I stopped by his apartment to see how he was doing. His head was wrapped in a bandage; the Caddy was a lot worse off. But a couple of nights later, he was back at work and laughing about the whole episode.

After a couple of years at the English pub, I took a bar job in Bergen County, New Jersey, at a restaurant called the Talk of the Town. Several times Joe came down to visit, and every once in while, I'd drop by to see him at the pub. But saloon friendships disappear quicker than cigarette smoke, and soon Joe became another shrug in my life.

The bar crowd at the Talk of the Town was a whole lot younger and hipper than the one at the pub. It was the mid-1970s, and along with Brooklyn, Bergen County was the epicenter of the disco craze. Though Gloria Gaynor and Donna Summer dominated the jukebox, I held fast to Sinatra and late-night solitary drinking. I also picked up a nasty habit of trying to kill my hangovers with a vodka or two in the morning. The only thing that would alleviate the pain was a drink. But that morning drink would, more times than not, set in motion a daylong drunk. Once I started, I couldn't stop.

I remember one morning when I began drinking at a place not too far from where I worked. I was the first customer; the bartender was still cutting lemons and stocking the beer refrigerators. I drank through lunchtime and into the afternoon. I barely remember the happy hour crowd filling the bar. I don't remember getting behind the wheel of my car early that evening. Later, in the hospital, I was told that I ran a stop sign and plowed broadside into a station wagon. Both cars were demolished. A man, his wife, and their teenage daughter occupied the other car, and by some miracle none of them had so much as a scratch. I remember coming to in the emergency room. I'd gone clear through the windshield and practically scalped myself. Behind the doctor, who was unsteadily holding a needle and catgut thread, and backlit by the operating room light, was my father. He had received word of the accident and hurried down to the hospital. His long, tough cop face was tight with anger and frustration. But his eyes were helpless with tears of compassion as he watched the doctor, who, my father later said, smelled of scotch, sew me up like a softball.

After a week or so of convalescence, I went back to work behind the bar. Like Joe had, I wore a big bandage on my head and tried to joke off the head dressing, and the scar underneath. I'm just a lousy driver, I quipped. But no one was laughing. And when I poured myself a drink behind the bar, the looks on the faces of my good customers turned from concern to bewilderment. A few nights later I missed my shift because I'd drunk that day away trying to beat a hangover. My boss fired me the next day. That evening I sat in yet another bar. Though far from sober, I couldn't get drunk. The booze was no longer working. I remember that night looking in the backbar mirror and being repulsed at what looked back at me. Inside my head, a shouting match of self-hatred was taking place, one voice louder than the other.

Maybe it was all those prayer candles my mother lit that helped me see that the guy I was looking at in the mirror needed help. I have no other explanation, really, for why one moment I was sitting at a bar consumed with self-loathing and a little while later I was signing myself into the detoxification unit of a mental health clinic. I can't for the life of me recall how I even knew about the detox. I do know that my decision to go to into detox came not a moment too soon. Even though I would drink again, my action that night stopped the free fall. There were frequent moments during this time of my life when I wanted to die more than I wanted to live. For a blackout drinker with a driver's license, that's a wish easily fulfilled. Word of my hospital visit also made its way to Elaine's. To this day I don't know if it was Tommy or Brian who told Frank about my detox stay. But somehow Frank found out. It was then he decided to slip a program brochure in my back pocket and see what happened.

Chapter Eight

PINPOINTING THE EXACT MOMENT your life path shifts is a pretty exact science for an alcoholic. Putting the Tango to my lips and finding the program pamphlet in my pocket were my two biggest plot twists—at least in the first half of my life. But the way my career at Elaine's changed was far more subtle—subtle when you take into consideration the abrupt language of the saloon.

It was about eight o'clock and a weekday evening and the year was 1988. Elaine was doing the checks, and there were only three or four tables up front. But the bar was halfway decent, almost full. A waiter, I think it was Carlo, but I'm not sure, came up to the service end and ordered a bottle of Italian red. It was a simple mistake on my part; I pulled a Barolo, which sold for about thirty bucks, instead of a fifty-dollar bottle of Brunnello, which Carlo had ordered. Elaine looked up from the checks, her glasses pushed up on her forehead, and with a hiss said, "What the fuck's wrong with you? Pay attention." Now Elaine's colorful use of language was never an issue for me. I'd been in the saloon business so long nothing shocked me. I even worked a couple of nights in a bar that had a live parrot who owned a sailor's vocabulary. I was also fully aware that Elaine's command of the language was part of her personality, that she was truly egalitarian when it came to her malediction—I'd heard her take the same tone with movie star and bar mook alike. But what got me, what pushed me over the edge, what would be the about-face in our relationship, was she said it loud enough for the bar customers to hear.

It wasn't the first time Elaine had embarrassed me in front of people, either. She did it a lot. I don't even know if she realized she did it so much. But this time was different. I was sick and tired of my life, my job, not getting the cash and prizes I thought all of my friends in the program were receiving, and especially I was sick of my boss talking to me like I was a dog. I began to burn, slowly at first, but then my head got so hot I couldn't get the words I was about to say straight. Screw it, I said to myself. Whatever comes out comes out. She wants to fire me, let her fire me. "That's the last time you're going to talk to me that way," I said, standing right in front of her, my voice crackling like a wood fire. "If I'm stuck working in this joint, our relationship is going to change."

Okay, I guess it played a little louder in my head than it does on the page. But the real evidence of the importance of that moment is how my life proceeded afterward. Of course, things didn't change all at once. Elaine's immediate reaction was hardly any reaction at all. She looked at me quizzically, as if she wasn't altogether sure she'd heard me right, then went back to totaling dinner checks. But later that night, as she sat at table 4, I caught her looking at me. Though her expression was still more one of bewilderment than one of respect, I had captured her attention. Frank, who had lived about a dozen lives, once did a stint in the Coast Guard. Sometimes he would throw advice my way in the shape of a life preserver. Just the slightest variation in course, he would say, greatly changes your destination. I bumped into Elaine that night and altered my heading forever.

It wasn't like Elaine waved her arm Vanna White style at the book jackets on her wall and said, "You, too, could be a writer, Brian." In fact, I don't ever remember Elaine championing writing as a career choice for anyone. If the truth be told, the woman who ran the most celebrated literary gathering spot of the late twentieth century wasn't all that impressed by writers—at least by my lights. She saw them as lacksters and children, and Elaine's as more of a rumpus room for them than a salon. No, Elaine wouldn't have been an advocate of a writing life for me. But what she did begin to share with me was advice grounded in reality, counsel that was a century old, experience that had seeped through tenement walls on the Lower East Side and, later, through the blocks of the apartment houses on the Grand Concourse or Ocean Parkway or, in Elaine's case, in Jackson Heights, Queens. Simply put, Elaine became for me what she was for a legion of writers. She became my Jewish mother—and the most influential friend and teacher I've ever had.

Of course, the relationship between me and my boss wouldn't have gotten off the ground had it not been for the appearance of something the restaurant had been missing for quite some time: customers. In 1988 a feature story about Elaine's in the *Daily News* proclaimed: "The once queen of the New York night is dead." It was a Mark Twain moment if there ever was one. That year the restaurant celebrated its twenty-fifth anniversary, and my boss decided to throw a party. She hired Bobby Zarem to do all the arrangements.

Rotund and bald on top, Bobby had hair wings on the sides of his head that, if the wind was blowing, made him look like Krusty the Clown. He could be neurotic, and in moments under pressure—which could mean anything from orchestrating the opening of a big-budget movie to deciding whether or not he should butter the Italian bread—he'd twirl his locks and let go with a stream of expletives. Yet in the next minute his voice would be as soothing as Southern cooking. A story about Bobby's neurosis found its way to London. A neophyte publicist from that city had accompanied a film producer client to New York to meet with Bobby. When the client took sick, the publicist rang Bobby anyway. According to *The New York Observer,* the conversation went like this: "What's your name?" asked Zarem. "Matthew Freud," the publicist said. "Any relation?" Bobby said. "Great-grandson," he replied. "My shrink's been out of town for two weeks," Zarem said. "I need to see you at once." The London publicist, who really was the great-grandson of Sigmund Freud, then went over to Bobby's office, where they chatted for two hours about Bobby's relationship with his mother.

Growing up in Savannah, Georgia, Bobby led a genteel existence. His father had a successful wholesale shoe business. Having tacked together information from Elaine and Bobby himself, I imagined Bobby's childhood as one of riding horses and piano lessons. He has two brothers. Danny, the oldest, ran the exclusive men's clothing store where Elaine shopped for staff Christmas gifts and Harvey became the head of plastic surgery at the UCLA medical school.

Bobby once told me that his desire to become a press agent was born when he saw Burt Lancaster and Tony Curtis in *Sweet Smell of Success.* His first PR job was a short stint with Columbia Artists Management, after which he joined up with the show business giant Rogers & Cowan. There it was said his pitch letters became legend. One began: "This movie reeks of Oscar." He credits Elaine for encouraging him to go out on his own. In one news story, he even said that Elaine wanted to back him financially. The story didn't say whether or not Elaine did back Bobby, and I never heard anything about it. But, with or without Elaine's pocketbook, it didn't take Bobby long to climb to the top of his profession, the second oldest profession, one might say. In the late seventies, *Newsweek* magazine dubbed him "superflack."

When his neurotic side showed, Elaine would call him "the big baby." In the winter, he'd wear a ski parka over an ill-fitting sports jacket that, eventually, would find itself rolled in a ball and stuffed under his chair. He wore khakis and Reebok sneakers. He was in the joint just about every night, and when he wasn't, he'd call Elaine on the pay phone to check in. When he did call, Elaine would pull up a chair under the phones and read to him the columns out of the next day's *New York Post,* which would hit the newsstand next door about midnight.

Aside from their Oedipal connection, my boss and Bobby's relationship was mutually beneficial. Just as Walter Winchell needed the Stork Club, Bobby needed Elaine's for its cache—it was a place where he could hold forth and be seen. Elaine welcomed the press Bobby generated for her. Plenty of people thought she paid Bobby for the publicity, and in a barter sense she did—Bobby's dinner checks were promotional. But, to my knowledge, there was no cash involved in their business together. At root, the financial part of their relationship mattered little. Bobby and Elaine were good for each other, and even during the barren years, Bobby brought some needed color and celebrity to the joint. But even Bobby's connections couldn't seem to stem the downward spiral Elaine's was experiencing in the mid-eighties. It was during that time that plenty of Elaine's supposed friends turned their backs on her. And, despite Bobby's best efforts, items about Elaine's in the papers most times had a sarcastic, funereal tone. Those who turned their backs and wrote her off, however, didn't know my boss.

Bobby had a vivid imagination when it came to promotion. For the opening of *Tommy,* the movie rock opera by the Who, Bobby persuaded New York City to let him use a midtown subway station for a black-tie dinner. For the movie musical *The Wiz,* he took over the pool room terrace in the Four Seasons restaurant. There the band he'd hired played from inside the pool (without amplification, I would imagine). Maybe Bobby's biggest coup was taking over the PR for a low-budget documentary about a little-known Austrian bodybuilder. For the opening of the film *Pumping Iron,* Bobby arranged a small luncheon at Elaine's and assembled a guest list that rivaled opening night at the Metropolitan Opera. In attendance were George Plimpton, Paulette Goddard, Andy Warhol, and Jackie Onassis, none of whom, I would presume, would have then known Arnold Schwarzenegger if he'd bench-pressed them. But a wire-service photograph of the Arnold with Jackie O made papers all over the country, and Schwarzenegger stepped that day into the realm of popular culture, from which he has yet to depart.

But Bobby wasn't bulletproof. He had his share of flops. One movie opening party at Elaine's he had an actor in Roman soldier's garb ride through the front door. The horse wasn't in the joint more than thirty seconds before it did its business near the buffet table. The movie didn't fare any better.

For the twenty-fifth anniversary of Elaine's, though, Bobby was not taking any chances. He sent out some twenty-five hundred invitations. It was overkill dictated by Elaine's slump. Of the twenty-five hundred invited guests, one estimate had it that two thousand showed up. By six-thirty, the time the invitation said the party started, a suggestion that if one is to be chic is never followed, the restaurant was as packed as a rush-hour 6 train. The crowd spouted from the door onto the sidewalk, even into the street. And this wasn't a flavor-of-the-month crowd. There were no Wall

Streeters, no garmentos, no *Bonfire of the Vanities* "social X-rays." Gathered was the real merchandise: the heads of every major motion picture studio, the editors of just about every major magazine. There were movie stars and literary stars and sports stars. But above them all, at least by my estimation, were the stars of Elaine's best era, the sixties and seventies, including Steve Rubell, Carl Bernstein, Joan Didion, Paloma Picasso, Bianca Jagger, Tony Hendra, Brooke Shields, Halston, Terry Southern, Nora Ephron, Robert Altman, Tommy Tune, Ahmet Ertegun, Sidney Lumet, Sydney Pollack, the playwright John Guare, and even Raquel Welch, who, at fifty, might not have been able to stop traffic, but she could slow it to a crawl.

Without a doubt, however, the best-looking woman in the place that night was aflame in a red dress that flared at the knees like a tango dancer's. (The artist Joe Eula captured her perfectly in a poster for the party; however, he made a small mistake. In big block letters he painted ELAINE'S CELABRATION. Eula told people who asked: "Italians would pronounce it that way." Elaine laughed it off. "It's perfect," she said with a deep chuckle.) Elaine's hair was luxurious thick, black waves, styled by Sabo, the peculiar Romanian hairdresser. (The husbands of all Sabo's customers were sure he was gay. What they didn't know didn't hurt them.) But Elaine's most radiant feature that night was her eyes, which, even behind the thick lenses of black-framed glasses, shone like French-polished mahogany. They also glimmered, at times, with tears of gratefulness. Elaine cried with the regularity of a comet. To see her eyes watery was a moment that is imprinted in my memory.

Though the night was nearly magical, it wouldn't have been Elaine's without at least one dustup. To mix religious metaphors, Jackie Mason's career had just pulled a Lazarus. His one-man show on Broadway was a huge hit, and he was in the restaurant almost every night after it. Although I didn't know too much about their history, my boss had to have liked Mason, because she let him get away with not spending a lot of money. Though he'd come in with as many as ten people, his parties rarely ordered anything to eat. They didn't even drink that much. Mason himself would order "tea in a glass," an old Jewish custom that didn't sit that well with Elaine Kaufman. Still, for some reason, maybe out of ancestral deference, Elaine put up with the comic.

The night of the anniversary party several local TV reporters were camped on the sidewalk outside the restaurant. One of them interviewed Mason. During the course of the interview, the comic was asked what he thought of Elaine's food. Mason said something to the effect of "Are you joking? I wouldn't eat here on a bet." Elaine knew, of course, that it was Mason's nature, or his act, to be abrasive. And had he softened his remark with a disclaimer that he was joking, Elaine might have let it pass. That same night Jerzy Kosinski told a reporter: "You don't make it as long as Elaine has by serving good food. You serve good people." But it wasn't Mason's wont to turn a phrase; he was just looking for the laugh at Elaine's expense. That was a mistake.

The reporter happened to work for the station that Elaine watched most evenings before getting ready for work, and she was watching when the station aired the Mason interview on the next evening's newscast. I don't know how Mason found out that Elaine saw the interview. All I know is that the comic was conspicuously absent from the restaurant for a few nights. Then, by messenger, a letter was delivered. Jackie Mason's apology was written in white ink on black stationery. The handwriting was an ornate loop, and practically flawless, like that of a Benedictine monk. It was two pages long. Elaine hardly glanced at it. Instead, she took a thumbtack and stabbed it to a bulletin board that hung behind the cashier's station at the end of the bar. The letter stayed there for weeks. Months. Elaine never, that I heard, said one word about it. And I never saw Jackie Mason in the restaurant again.

But Mason's attempt to get a laugh at Elaine's expense was the exception that night. The outpouring of affection, the sheer number of people who came to help her celebrate, moved my boss in a way I had never seen before. At one point, I looked over at her seated at table 4. Customers new and old swarmed around her. On a face that had for me held only simpering expressions, a sweet little smile was affixed. I knew she was perfectly happy.

In the years following the anniversary party, and no doubt partly as a result of the publicity the party generated, business at Elaine's steadily gained momentum. As it did, I saw a distinct change in my boss. Some of the change was purely cosmetic. For years Elaine had a dressmaker from whom she would buy her outfits. The couturier might have been cutting edge at some point in her career, but by the time I started at Elaine's, she seemed to have run out of ideas. The smocklike dresses Elaine wore had balloon and silver lightning bolt patterns. Though far from threadbare, they had the sheen of being dry-cleaned once too often. It wasn't that Elaine couldn't afford new dresses. She certainly could. With business slow, she just didn't give her attire that much thought. But as the business grew, a new wardrobe emerged. And although Elaine still favored the rather garish look of a recent Lotto winner the dresses echoed her newfound vibrancy.

But Elaine also made more foundational changes. By then I knew her well enough to know how much courage it took for her to get rid of the South American chef. I also knew, when she took me into her confidence about her decision, that event marked a huge step forward in our relationship. I remember coming into work the night before Elaine let the chef go. She was practically white with fear. She had one cigarette in her mouth, another in the ashtray. She told me she had had an extra session with her shrink that afternoon and was going back the next morning. It was the first time she'd talked to me about her therapy, and her candor was disarming. I said something brilliantly supportive like "It will all work out," and she nodded with her chin tucked to her chest like a six-year-old getting the first-day-of-school-is-going-to-be-fun speech from her father.

Though Elaine might have been an emotional wreck about firing the chef, in replacing him she was steel-cold business. To help find someone to run the kitchen, she called several well-known and successful restaurateurs, including Drew Nieporent, Robert De Niro's partner in the Tribeca Grill. The chef Nieporent suggested, however, was far too expensive. Elaine's is a relatively small restaurant, with a capacity of less than one hundred and fifty. There just aren't enough seats to support a six-figure-salary chef. Finally, Elaine decided on a Culinary School graduate; her thinking was that she would catch someone on the way up.

Peter Dulligan improved the food and presentation dramatically. For years, the silverware in the place looked like it had once belonged to a frat house—there wasn't a matching fork and spoon in the drawer. After Dulligan arrived, Elaine bought beautiful oversize platters and cutlery. One afternoon when I'd come in to set up, she was at the end of the bar looking at tables and chairs in restaurant supply catalogs. She told me her dream was to redo the whole place and pointed out pictures of several of the styles she liked. She dipped her hand in her pocket and pulled out a rubber-banded wad of cash, a couple of credit cards, and some Lotto tickets. She slid out one of the Lotto tickets and laid it on the bar next to the catalog. "This is what I'll do with the winnings," she said, tapping the picture of one of the more ornate styles of chairs. It wasn't like Elaine couldn't afford to buy the chairs without the help of a Lotto windfall. As a businesswoman, she just knew it was far too foolish an investment.

Elaine's comeback may have been completed in the summer of 1992. From then presidential candidate Bill Clinton's unscripted prenomination stroll from Macy's to Madison Square Garden to his acceptance speech at the Democratic National Convention on the steamy night of July 16, the joint was "lousy with Democrats," as the gossip columnist Joanna Molloy said to me at the bar—and this despite the fact that New York City picked the week of the Democratic National Convention to repave Second Avenue. Limousines headed for Elaine's had to park blocks away. But instead of impeding business, all it did was create a futuristic scene right outside the restaurant.

The night of the nomination, the temperature climbed well into the nineties. Out in front of the restaurant, city workers, more than earning their double overtime, wore galvanized yellow suits with full hoods and plastic face visors. A gargantuan contraption that looked like a huge praying mantis with its legs spread sprayed tar across the width of the avenue—the steam off the fresh-cooked pitch was as thick as London fog. At one point that evening, as I was working the busy bar, something outside Elaine's front window drew my attention. I watched as the figure strode through the tar smoke: a giant wearing a leather jacket with a cigar the size of a rolling pin between his fingers. The guys in the yellow space suits knew right away who it was; their rubber-gloved hands pointed at him in recognition. The Terminator acknowledged them with purposeful nod.

Inside, he sat with his wife, Maria Shriver, who was covering the convention as a reporter for NBC. Her husband wasn't yet a politician, not even a full-blooded Republican. I believe Ann Richards, the former governor of Texas, a longtime Elaine's customer and chairwoman of the convention, was sitting with them. Elaine made her way over to their table. It had been fifteen years since Bobby Zarem had arranged the picture of Schwarzenegger with Jackie Onassis in Elaine's. In those fifteen years, Arnold had become the highest paid actor in Hollywood: $12 million a picture, with a slice of the profits and say in production. Elaine's fortunes had not had the same celestial arc. I remember giggling at the physical differences between Schwarzenegger and Elaine. It was hard to imagine they were from the same species. But that night I would have bet my tip cup that the biggest muscle at the table belonged to my boss. I could practically hear her heart beat from behind the bar—even in the din of the busy restaurant.

There were a few times that I remember when Elaine herself seemed to doubt a comeback. At the end of those nights, she would look at the numbers of the minuscule take and mumble, "Oh, shit." But the next night around nine o'clock, she would make her entrance with her coat barely clinging to her shoulders and flowing behind her like the cape of a mad queen. Once inside the restaurant, she'd shrug the garment off, and Jack, or Carlo, or one of the other waiters would deftly catch it before it hit the floor. She would will the business back, her expression read. As I glanced at her sitting with Schwarzenegger that night, the restaurant humming around her, I knew she had done exactly that.

Chapter Nine

E LAINE STARTED TO CALL ME "Bri" and began to share some of the gossip she gathered from her travels around the dining room. One night she called me down to the end of the bar and told me that the writer wife of a well-known journalist was "schnockered" in the back and telling everybody about the unfortunate brevity of her husband's phallus; another time my boss whispered that the girlfriend of a regular was in the ladies' room stall with a first baseman who frequented the place.

As I've already mentioned, Elaine's restaurant has always been known as a men's club (still more on this later). Of Elaine's closest relationships among customers, almost all of them were men, many of them writers, and most of them married. This dynamic provided my boss with an enormous wealth of marital information, all of it one-sided, and all of it entertaining. And, no matter how damning the evidence to the contrary, Elaine always took the man's side. There was one writer who lived in the neighborhood who would come in late at night with his basset hound. Walking the dog, of course, was pretense to get to Elaine's and have a couple of snorts. Invariably, as the hour grew small and the basset hound was snoring under the table, the phone would ring. You could practically set your watch by it. Elaine would wave to me to pick it up, and I'd have to swear to the irate wife of the writer that, no, we hadn't seen her husband that night. As I'd hang up the phone, Elaine would issue a deep chuckle and acknowledge my act with a little nod.

Though my relationship with Elaine began to improve, on slow nights, while I was tending bar and Elaine was doing the checks, there would be long, languorous stretches when both of us struggled to find some interest we shared. There was always the business to talk about, and with business improving, there was plenty of material. But the truth was, we were completely mismatched. I was a suburban kid, while she was as New York City as a pushcart vendor. I was Irish Catholic, she was a nonpracticing Jew. I was tall and skinny, she was short and fat. Among her friends, she counted artists, actors, and ballet dancers. My friends played softball and went to Jets games. Although Elaine had a working knowledge of the program from Frank and several of her customers who ended up having to put the plug in the jug, it was against her nature as a saloonkeeper to be overly supportive of an organization whose basic tenet was sobriety. It wasn't that she was antiprogram; she just didn't want it to catch on in her saloon any more than it already had.

As far as her personal life, Elaine was very guarded in the beginning of our relationship. There were a few instances early on when she would talk of her childhood, like when she told me that she got in trouble at Evander Childs High School for reading the gossip columns in the *Daily News* under her desk. But for the most part, she kept her more intimate information under wraps—literally. An image of Elaine sitting at the cashier's station with her arms folded tight to her bosom comes to mind. She'd sit that way for what seemed like hours, the pose interrupted only when she needed to add to one of the checks.

Now and then, Elaine would tell a story, and I'd listen intently, especially getting a kick out of the names she stitched into her tales without the slightest intention to impress. For some reason, one night we got on the topic of California. I think Elaine told me she was there only once, when she visited Cass Elliot. For a guy my age, the mention of Cass Elliot would have been a satisfying ending to the narrative. But Elaine's whole point was that the iconic singer from the Mamas and the Papas had a watercooler in her kitchen—a fact that just tickled Elaine to death.

But the paradox was, as much as I enjoyed listening to Elaine, I was that much and more unhappy in my job. In some ways, Elaine's budding friendship with me fostered the feeling of being trapped—the downside of having a Jewish mother. It was safe and warm in her good graces, nestled, metaphorically, within her ample bosom. But it also became claustrophobic. This push-pull caused an ongoing debate in my head—a place where, as is said often in the program, I had no right spending any time.

In the late 1980s, Elaine gave me a promotion of sorts to the cashier's job. Partly, she needed to fill the position, and partly the job was meant as an appeasement. Elaine wanted me to be happy working for her.

As cashier, I wasn't on my feet for the whole shift, and my new position gave me dominion over the waiters. But I didn't make nearly the money that I had behind the bar—as Elaine's business increased, so did the bar tips. I could've made twice the money, though, and still been intolerable. I was every bit as surly to the waiters as Elaine at her worst. I was angry at what I viewed as my predicament. Though I didn't know this then, my predicament wasn't that I was trapped in a job I hated. I wasn't bitter because my dreams had fallen through. My unhappiness stemmed from something that was much more overwhelming but was then so subtle the fully formed thought never entered my consciousness. On the shelves behind me were every imaginable brand and bottle, and softly they called. Right in front of me, night after night, the art of drinking booze was displayed in its most exciting, romantic form, or at least that's how my alcoholic mind interpreted it.

At Elaine's I was soberly unhappy, like Gatsby at his parties. Sure, there were displays of the ugly side of alcohol consumption. One night the wife of a legendary New York City detective puked right on the bar in front of me, and other drunken customers made fools of themselves on a nightly basis. But the bar I worked behind was on the East Side of Manhattan. It was the big leagues, and it attracted professional drinkers who could hold their liquor and tell jokes or make passes at girls until the lights came up at closing time.

About two o'clock one morning, a group of regulars—a couple of bar owners and a Wall Street guy or two—were gathered at the corner of the bar. They had been drinking for hours. I remember thinking they looked as though they had just showered, shaved, and changed at the health club. Frank, my sponsor, would always say that the percentage of alcoholics in a bar increases dramatically as the night wears on. At midnight it might be that 50 percent of the people there are alcoholic, and at two in the morning it's 95 percent, he'd say. But so what, I thought as I saw them laugh and sparkle at the end of the bar. I wanted to be able to drink like they did, and I was angry as hell that I couldn't. The healthiest thing I could have done was to move on, take any job outside the bar business. There was far too much temptation in a saloon. Instead, for reasons that are rooted in my alcoholism, I stayed rooted in my misery and blamed everyone in Elaine's for my unhappiness.

One night I picked up the house phone and didn't recognize Bobby Zarem's voice on the line. He reacted with a string of obscenities. Sometime later that same night he walked into the restaurant with Kirk and Anne Douglas, but I wouldn't have cared if he were with Mother Teresa. I met him just inside the doorway. "You ever talk like that to me again and I'll knock you on your fat ass," I said as I poked Bobby in the chest. The Douglases made a beeline for Elaine, who was sitting a few tables away. Bobby was stunned and tried to sidestep around me. As he moved, so did I, blocking his way. I don't know whether I would have punched him, but I sure as heck was mad enough to. I could feel the heat in my face. I must have been the color of a neon sign. A waiter named Michael, who had watched the scene play out from the wings, came and ushered Bobby past me.

Maybe Bobby did deserve the bracing, but my anger wasn't about him. The fact was, I was surrounded by booze and I wasn't allowed to drink it. Not the healthiest predicament for a sober alcoholic to be in.

Chapter Ten

In looking back, I don't know how I justified my altercation with Bobby—or my overall behavior at Elaine's—at my meetings. Frank still acted as my sponsor, although I was calling him infrequently. And though Frank's counsel was sound in many ways, he wasn't the best person to talk to about anger—and especially anger in Elaine's. He'd been involved in some legendary brawls in the restaurant himself—one when he hid in the basement to evade the cops who came to arrest him. For me, it was almost as though I was living a double life: sober and serene in church basements and absolute madman at work.

My sober friends would stop by the joint every once in a while to say hello, to try to boost my spirits. As Elaine continued to warm to me, she even, now and then, broached the subject of the program, usually by outing people she'd known who went into it (early on in my time in the restaurant, on the rare occasion a customer tried to buy me drink, she would yell across the length of the bar: "Don't bother, he's AA!"). Still, she didn't embrace the "give it ups," as one customer called my sober buddies. In the program, however, my job drew much interest. My friends never tired of my Elaine's stories. One New Year's Eve, about twenty program pals walked into the restaurant. They were on their way from a meeting to a midnight run in Central Park. They took up the whole bar for half an hour, ordered nothing—not even Diet Cokes—and then left. Out of deference to me, Elaine didn't say a word to my gang, though I swear she pulled a muscle keeping her mouth shut.

The fact of the matter was, I wasn't living a double life. I was angry all the time. At Elaine's, I didn't try to hide my displeasure. I could rage all I wanted and nobody would notice. In the church basements, my emotions simmered under a placid facade. In Elaine's, the worst that could happen was someone would hit me back. Keeping these feelings secret in church basements, a place where I might have gotten help, had consequences that were much worse.

For years while I was in the program, the thought of drinking never entered my mind. Such is the power of meetings. Booze presented no temptation at all, I thought. When people in the program asked me how I tended bar sober, I often remarked that I might as well be selling shirts for all the thought I gave it. But my alcoholism was patient. It sat there, contained in a pretty array of bottles, like an evil genie, waiting for a rub. It would wait as long as it had to. As my years at Elaine's went by, alcohol just bode its time. There was a woman in the program with whom I had a brief friendship. When she found out I tended bar for a living, she nearly dropped the cup of tea in her hand. "You have to leave your job," she said in a formal English accent. "Must leave it this moment!" I tried to explain that I had done nothing else in my adult life. "The only other thing I know is horse racing," I said with a nervous giggle. "But I'm a little too tall to be a jockey." She looked me directly in the eyes. There was no humor in hers. "If you continue working behind a bar, you will drink again," she said unequivocally. "And if you drink again, you will either die from it or wish you were dead."

I shrugged off her Shakespearean warning as a bit dramatic. I thought she was buttoned too tight. But every so often over the next few years at Elaine's, her words would come floating back into my consciousness. They say in the program you're either moving toward or moving away from a drink. Working behind the bar, I had never really moved away from one—booze was always an arm's length away. The English lady had predicted my future.

On the one hand, Elaine had trouble understanding how anyone could be unhappy working in a restaurant, especially her restaurant. She would recount for me her early days in the business, working in the Harlem restaurant, even for Alfredo, and her eyes would sparkle at the memories. She knew, right off, that she'd found her life path. And, for the next forty-something years, she had not once veered off the path. I never heard her come close to saying she was fed up with the business. Later in my time at the restaurant, when Elaine's hair showed the first strands of gray, she never mentioned retiring.

I once knew how she felt. When I first stepped behind a bar, I had the same feeling: working saloons was something I could do forever. For one thing, I loved how fast the money was, an unending spring. It didn't matter if you had only lint in your pocket at the start of your shift, by night's end you could have plenty. When I was eighteen, nineteen, I was making eight hundred dollars cash a week. Take home. In 1973 that was an enormous amount. I bought new cars for cash, clothing for shifts. I left tips so large bartenders would run out the door after me thinking I'd made a mistake and I gave it not one second thought.

But it was more than just the money that kept me coming back night after night. It was a constant state of escape, a different planet.

No part of my outside world walked into the bar or restaurant with me. When I was at work, I had no troubles, no insecurities. I was never lonely. I didn't even have deficiencies. Elaine, I knew, felt the same. I remember overhearing her tell a customer at the bar one night why she never went on long vacations, and why, even on her brief trips, she was always in a hurry to get back. "Anywhere else, I'm just another fat Jewish broad," she explained. "But here, I'm Elaine."

For both of us, however, our saloon personae were fantasies, suits of armor that both deflected words that could hurt and kept our real feelings from coming out. When I got sober, the suit became too hot, too clumsy to wear. Under the armor, I wore nothing. Being naked to the world is hard enough anywhere. In a saloon it is particularly difficult.

Chapter Eleven

WOULDN'T HURT if you opened a book now and then," Elaine said to me one night. My boss had a way with words. She had been telling a story about Peter Malkin, the Nazi hunter who captured Adolf Eichmann. Malkin had been in for dinner the previous evening. I had no idea who she was talking about. Though her suggestion stung, she had a point. Here I was surrounded by a literary diorama and I was reading nothing more illuminating than the *New York Post*. So, I took her suggestion and, for the first time in my life, began to read in earnest. Customers whom I'd watched, night after night, walk through Elaine's front door wrote some of my early literary choices. Hunter S. Thompson's *Fear and Loathing in Las Vegas* was the first. That Carlo the waiter and I had to put Thompson out with a tablecloth one night after the writer, armed with 151 rum and a Zippo, tried to make himself into a human flamethrower only made the reading experience that much more satisfying. I half-expected an official visit from Dr. Gonzo at the bar. Terry Southern's *Candy* was another inaugural pick. One night, someone left a copy of his and Mason Hoffenberg's teenage sex fantasy on the bar. As I laughed out loud at Dr. Krankheit, his champion of "self-gratification," I could almost hear Southern, all hair and cigarette smoke, laughing along with me from back on table 9. For me, reading the Elaine's writer was an interactive experience. It was not Tom Hanks's Southern affectation telling me the story in *Forrest Gump* but the author Winston Groom's own Alabama drawl, laced with the bourbon I had served him. It was George Plimpton's Harvard argot in my ear when I read *Paper Lion* or his April Fool's Day farce of Sidd Finch, the lefty from Tibet.

Though Elaine's suggestion that I begin to read the books of her living library was said extemporaneously, the next chestnut she handed me had a bit more thought and planning behind it. Still, the suggestion was not sugarcoated:

"Don't be a putz. Go back to school," she said.

There was brilliance in the simplicity of this suggestion. My going back to school was the perfect solution for both of us. For Elaine, it meant no separation anxiety over my leaving the restaurant for quite some time. As I had only about twelve underwater basket-weaving credits from a fall semester at Rockland Community College in 1972 and my truncated attempt with the nuns at St. Thomas Aquinas College, my graduation date hung somewhere way in the future. Working nights at Elaine's was the perfect job for a college career. For me, the idea of completing college gave purpose to my life, something to work for, a real, obtainable goal.

So, at the age of thirty-five, I applied to Fordham University.

I chose Fordham for several reasons. Frank, my sponsor, had gone there. And, at the time, Fordham offered "life experience" credits for older students returning to school. But the main reason was my mom. For those of Irish Catholic descent with roots in the Bronx, Fordham is the ultimate in higher education. It's as Ivy League as we B.I.C.'s (Bronx Irish Catholics) are allowed. On Fordham Road, the Rose Hill campus of the university is eighty-five acres of undulating, lush green grounds shaded with elm and maple trees. The buildings are stone, and Gothic in design. When thinking of the Bronx, most people conjure images of burned-out buildings and graffiti-covered elevated subways. But Rose Hill seems to belong to a bucolic New England town. Of course, I didn't have the heart to tell Mom right away that I would be attending classes at the school's Lincoln Center Campus in Manhattan (not a bad location, either). When I did tell her, the variant did little to dull her glow.

In the beginning, I felt more than a normal first-day-at-school anxiety. Most of the nontraditional students at Fordham attended classes at night. Because I worked at night, I sat in classrooms during the day surrounded by eighteen- and nineteen-year-olds. I showed up with everything but a protractor and a Spider-Man lunch box. I also brought with me the habit I had acquired at meetings of sitting in the front row and paying attention to the speaker or, in this case, the teacher. Though I was nervous, and felt enormously out of place, I was also excited. Having explored the course catalog, I took electives like Religions of the World and French Film and core courses like Western Civilization and Psychology (I figured I had already taken Psych 101 as a bartender). Almost as an afterthought, I took a class called First-Person Journalism. The teacher's name was Elizabeth Stone. She was just a few years older than I was, and I liked her right off. A Brooklyn kid and a Berkeley student of the 1960s, Stone still held dear to a rebellious attitude, though she now wrapped it in the loose leaf of academia. I also liked the way she needled students, even when I was the target. Several jokes she told at my expense went over my head so fast they left a crease.

For school, I bought a word processor that had an early version of spell check with a limited dictionary. The dialogue box would read "no suggestion" for the simplest misspellings. It would also highlight mistakes. It seemed like every other word in my homework lit up. I wrote like e. e. cummings on a bender. I misused and misspelled the simplest words. I had to check just about every word with the dictionary.

I can't remember the parameters of my first assignment in Stone's class, but I do know that I wrote about my first day back in college and the enormous anxiety I suffered. I also had anxiety writing the assignment. Though I had trouble putting my feelings down on paper, the anxiety over expressing the anxiety I felt actually translated pretty well to the page. I told about being in the wrong room for my first class. How I hadn't realized the school had changed room assignments. I compared my feelings with those I had as a child when I was lost in Alexander's department store and an announcement came over the loudspeaker system: "Anyone losing a small boy who answers to the name Brian, please come to the security office on the main floor."

Without my knowledge, Stone handed the piece to the editors at the school's newspaper. I was thrilled when I found out it was in the Fordham *Observer* that same week. With the glee of a fifth grader, I cut it out and brought it to work. Elaine read it under the green banker's light at her end of the bar. Without saying a word about it, she walked over to Gay Talese and, with a fleshy hand, slapped it on the table in front of him. "Read this," she ordered. I was so embarrassed my ears were red. I turned and slowly counted the quarters in the register drawer. Before that night was over, the sportswriter Mike Lupica and the playwright Sam Shepard had, with Elaine's formidable presence hovering over them, evaluated my nascent prose. It's a wonder I ever wrote another word.

Maybe it wasn't so far-fetched. My mom was a letter writer. Her envelopes were addressed to places as close as her sister's in the Bronx or, on parchmentlike airmail stationery, as far away as her Irish cousin's in County Kildare. She would start with a draft on scratch paper that would end up with sections crossed out and others added in the margins. From across the kitchen table, I'd watch as she transcribed her edited version onto the good stock. If a mistake was made, she pursed her lips and let out a *tsk,* then drew one neat line through the faulty phrase. Her handwriting was an ornate, forward-leaning loop, which, like her tone and the twinkle in her eyes, was lighthearted and soothing.

My father wrote on the NYPD-issued Underwood typewriter he gave me. For a couple of decades, his literary endeavors were limited to crime reports called DD 5s. When he retired from the police department, he took the Underwood with him (I don't think the NYPD missed it). At home, he wrote letters on behalf of fraternal organizations like the Ancient Order of Hibernians or the Knights of Columbus. After a teammate of my older brother's died of injuries sustained during a high school football game, my father went on a letter-writing campaign to local businessmen and politicians, including the then U.S. Senator from New York Jacob Javits. Ultimately, my dad was able to enlist enough community support to effect changes in safety regulations for high school football equipment. For years, Dad had interpreted his detective's investigative notes on murders, rapes, and robberies, and turned them into crime-scene reports, short stories of short-lived lives. As he wrote them, he kept an open dictionary within his long arm's reach. As a result, my father's writing was lean, forceful, and erudite.

But, if I inherited writing talent from either of my parents, it took me a long time to own it. Each time I would attempt a written assignment, I would be overwhelmed by my lack of grammar fundamentals. More than once, I thought that I had embarked on a senseless journey. I even once grumbled to Elaine about my inadequacy.

"Just tell the story," she said. "They have editors for the rest of the crap."

I took as many writing courses as I could. And though I never really made up for all that lost time when I was flipping baseball cards in grammar school and drinking beer in high school, I kept Elaine's advice in mind, and for the most part, it provided a steady stream of A's and B's.

By the second semester of school, I'd chosen media studies, Fordham's version of journalism, as my major. I fell in love with Damon Runyon's life story. I liked the old sportswriters, like Red Smith and Jimmy Cannon. I read current and back columns by Jimmy Breslin and, of course, Pete Hamill. As it happened, I had plenty of other ink-stained role models in the flesh.

Chapter Twelve

B Y THE EARLY 1990s, on any given night, there would be upward of a dozen newspaper reporters hanging from Elaine's bar rail. Some of these were tabloid legends, like Steve Dunleavy and John Cotter, a metro editor for the *New York Post* who perhaps more than anyone made that paper fun to read. But the reporter to whom I was most drawn, maybe because of his youth, definitely because of his humor, was Mike McAlary, a columnist who worked alternately for the *Post* and the *Daily News*.

In his early thirties, McAlary had a square head of curly brown hair that topped a constantly furrowed brow and a brush of a mustache better suited to a Prussian. Brash, unpredictable, and fearless, one night, at about two in the morning, he entered the front door of the Elaine's via two perfectly performed cartwheels and a dismount worthy of Olga Korbut. McAlary loved controversy, and his lived on the front page or, as he called it, evoking an old newspaper term, "the wood." Around this time there was a full-fledged war among the three New York City tabloids. McAlary's allegiance to his employer was as thick as the paper on which his paycheck was printed. He seemed to dash from *Newsday* to the *Daily News* to the *New York Post* as if he was legging out a triple. But whatever paper his byline happened to adorn, they got their money's worth. He had left *Newsday* to work for the *Daily News,* filling a hole caused by the departure of Jimmy Breslin, who had left the *Daily News* for big dollars at *Newsday.* Soon after McAlary slid into the *Post* (he quit the *Daily News* during a strike), Breslin wrote an unflattering column about McAlary's new boss, the *Post*'s publisher, Peter Kalikow. Not one to shy away from a fight, McAlary dedicated his next column to his most personal thoughts about Breslin: "He doesn't even make up stuff as well as he used to," McAlary wrote. "After George Steinbrenner and Ed Koch, Jimmy Breslin now rates as the third-largest self-important blowhard in the city." But that was in print. In person, McAlary once said he was in awe of Breslin.

New York City cops both loved and hated McAlary, because he displayed in his columns the perfect balance of loving and hating New York City cops—his exposé of a dirty cop ring in Brooklyn's Seventy-seventh Precinct culminated in his book *Buddy Boys.* People said stories seemed to find McAlary, but the real reason he got so many scoops was he was always working.

A few times, McAlary and I played golf together. On one of these occasions, at a golf course near where I grew up, I was lucky enough to have had a hole in one. After the round, I called my father and invited him to join in on the obligatory round of drinks I was to buy (sober at the time, I had a Diet Coke). As McAlary's luck would have it, the columnist sat at the bar next to two New York City cops who that very day had been suspended for vigilante actions against drug dealers. Essentially, the cops had been working on their days off. In the upside-down world of the NYPD, this was worse than not working when you were supposed to. With a few beers apiece in them, the disgruntled policemen started telling their tale. My father, the old squad commander, marched right over and lectured them on the evils of talking to the press. But his words came a little too late. The next day the two "Cowboy Cops," as the headline shouted, were front-page news, and no doubt my father shook his head as he read it.

Probably because he was always following the scent, McAlary was prone to the occasional hoax. Alex, a bartender Elaine hired when I moved to the cashier position, reeled him in good one night. Knowing he was within earshot, Alex started telling me about an unusual murder that had occurred in the neighborhood the night before. The victim, Alex began, was found in their bathtub filled with milk and covered with Cheerios. Moon-mad with curiosity, McAlary almost climbed in Alex's pocket asking questions. "Well, the cops think it's the work of a cereal killer," the bartender coolly replied.

For the restaurant, the presence of news reporters was very good news indeed. During the business dearth of the mid-eighties, Elaine's was rarely mentioned in the columns. But now, because gossip writers like Michael Shane from *Newsday,* Joanna Molloy from the *Post* and later the *Daily News,* and even Richard Johnson from the *Post*'s "Page Six" began to frequent Elaine's bar, the restaurant was again part of New York City's print gossip lexicon. For a while, I fancied myself a kind of mole for the columns. I remember once calling a gossip columnist about Louis J. Freeh, the then new director of the FBI. Freeh had been in for dinner with a lawyer who I knew had shared the same table with more than one mobster client. Woody Allen, once a fixture in Elaine's, reappeared after a considerable absence—one week coming in four times in a row for dinner. (Like many of Elaine's old customers, Woody had just tired of the bad food.) That week I called the editor of the *Daily News*'s "People" page and told him of Woody's renewed patronage. A piece ran in the Sunday edition of the paper, complete with pictures of Elaine and Woody. Elaine thought Bobby Zarem had placed the item. But Zarem came in that night and told her he'd had nothing to do with it. While Elaine and Zarem were at the end of the bar trying to figure out who the source was, I asked if she was happy about the publicity. "What do you think?" she said sarcastically.

"Good, 'cause I called it in," I said, then winked and walked away.

For many years, throughout the 1960s and '70s, Elaine's restaurant had more publicity than it wanted, if such a state exists. Press for the restaurant came inexorably, like Fords off an assembly line. As I mentioned earlier, that file drawer in the clip morgue of the *Post* was testament to Elaine's popularity. Elaine's sister, Edith, had a collection of the restaurant's news clips. She saved the items, stories, and profiles in leather-bound photo albums which were at least two-feet square. According to Edith, the collection included every story ever published about Elaine and the restaurant. Stacked on the floor, the albums were at least three feet high.

But for the most part, the press that Elaine's had generated in the past was celebrity fueled: who was in, who said what to whom, and so on. By the early 1990s, however, it more than just gossip that got Elaine's mentioned in the papers.

When news happened in New York City, the reporters who covered it, the cops who investigated it, even the criminals who participated in it, came into Elaine's to talk about it. In 1994, New York City's mayor, Rudy Giuliani, made William Bratton his police commissioner. One of the first moves Bratton made as commissioner was to appoint John Miller as his deputy commissioner of public information. Miller was a well-known and well-liked local TV reporter and a regular customer at Elaine's. The first night Miller brought Bratton into Elaine's, the new commissioner looked like a candidate for president working the room at a press function. As it happened, that night there was a newspaper or TV reporter at practically every table. As he walked past the bar to a back table, Miller whispered each reporter's name to Bratton. The commissioner made it a point to stop at each table and address the reporter by first name. It was a brilliant piece of press relations. Though Bratton had been the New York City Transit Police Chief, his Boston twang might have marked him as an outsider and an easy target for the local reporters. But from that first night in Elaine's until he stepped down as police commissioner, Bratton enjoyed a honeymoon with the New York City press corps. (It also didn't hurt that he oversaw a huge drop in the crime rate.)

The commissioner became a semiregular, sitting at a back table until very late, sipping a Baileys Irish Cream. Bratton's deputies, including the dapper Jack Maple, the same Maple of the brief Phil Spector friendship, however, were in all the time. Maple had worked for Bratton in the Transit Police Department. When Bratton went to the NYPD, he brought Maple along as a deputy commissioner. Although Elaine was wary of Maple at first—thought he was "too much of an act," in her words—she quickly warmed to him and would eventually count him as a close friend.

Maple looked like the bulldog in the felt dogs-playing-poker painting. He had a pug nose, jowly face, and bald head that was at most times topped with a bowler or straw hat. He often wore seersucker suits accented with a bow tie and saddle shoes. Years later, Maple would be the inspiration and technical adviser for a television show called *The District,* which starred Craig T. Nelson playing Maple. There was plenty about the real Maple that seemed made for TV.

Popular conception has it that the jaunty deputy commissioner had partly conceived the idea of Rudy Giuliani's crime-fighting strategy on a napkin at a back table at Elaine's. Maple might have, but he also plotted it on the bar, on the front table, and in many other spots around the restaurant that gave him an audience. Like a kid with toy soldiers, he schemed out manpower distribution in precincts throughout the boroughs using salt and pepper shakers, stirrers, and lemon peels.

Maple scoffed at the idea that the end of the crack cocaine epidemic had anything to do with a drop in crime, and he said exactly that to me. It was his opinion that his strategy was responsible for New York City's then plummeting crime rate. Societal, demographic, and economic influences had only a nominal effect. There were times that the vantage from behind the bar at Elaine's afforded the best insight into people's character. I liked Maple enough before he was given the big promotion but thought his ego was inflated after he was made deputy commissioner.

Early one evening, a thick, middle-aged guy with a ruddy complexion and a buzz cut sat at the empty bar and ordered a club soda. Politely, he asked if I expected Maple in that night. As it was common knowledge that the deputy commissioner was in every night, I said yes. At first I couldn't place the man. Then it dawned on me. He was a casualty of the deputy commissioner's new system.

Maple's brainchild was called "compstat." Regularly, and sometimes with little or no notice, Maple and several of his top officers, armed with computer statistics, would spring meetings on precinct commanders. During these meetings, Maple was known to go out of his way to humiliate a commander who had to defend negative arrest statistics that were sometimes out of his control (*The District* re-created these meetings in several episodes). One time Maple arranged for the image of Pinocchio to appear on a screen behind a popular commander who was presenting his statistics. Though Maple later apologized for the stunt, I remember how he bragged about it in Elaine's the night after it happened.

The guy with the buzz cut waiting at the bar had been suspended by Maple after one of these seven A.M. compstat meetings, and in a very public way. The story made the papers. I believe the man had been at a "racket," a retirement or promotion party, the night before and had only a few hours' sleep. That morning a compstat meeting was sprung on him, and Maple smelled alcohol on the man. At the bar, the captain waited, stirring the same club soda, his eyes fixed in a dead-cold stare, for a couple of hours. As it turned out, Maple didn't show that night. I often wondered what would have happened if he had.

There is no doubt in my mind that Maple was a good cop. One story about his underground exploits was told many times. Maple discovered that a leather goods store in the Times Square subway station was doing a brisk business selling pistol holsters to young toughs. The subway cops then found a good place to watch the transactions. Invariably, when the customers were out of the store, they would try the holsters out. As soon as their guns were visible, Maple's men would swoop in and bust them for firearms possession. Maple was a good cop; he might have even been a crime-fighting innovator, and certainly the colon cancer that ended his life took him too soon (he died in 2001). Still, whenever I think of Jack Maple, I can't help but remember the look in the eyes of the guy with the buzz cut.

But if Maple was abrupt and abrasive, his partner, John Miller, was subtle and smooth. He began his news career as a kid on a bicycle with a police radio strapped to the handlebars. As a young reporter for WNBC, a local New York affiliate, Miller one day knocked on the door of the Bergin Hunt and Fish Club in Ozone Park, Queens, and asked to speak to the proprietor, one John Gotti. The godfather admired Miller's courage, and, from then on, Miller's information on Gotti's career was days before anyone else's.

When Miller got the job as the deputy commissioner of public information, he acted like he'd hit the cop buff lottery. He was in

Elaine's the night he was issued the badge and gun, and he proudly showed them to a young couple seated at the next table.

Miller's media savvy helped make William Bratton one of the most popular New York City police commissioners ever, and in January 1996, Bratton garnered the cover of *Time* magazine, an event that Mayor Rudy Giuliani wasn't exactly thrilled with.

Though a good part of the credit for Bratton's success in New York has to go to Miller, the newsman turned cop flack might also have been partly responsible for the commissioner's brief New York City cop career. It seemed that Miller always had a beautiful lady on his arm. One night, he was in the restaurant with a gorgeous brunette. He left with her about one in the morning. A couple of hours later, Elaine and I stood on the sidewalk while Carlo pulled the metal gate down over the front of the restaurant. Across the street was Miller's car. It was a police-style Crown Victoria. Though it was a clear, dry night, the windows of the Crown Vic were steamed like someone was taking a shower inside. Elaine giggled as we watched the car bounce up and down like one of those Chevies on the Barrio.

Anyway, when Bratton was appointed commissioner, Rudy Giuliani's press secretary (and, later, chief of staff) was a young woman named Cristyne Lategano. For a brief period, Miller and Lategano became friendly. They shared a cozy table at Elaine's on several occasions. What would later be widely reported, and even portrayed in a television movie, was that Lategano's relationship with Giuliani was more than just professional. A gossip-page spy had clocked the mayor at a Madison Avenue boutique buying lady's unmentionables. Lategano's relationship with Miller came right before the rumors about her relationship with the mayor started. In any event, the Miller-Lategano liaison was brief, with Miller moving quickly on and leaving, most watchers believed, Lategano's feathers ruffled.

Soon thereafter the mayor's office issued an unofficial decree that no person in his administration was allowed in Elaine's. Giuliani said something to the effect that the restaurant represented the limousine liberals associated with his predecessor, David Dinkins. But, more likely, the real reason for the edict was plain old jealousy. Though Rudy's displeasure at all the favorable press his police commissioner was garnering at Elaine's had to have something to do with it, what was plain for us to see was the mayor was not about to be trumped romantically by someone under his employ.★

While all of this was transpiring, the New York Press Club was planning its annual Inner Circle event. Each year, the mayor would perform at the dinner in some kind of self-deprecating spoof. One year, Giuliani appeared in drag, an episode, it was said, that kept many reporters up with nightmares. The organizers that year thought it would be funny to surprise the mayor by bringing Elaine onstage. She was supposed to say something like "Why don't you stop being a bully and come by for something to eat?" As the whole body of the New York press was fully aware of the soap opera at Elaine's, the skit was assured of laughs. But when the mayor found out about the trap, he let it be known that, if Elaine was invited, he wasn't coming. If Giuliani was seeking revenge against Elaine's, his plan backfired. The highly publicized drama between Elaine's and City Hall only made it harder to get a table at the restaurant.

★Rudy's disfavor didn't have a negative effect on John Miller's career. For a while Miller went back in front of the camera. He was the last Western journalist to interview Osama bin Laden. He now works for the FBI as an Assistant Director.

Chapter Thirteen

THROUGHOUT THE EARLY NINETIES, the restaurant was packed every night, and everybody there—Tommy, the waiters, especially Elaine—was making money. When I first started at Elaine's, Tommy would count the receipts and hand Elaine the cash and numbers for the night. Invariably, on reading the disappointing figures, Elaine would pinch her shoulders to her neck and say, "That's it?" Tommy would yell down the bar to me, "Brian, give her the tip cup." Elaine then would smirk and slide the skinny night's receipts under the strap of her brassiere. But now I was handing her a horse-choker roll in a thick rubber band. She'd slide her eyeglasses up onto her head and read the numbers and whisper in the most understated of ways: "Nice." Elaine's billowy dresses always had slit pockets, and she'd stuff the roll in one of them and walk contently back to table 4, or sit at the bar and chat until three or four in morning. Sometimes she'd take Michael the waiter, some of the remaining customers, and me out for breakfast at the Greek coffee shop up the block, or down to Brasserie when it was open, and buy breakfast for all of us.

But any restaurant can do business. At Elaine's there was a kinetic energy, a palpable static electricity that was produced by celebrity, notoriety, and normal people rubbing up against one another. As in the rest of the country in the fall of 1990, the television at Elaine's was tuned to the Gulf War. But at the restaurant it was not unusual to see the Scud Stud (Arthur Kent) or Christiane Amanpour or Peter Arnett on furlough from their network duties and seated at a table beneath the images of smart bombs and Fourth of July–like explosions.

In 1993, when the World Trade Center was bombed, the FBI hero John O'Neill made Elaine's his unofficial headquarters. Full-faced, with gleaming black hair, O'Neill was a dandy in his Valentino suits. He was all man, though, and Elaine loved him and introduced him to the whole cast of her movie star customers, like Dabney Coleman and Michael Caine. O'Neill's high life at Elaine's did not, however, play well at FBI headquarters in Washington. But years before September 11, 2001, O'Neill raised the alarm about a Saudi-born terrorist named Osama bin Laden, a warning that fell mostly upon deaf ears. (In August 2001, O'Neill left the FBI to become chief of security of the World Trade Center. He died in the collapse of the towers.)

John Miller once said that Elaine's was fiction following fact following fiction. Nowhere was theory more in evidence than in the late nineties on Thursday nights. It was then some of the character actors from gangster movies like Goodfellas and The Godfather started to make a regular meet at the front tables by the bar. Some of these actors, like Tony Sirico and Dominick Chianese, went on to star in The Sopranos. Sprinkled among make-believe gangsters would be members of the Brooklyn Gambino family. One night, a guy with a face that had the warmth of a headstone was seated alone at the bar nursing a drink when a drunken couple came in and sat next to him. The couple began to shout at each other, an argument that hit a crescendo when the man said something very loud and very unflattering to his date. The declarative statement prompted the gangster at the bar to say something in the woman's defense. The man with the date, heavyset, late thirties, made the mistake of telling the wiseguy to mind his own business. Those were the last words to come out of his mouth that evening. The rest of the sounds he made were gurgles. The punch was frighteningly fast and effective. It knocked the heavyset fellow onto the floor and nearly out cold. But it didn't end there. In the next second, the gangster had his barstool lifted high over his head, his eyes measuring the length of the neck on the writhing man on the floor. Tommy jumped up on the bar and grabbed the stool. "Watch the light!" my bartending partner screamed. Tommy was more worried about the antique fixture that hung from the ceiling than the welfare of his customer. With a frost-like blast of an air conditioner, the gangster tented a crisp twenty and dropped it on the bar next to his half-drunk glass of scotch and walked out the door. Miller, who had left just before the altercation, told us that he had recognized the guy as a Gotti hit man.

It wasn't only gangsters who held forth on Thursdays. The cast members from *Law & Order,* like Jerry Orbach, Chis Noth, and Paul Sorvino, would be seated at table 7. Meanwhile, the real cops, Miller, Maple, and Bratton, sat in the back of the restaurant.

I couldn't wait to tell my friends at meetings who I'd seen in Elaine's the night before. I was thrilled each time Harvey and Bob Weinstein would come in with stars like Tom Cruise, Nicole Kidman, Jack Nicholson, or Leonardo DiCaprio. And Miramax was not Elaine's only Hollywood connection. When New Line Cinema was the brash startup, the moviemaker held release parties for the Nightmare on Elm Street films at Elaine's. On table 21, they would set up laptop computers that gave them real-time national attendance figures for opening night. Robert Englund, who played

New Line's cash-cow character Freddy Krueger, became a regular customer.

I also got a charge out of the return of Woody Allen as Elaine's premiere customer. Long before I began working at the restaurant, I was one of those people who each autumn lined up at the Beekman Theatre in Manhattan to catch the first showing of his "fall release." I knew by heart lines from *Stardust Memories* and *Broadway Danny Rose*. When Elaine would see Woody walk in the door, she'd slide off her stool at the end of the bar and say, "Watch the power show." Arm in arm, Elaine would walk Woody past the famous writers, actors, and directors whose eyes implored the director for acknowledgment. None ever came. One time Sydney Pollack touched Woody on the arm as he walked past, and Woody almost jumped out of his shoes. Another night, when the director was sitting with Mia Farrow and some friends, a Japanese tourist walked over and, without asking, snapped a picture. It was as though he was photographing a zebra in the zoo. Woody sat there in frozen horror.

The one and only time Woody ever talked to me he asked me the score of the Knicks game on TV (he didn't look at me when he asked the question). I was so excited I almost telephoned my mother. But even though Woody had all but ignored me, my close proximity to him at Elaine's made me feel as if we had a kinship. Who else knew that he wore a white Cascade laundry dishwasher's shirt after Carlo spilled a bottle of wine on him? Who knew about the night he waited out in front of the restaurant for a pizza to sneak in past Elaine? And he used me and the rest of the staff of Elaine's as extras in *Manhattan Murder Mystery*. The scene shot in the restaurant had Woody, Alan Alda, and Diane Keaton, and, if you look closely, my left arm.

The other thing that Woody and I shared was a love of sports, and Elaine's connection to the sports world dated back to the late sixties and early seventies when the New York Knicks were an NBA power, and when Woody, the number-one Knicks fan, began hanging out in the restaurant.

By the seventies, Elaine had forged a friendship with George Steinbrenner. They became so close, Steinbrenner gave Elaine a World Series ring each time the Yankees won. One of them—from 1978, I think—she had made into a pendant that she wore all the time.

Elaine's in the seventies also had an international sports connection as the unofficial headquarters for the North American Soccer League. Ahmet Ertegun owned the Cosmos, a team that fielded world superstars like Georgio Chinaglia, Franz Beckenbauer, and Pelé. When Pelé came into the restaurant, as he did often, the kitchen would come to a dead stop as the cooks and dishwashers would sneak out to the dining room for a peek at the star.

With the restaurant's resurgence in the nineties, and thanks to Bobby Zarem, Elaine's again became a sports mecca. Though it was my belief that Bobby couldn't tell the difference between a first basemen's mitt and a flounder, he certainly knew how to wine and dine ball players like Hernandez, David Cone, and Cal Ripken. Bobby came in with Ripken nearly every time the Orioles played the Yankees. When Ripken was closing in on Gehrig's consecutive-games-played record, a caravan of autograph hounds would follow him all the way from the stadium to Elaine's, where they would camp out front and wait for the star shortstop to come out. Ripkin always signed.

Elaine's also had a close connection to Madison Square Garden. Monie Begley, who was in the restaurant nearly every night, was then the head of publicity for the Garden. In the mid-nineties, when the Knicks were more than just decent, Monie would scour Elaine's for celebrities to fill courtside seats when the games were on national TV. One day she had two tickets on the court for

Elaine and me. At the time I was a season ticket holder—my seats up in the rafters. I told Monie I would take Elaine to the game, but I couldn't sit next to her. The grief I would get from my pals four levels up would be intolerable, I said. In the middle of the first quarter, I found Elaine through my binoculars. The seat next to her, my seat, was at first empty. The next time I looked, there was a younger woman with short blond hair sitting there. That night in the restaurant, I asked Elaine who took my seat. "Madonna," she said with a shrug.

Maybe Elaine's favorite sports celebrity was Pat Riley. The first time I saw Riley in the restaurant the Knicks had just made it to the NBA finals against the Houston Rockets. Riley, who looked more like a movie star than the movie stars in the joint, received a standing ovation from the whole restaurant—the only time I ever saw that happen. A photograph of Riley giving Elaine a smooch hangs on the back wall.

Though Riley's appearances rate right up there, the biggest sports nights in Elaine's occurred in 1994, when the New York Rangers became the champions of the NHL, and 1996, when the Yankees won the World Series against the Atlanta Braves. About two in the morning of the night the Rangers won, Monie showed up with winger Adam Graves, coach Mike Keenan, and the Stanley Cup. Word that the cup was in Elaine's went quickly around the neighborhood, and soon the bar was four deep. Elaine told me to open a couple of bottles of Cristal. Customers were lined up to the kitchen while I held the famed cup and poured champagne into their open mouths.

In 1996, when the Yankees beat the Braves to begin the team's run of World Series victories, Second Avenue outside the restaurant was a sea of fans. Not only was it common knowledge that Elaine's was Yankee territory but Cronies, a restaurant just down the block, was a favorite of Derek Jeter's. Worried that the crowd would try to force its way into the restaurant, Elaine asked me to watch the door. I did. At one point, nature called. I locked the door and asked a woman who was a regular "to keep an eye out for friendly faces." She apparently thought that George Steinbrenner's face didn't fit my criteria. The Boss elbowed his way through the crowd and pulled at the locked door several times, but she wouldn't let him in. Steinbrenner ended up celebrating the World Series victory at P.J. Clarke's, and the story of him being locked out of Elaine's was in the *Daily News* the next day.

It's obvious that I got a thrill out of my close proximity to fame. I liked the fact that movie stars like Matt Dillon and Albert Finney knew my name. I liked that Keith Hernandez would come sit at the bar to talk baseball. I liked that in Elaine's we had the inside story on City Hall and the NYPD. Sometimes, when I'd see folks reading *People* or "Page Six" on the subway, or think about the fans of star-driven gossip sheets across the country, I'd feel a sense of self-importance—a behind-the-velvet-rope attitude. But, truth be told, I was the same as any devotee of *The National Enquirer* or *Star.* I thought my existence small compared with those of the celebrities who inhabited Elaine's. Now and then I'd realize the reality of the situation: that it was only my job in Elaine's that allowed me to brush up against celebrity. In those moments, I longed for my own life to shine. The search for that inner light produced some strange routines.

Chapter Fourteen

Throughout the course of my sobriety, I integrated a number of disciplines into my life that ranged from healthy to the absurd. I gave up smoking cigarettes early on and began to run, at one point logging nearly fifty miles a week. At a hundred and eighty-five pounds, I weighed about the same as I had as a senior in high school. In a little over one year, I completed three marathons: the New York City Marathon twice and one Long Island Marathon. For long periods of time I wouldn't eat sugar or red meat. I saw a massage therapist once a week, and every other week had an acupuncture treatment.

For years, I was in both group and individual therapy that included regression and past lives. In one session, I believed that my therapist and I had uncovered a past life in which I was a pirate and forced to walk the plank. I meditated for up to an hour each day to the recorded sounds of ocean waves. For periods of time, I listened to an array of self-help tapes. During the New Age craze of the eighties, I visualized my chakras, carried crystals, and hung dream-catchers. I cared for my inner child. I read John Bradshaw,

Marianne Williamson, and Shakti Gawain. I had a bookshelf filled with self-help titles such as *I Deserve Love, Feel the Fear . . . and Do It Anyway,* and *The Inner Voice of Love.* I read daily affirmation books. I read Louise Hay. I really thought I could align the universe. I thought I deserved its abundance. I once met with a Santeria white witch.

At one point I expanded my twelve-step dossier. I began going to meetings to address what I believed was a dormant gambling problem, even though I hadn't been to the track in years. I was swept up in a movement that blamed parental alcoholism for much of the adult child's problems, in spite of the fact that neither of my parents was an alcoholic.

In retrospect, I don't know how much difference the crystals made. My guess is the only thing the dream-catchers caught was dust, and, in looking back, I see that the white witch wasn't all that much of a witch. Though I spent considerable time doing it, blaming my parents was ridiculous and an excuse. Still, it was during this endless search that I found the root of my unhappiness— and some insight into Elaine's.

With Elaine's blessings, and paid for by group carrier insurance she had for the bar staff, I went to a rehab that dealt with the core family issues of adult children from alcoholic families. It had once been a resort hotel in the rolling hills outside Reading, Pennsylvania. And, in spite of the preponderance of stuffed bears, it had that Jack Nicholson *The Shining*/Eagles "Hotel California," not-everyone-who-checks-in-is-going-to-check-out type of feel. Much of my remembrance of that first day is influenced by extreme anxiety. One of the rituals of the rehab was to photograph you on your way in and again on your way out. The difference in my photos was remarkable.

I was assigned a room that was small and monastic with two single beds. It was, as these things tend to be, a little uncomfortable when my roommate and I started unpacking our things. There wasn't much conversation. Dressed in a heavy plaid shirt-jacket, jeans, and work boots, my roomie reminded me of the seventies crowd at Chuck's Pub. He was in his mid-twenties, with shaggy hair and a mustache that curved around his mouth like a parenthesis.

After a brief introduction, I didn't speak to him again until we were back in the room following orientation and dinner. Naturally, I was uncomfortable with a stranger in a bed not three feet from me. I stared at the ceiling. The floor creaked in the hallway, a steam pipe rattled. In New York, my second-floor apartment faced the street. At night, I'd hear shouts and the wail of sirens, horns and the blast of boom boxes. For me, trying to sleep in silence was how trying to sleep on the median of a six-lane highway would be for someone else.

Finally, maybe after an hour or so, I fell off.

I couldn't tell you if it was five minutes or two hours later when I heard him scream. The sound was high-pitched and frightened—that of child. My eyelids snapped wide open. My roommate was standing on his bed, wearing pajamas, his hands clenched in fists, with his arms straight and tight to his sides. The look on his face was utter terror. He continued to scream for maybe thirty more seconds. Then he fell completely silent. He lay back down and pulled the covers up over him. The next thing I heard was the peaceful, rhythmic breathing of a sound sleep.

I didn't sleep the rest of the night.

The next morning, he washed and dressed. We walked together to the cafeteria and ate breakfast at the same table. Although several times my roommate caught me sneaking a glance, he responded only with a small, wistful smile. That morning, we were broken into groups of five or six. My roommate and I were separated. I saw him again at lunch. Holding a red plastic tray, he came up to me on the line. Sheepishly, he asked in a whisper if anything had happened last night. I didn't want to embarrass him. But he could see in my eyes that something had. He then told me this story:

In his childhood, his father had owned a pickup truck. At night, when he was in bed sleeping, he would be awakened by the gravel crunching under the wheels of the truck. He could tell by the slam of the truck door whether his father would come into his room and kiss him on the forehead or, stinking of bourbon, pull him out of bed and beat him mercilessly. Now, at age twenty-five, he would still hear that slam in his dreams. He told me he came to the rehab because he was about to be married. He said his fiancée had demanded he seek help.

My own story was vastly different, yet for some reason I identified with my young roommate. My father never beat me. As matter of fact, after my brother Tommy and I buried in the backyard a switch he'd once swatted us on the bottom with, Dad never touched us in anger again. Yet there was something about my alcoholism that was all about a scared little boy. I didn't come from a broken home. There were plenty of fistfights between my brothers, and screaming matches between Mom and Dad, but my mother loved me with a fierce passion and protected me from the fray. Though we were far from rich, there was always enough: enough to eat, to wear, to play with. The irony of it was, I was frightened to be alone, but I wanted nothing else. As in a recurring childhood dream, I wanted to fly, but not so high that I couldn't see my life.

One day, when I was about ten, there was a blizzard. The next morning, with drifts up to my waist, I walked into the woods at end of my block. The land was a Jewish day camp in the summer, hundreds of acres of forest and trails and streams. I remember trudging along the bank of a winding stream until I broke out of the woods into a clearing. I practically had to lift my knees to my chin to walk through the snow. Finally I made it to the middle of the snowfield. All sound was muffled. I let myself fall backward, the drift gently catching me. I felt totally and comfortably isolated from the world. I would feel the same way countless nights sitting at a bar with a drink in my hand, no matter how many people were around me.

During the five days I spent in Pennsylvania, I got to know that lonely child better than I ever had. Snicker all you want, but there is something spiritually basic about loving the innocence within you. I also found out that my dreams took root in that innocence. In one exercise, I told my group that the perfect life I envisioned had a house on a rocky shore and a windowed writing room from which I could watch the waves break while I gathered my thoughts for the page.

My last night at the rehab, I stood on the porch of the old resort and looked up at the brilliant December canopy of stars. I felt like I had a ten-year-old's heart, one filled with awe and expectation. It was as close to God as I ever have felt. But New York City has a way of aging your inner child quickly. Soon, I was back behind Elaine's bar and a million miles away from that Pennsylvania night. Like a comet, I had brushed the face of God, only to hurtle by.

But it was no coincidence that after the rehab I began to see that Elaine and I were not so dissimilar. At some point in our lives, we had both come to the erroneous conclusion that we were fated to certain loneliness. How much of that belief formed in our childhoods I can only guess. But I'm pretty certain we shared an adult disappointment that convinced us it was so: Elaine had her Alfredo. For me it was Carol.

I met Carol before my time at Elaine's, when I was working in a country-and-western-themed restaurant in midtown Manhattan. There she played fiddle in an all-girl country band. Carol had long brown hair with matching brown eyes and wore off-white overalls. Though she could set the fiddle on fire, she was actually

Juilliard-trained. Early in our romance, I took her to a Jets football game that was played on a Monday night. I got horrible seats—up in the top deck of Giants Stadium. The guy sitting next to her was shirtless and painted green. Our whole section was drinking like it was a bachelor party. Quiet for most of the first quarter, Carol leaned close just before halftime and whispered: "I might be the only person in this whole place who plays the violin."

Many nights back then I sat in smoky clubs watching her perform. I loved the way she loved her music even when that love excluded me. She spoke a language with her fellow musicians that I didn't understand and one she never tried to explain. Still, there were plenty of times in her place in New Jersey or in my apartment when we shut the rest of the world away. I was a full foot taller than Carol, and we'd find inventive ways to kiss and hold each other. Sometimes, she'd stand on my feet like a little kid, or I'd stand on the street and she'd stand on the sidewalk. Sometimes, she'd just leap into my arms and I'd hold her by the butt. We called each other "Shoes," just because we liked the way it sounded in baby talk. There were trips to the mountains, the seashore, and a week on Saint Thomas. The first night on that Virgin Island, in front of our hotel, we climbed into a van thinking it was a taxi. We asked the driver to take us to good place to eat. We ended up at the man's house, eating a home-cooked meal of local fish his wife prepared.

But for nearly six months, I kept my program life a secret from Carol. Obviously, I still carried shame about being an alcoholic. I also carried, from my car accident, the scar that reached around my forehead. I told Carol about the accident but conveniently left out the fact that I was drunk when it happened.

At the time, I was living in a tiny one-bedroom on the very eastern end of Seventy-ninth Street. I could throw a softball from my fire escape into the East River. It was a fourth-floor walk-up in a building that was once a sanitarium; the walls were literally a foot thick. Carol called it "my tree house." She grew up in a middle- to upper-middle-class town in northern New Jersey but just adored New York City. Many nights, after her gig in the cowboy bar, the Lone Star Café, or one of the other country-and-western joints in town, she'd spend the night with me in the tree house. One night, unexpectedly, she rang my bell. The next morning I was to lead a meeting just up the block. Then held in a room above a Moravian church, this particular meeting was the marquee program gathering in Manhattan—the "Hollywood" meeting, as I used to call it. It was not unusual at all to sit next to the latest star who had just been spun out of Betty Ford or Hazelden.

Carol and I were still wrapped in covers twenty minutes before the meeting was to start. I didn't know what kind of excuse to give her to get me out of the apartment alone for an hour. Finally, with the clock ticking close to ten, I said I had to meet some friends about something and I'd be right back. Not the cleverest of ruses, I'll admit.

"I'll come with you," she said, with bright, brown, morning eyes.

"I'll be right back," I reasoned.

"You don't want me to come?"

"It's not that, it's . . ."

In the next moment we were walking out the door together and I was trying to bring her up to speed on about fifteen years of my drinking and three years of my sobriety. Bemused, she had no idea what she was about to walk into.

The room was packed to capacity, a hundred or more people sitting in folding chairs. I climbed the platform and sat behind a podium equipped with a microphone. Squeezed in a seat in a corner, Carol looked astonished.

I began my qualification, as the program calls the talk each of us does in front of the room, with the story about Joe Caso and John Sisler. The room laughed at my Dean Martin line, the one about drinking vodka and Tang in space. Carol hung on every word.

After the meeting, we walked with some of my program friends to a coffee shop nearby. Frank, who was still working at Elaine's at the time, was with us. For most of the time, Carol sat quietly, taking in the obvious affinity we program people have for one another. Several times I felt her stare. When I looked at her, she wore an incredulous expression. How could I have kept this from her? her eyes asked. Under their glare, my excuse for not telling her seemed ridiculous.

I promised her, and kept the promise, that I would keep nothing from her again. I told her every secret I had. I told her I had some sexual confusion. She said everybody has some confusion, make up your mind. I did. I wanted her. Because I no longer held anything back, there were moments over those two years when the honesty between us was too painful, moments when circumstance and confusion would doom our relationship that very second. There were also moments when I was sure we'd spend our lives together. But by the end of those two years, it became clear that Carol was moving on. She had joined a program of her own, one that helped family and friends of alcoholics. She even had a sponsor—a big Broadway star, who wasn't fond of Carol's relationship with me from the start. Carol enlisted relationship advice from the sponsor-singer, who gave the situation little deliberation: "Break up with him," she said rather coldly, perhaps believing that if I had been capable of withholding my program membership from Carol, I couldn't ever be trusted. Carol also befriended a man from her program. He had thinning reddish blond hair and rode a bicycle. One leg of his trousers was always clipped tight so it wouldn't get caught in the chain. Several times when I'd go to meet Carol after her meetings, she was with him. I remember thinking that she laughed a little too easily at his remarks, that he held her gaze a bit too long.

The love of my life exists only in memory. I was twenty-eight when I met Carol, and the romance lasted only three years. It was maybe a year later when I finally accepted that it was over. I took her picture out of the frame that sat on my bookshelf and gathered all the letters and cards from her I'd collected over the years. With the package under my arm, I walked late one night to the promenade on the East River. One by one, I gently dropped each of my mementos of Carol into the roiling blackness below. As in the ending of a saccharine TV movie, her picture momentarily stayed on the surface before the current swallowed it.

It was not too long after that midnight ceremony that I took the job at Elaine's. I also moved from the tree house to an apartment on Eighty-sixth Street. It was a sprawling three-bedroom over a drugstore that Randy and I shared. One morning I awakened to see my room filled with smoke. I leapt from bed and pulled on some jeans, then crawled down the hallway toward Randy's room. Halfway there, flames shot out of the floor. With no recourse, I stumbled back out of the apartment and furiously knocked on my neighbors' door. The elderly couple were still half asleep and dressed in pajamas. Together, the three of us hurried down the stairs and into the street.

The fire was several alarms and gutted most of the building; Randy's room was completely destroyed. For almost two hours, I didn't know if my roommate was alive or dead. Fate was on his side. That night was the first Diane, his girlfriend and later his wife, let him stay over.

I went to work at Elaine's that evening wearing the same jeans I'd worn running out of the building. You could smell the smoke on them. Just before I walked into Elaine's door, I noticed Carol's car across and down the street. She was slumped in the seat, as though her feelings for me embarrassed her. Only when I opened the door of her Toyota did she finally turn to look at me. Her eyes were swollen and red. Somehow she'd found out about the fire but knew few of the details and feared the worst. She climbed out of the car and stood on the sidewalk and I stood on the street and we held each other that way forever—at least that's the way it stays in my memory. The moment is frozen there.

Still only thirty-two, I knew there would be other romances. There were. But in none did I feel the way I felt about Carol. As the years when by, I began to consider that I'd blown my only chance at true love. As I write this, it seems ridiculous, melodramatic, that sentiment. It would be if it had not been true. The dissolution of Carol and me folded neatly into a growing stack of disappointments in my sobriety. In a convoluted way, I started to blame my sobriety because I couldn't medicate myself by drinking those echoing feelings away. Instead, I railed against them with outbursts of anger.

Elaine dealt with her echoes by eating until she had wrapped herself in an absurd amount of insulation. Neither of us had a problem attracting people into our lives. Elaine's restaurant had been in business for those many years because and only because of her ability to attract people. I've always had plenty of friends. But neither of us would let anyone get close. Maybe it was in that misery where we began to enjoy each other's company.

Sometimes my boss would call in the early afternoon and ask if I wanted to go to lunch. Sometimes we'd go to the movies, the "waiters' show," she called it. When I asked what she meant, Elaine explained that many waiters in the big midtown and hotel restaurants worked split shifts. They'd work lunch, take a couple of hours off, and then work dinners. The downtime was spent either at the track or at the movies. "The married ones usually went to movies," Elaine said with a chuckle. One day we went to the Carnegie Deli for corned beef sandwiches. It was Christmastime, and the line of tourists to get into the restaurant stretched a block. My boss marched right in the front door and over to the cashier and said simply: "I'm Elaine." The man was properly impressed. "Cloth napkins for these two," he yelled to the waiter. Under the envious stares of the tourists, a waiter carrying two cloth napkins by the corners led us to a table.

Elaine's company was wonderful, especially away from her restaurant. During these chats, she could be funny, self-deprecating, and endearingly shy. Though never completely unrestrained, Elaine would divulge snippets of her past that, when pieced together, gave insight into her formative years. Her father had owned a dry-goods store during the 1920s on the Upper West Side. The store was profitable, and the Kaufman family lived in a spacious six-room apartment in Washington Heights. But the Depression ruined the business, Elaine told me. Her father had to close the store and move his family out to South Jamaica in Queens, far from the affluence of upper Manhattan. One of Elaine's earliest memories was of her mother telling her father to go out and peddle socks in the street. Her father, once a proud man, had been broken by the loss of his business.

When Elaine talked of her father, it seemed that she had conflicted feelings. There was something in her voice, a subtle inflection, that both defended him and revealed her disappointment in him. She often used the word *unassuming* to describe her father, but modesty is an attribute that is hard to imagine given the circumstances of the man's life. In her adulthood, Elaine had the same confused views of men. She saw a quick temper as an attractive quality in a man. Her favorite waiters, Frank, and most of the tough-guy writers who surrounded her every night—and me, too—all had a low boiling point in common. But she saw sensitivity in a man as a

flaw. There was one waiter, a Spaniard, who was terrific with customers, but Elaine rode him unmercifully and eventually fired
him, only because he was soft-spoken and afraid of confronta-
tion, especially with her. She picked on men who were milque-
toasts. But, as I had found out, most of Elaine's anger toward men
was pyrotechnics. All she wanted out of a man was for him to act
like one.

Most times, however, I left the amateur analyst in me at home
when I was with Elaine and just enjoyed her stories. She once told
me that, as a teenager, she'd worked in a collectible stamp stand in
Times Square. There she would display the stamps on the crook
of her thumb and forefinger with the grace of a ballet dancer.
Nearly every night she would rush from work to see a Broadway
show or drama, paying just two dollars for a standing-room ticket,
then palm the usher with a buck or two and be given a seat. Along
with her devotion to Marlon Brando and *Streetcar,* she loved Ethel
Merman in *Annie Get Your Gun* and Tennessee Williams's *Cat on a
Hot Tin Roof.* She saw every one of Jerome Robbins's shows.

One day, Elaine called me to say she had tickets for a matinee of
Les Liaisons Dangereuses by the Royal Shakespeare Company. We
sat in the first row, surrounded by an elegant and older daytime
theater crowd. In the scene where Alan Rickman writes a letter
on the writhing body of his lover, Elaine leaned into me and
whispered: "Look at all the blue-haired women squirming in their
seats." I remember thinking she looked a bit flushed herself. At in-
termission, she asked me if it was all right if we left to get something to eat.

Although Elaine was not the voracious reader some of her
writers made her out to be, she was an amazing listener. At the tables in her restaurant, Elaine absorbed the news of the day from
the primary sources. No one was more informed than my boss.
Reporters, writers, and sports stars loved talking to her. Because

of this quality, she had a unique mental catalog of information. Though she wouldn't be able to tell you Derek Jeter's batting average, she could tell you what George Steinbrenner's first impressions of Jeter were. Though she might not know the difference between a plié and an arabesque, she could tell you Nureyev's parents' names.

One night I realized that she listened to me.

It was just before Christmas, and I was talking about presents I usually received from my family. I said that, though my relatives' hearts were in the right place, most of the gifts were things I didn't need or couldn't use. Most times, I got shirts and sweaters two inches short in the sleeves and ended up throwing them out or giving them away. This particular Christmas, what I really wanted was a watch. So I asked Elaine if she thought it would be impudent of me to ask my family to pool their resources and buy me one. I wasn't even sure she was paying attention. When I finished my monologue she shrugged noncommittally; she didn't say a thing about my plan the rest of the evening.

The next night I came in to work, and Elaine waved me over to her table. She rooted around in her pocket and pulled out a watch. It had been in the bottom of her drawer, she said, and then assured me that "it was a man's style." Thin, with an octagonal face, the watch was as handsome as it was unique. On its back was engraved a two-digit serial number. Elaine said that it would need a link to fit my wrist and told me to go to the store where she'd bought it, on Fifty-seventh Street. There they'll put one in for nothing, she said.

I remember that, when Elaine handed it to me, she didn't, or couldn't, make eye contact. By then, I was aware of how much it took for Elaine to express affection. I wanted to hug her, but instead I kissed her on the cheek and spent most of the rest of the night with my hand in my pocket feeling the smooth watch face.

The next day, at the store, the woman behind the counter looked stiff and unhappy, exhibiting just the kind of countenance expensive boutiques like in their salespeople. She was surprised, even a bit suspicious, when I handed her the watch. "It was a gift," I said, feeling a rising warmth in my face.

I asked what the watch was worth, and the number the woman told me left me speechless—it was bigger than the one on the sticker of my new Jeep. But more than the worth, it was a connection to Elaine, her way of saying—without words—you're my family now. Her restaurant had always been her substitute family, though gaining entrance into her clan wasn't as easy as walking in the door, or even getting a job there. There's an old saw used by psychotherapists that goes something like, If your own family won't do, pick a new one. The watch was Elaine's way of saying she had picked me to be part of hers.

Chapter Fifteen

IN EARLY WINTER OF 1991, Elaine told John Cotter to hire me at the *Post*. "Give him a job as a part-time stringer," she said late one night. Cotter said no problem and told me to stop by the paper the next day and he'd introduce me around.

Cotter had a mouth full of teeth that looked like a twisted pack of matches. But with his mouth closed, his tousled mop of blond hair, and his boyish features, he had the look of a hip New England college professor. As metro editor of the *New York Post*, Cotter presided over the paper during a time when it began to build its reputation for irreverence, when the paper's headlines first made headlines, like the famous "Headless Body Found in Topless Bar." His was also the time when the rivalry between the *Post* and the *Daily News* was at its bitter best. When the *Daily News* owner, Robert Maxwell, mysteriously slipped off his yacht and into Davy Jones's locker in the Atlantic, several *Post* reporters wanted to run the headline "Victory at Sea." Only a last-minute veto from Cotter's boss kept those words from immortalizing the front page of that edition. Cotter took much of his inspiration from Fleet

Street. His weathered and cracked leather briefcase was bursting with the British tabs.

The *Post* metro editor would often roll into Elaine's about two in the morning. Most times he'd have Mike McAlary, Joanna Molloy, or one of his other charges in tow. Elaine loved Cotter, so did most people, so did I. At the end of the night, Cotter would wander over to me at the bar, his eyes in a drunken flutter like those of my old friend Joe the bartender, and whisper for a couple of unopened bottles of Amstel Light. Somehow he'd find room for the brews in his briefcase. He'd snap the set of headphones from his Walkman around his neck, readying himself for the U2 rock-and-roll ride home to Connecticut in the backseat of the car-service limo.

When I showed up at the *Post* the following day, Cotter had no recollection of his promise to Elaine or our conversation the night before. A man of his word (even a not-remembered one), however, Cotter put me on the schedule. I was to work Sundays—and Mondays when it was a holiday.

My first assignment was during the Gulf War in 1991. I was sent to St. Patrick's Cathedral on Fifth Avenue to cover Cardinal O'Connor's homily. O'Connor was a favorite target of the *Post*. At that time, you could almost count on the cardinal's, John Gotti's, or Donald Trump's picture being plastered on the front page of the paper. The editor on the city desk that day thought O'Connor would comment on the pending war.

I sat in a back pew. I would have been much more comfortable below sea level, in the basement. That is, if there was a meeting being held there. I was positive that the cardinal could hear the whir of my tape recorder. I couldn't help thinking how disappointed my mother would have been had she known that I was being a traitor to the faith. Out of the corner of my eye, I could see the statues along the wall, the splayed Pietà figure of the lifeless

Christ, the images fired into the stained-glass windows. I raised my eyes and looked at the crucifix behind the altar. Like in a scene from *The Omen,* the eyes of the icons seem to settle on me accusingly. Still, I soldiered through my task: scribbling notes and secretly hoping for a quote that would put the O'Connor story on the front page. By the time the homily was over, I was a wreck. I hurried out of the pew, stepping on parishioners' feet as I went. I darted out of the huge Gothic front doors and shielded my eyes from the glare.

At the time, I was in my second year at Fordham. My experience in writing for newspapers was limited to a half dozen feature pieces for the Fordham *Observer.* The thought of going back to the newsroom to write the story caused me overwhelming anxiety. Instead, I went to a phone booth a block from the church on Madison Avenue and called Elizabeth Stone, my teacher at Fordham. Over the phone, Elizabeth dictated a lead paragraph, which I copied word for word into my notebook. I then called the newsroom and was told, much to my relief, to head to the UN to get some quotes at a protest. But first I was switched to a writer to whom I unloaded Elizabeth's lead and O'Connor's quotes about the war.

That night I had to work at Elaine's. At about ten o'clock, Cotter, McAlary, Molloy, and Ken Moran, the outdoor columnist for the *Post* (who actually spent very little time outdoors) came into the restaurant to congratulate me. At first, I thought they were just talking about my first job reporting a story. Then one of them showed me the next day's paper. Under a headline and a picture of O'Connor, in dark, bold letters, was my byline. Apparently, the writer of the story gave me credit for it and didn't tell Cotter, or any of the other editors, that I hadn't actually written it.

I didn't know what to say, or what not to say. I knew my part-time job was a tryout, and a full-time position hinged on being able to perform. And the adulation from Cotter and McAlary felt really good. For one vaporous moment, I considered not telling them that I didn't write the article. I saw it as my chance to be done with the bar business for good, to be doing something that actually mattered (in the broadest sense of that expression). I also wanted to pal around with McAlary and Cotter. I saw them as swashbucklers—work hard, change the world, drink hard, and laugh about it. But just as quickly as the fantasy formed, it disappeared. I'd like to say that it was my inclination to be honest, but the truth is, I thought someone would catch me in the lie. As they were gathered before me, on the other side of the bar, with beers raised in toast, I told them I didn't write the story. Although there was some good-natured laughter, I could feel the chill as the spotlight moved away.

I would get other chances. Over the next couple of years, I continued working, on and off, part-time for the *Post*. I even got over a paralyzing fear of an empty computer screen and wrote a few of my own stories; one, about a disturbed man who was jabbing people with a screwdriver on crowded subway cars, even made the front page. The headline read: "Screwball on the Loose." But if I learned one thing about newspapering, it was that you need to have confidence—even if it's false bravado—to do the job well, and the truth was, I had very little confidence in my ability to write and especially to write on deadline. Still, I kept showing up at the paper when they called and prayed all the time for my big break.

There was writer with whom I became friendly at Elaine's named Bobby Drury. When I first met him, Drury was a contributing editor for *GQ* magazine, but he had once worked as a sportswriter for the *Post*. One night at the bar, Drury told me the story of how his writing career began. In his early twenties, Drury was a copyboy for the paper and, like me, did a few stories on Sundays and Mondays, when no one else was around. It was on Thursday, August 2, 1979, that Steve Dunleavy, then an editor for the *Post,* got word that the Yankee catcher Thurman Munson had died in a plane crash in Canton, Ohio. With the phone receiver still in his hand, Dunleavy looked around the nearly deserted newsroom and spotted Drury. That evening Drury was on a flight to Canton, where he wrote several front-page stories for the paper. Drury the writer never looked back. Though I was decades older than the copyboy Drury, I wanted to experience what he did. I wanted to be a writer.

Chapter Sixteen

I N OCTOBER 1991, John Cotter, just forty-eight years old, died in his sleep of a heart attack. Only a week or so before he died, the editor had jumped from the *Post* to the *Daily News*. Cotter left a couple of kids, who, with the exception of the orthodontist's work, were biological stamps of him—blond mop tops and youthful grins. But Cotter didn't leave any life insurance. His benefits were not in force. Elaine and Steve McFadden, a saloonkeeper who owned Ryan McFadden's, across from the old *Daily News* building, helped organize a huge fund-raiser for the family. I drove Elaine and Bobby Zarem to the wake, which was attended by a generation or two of New York newspaper people.

Now and again, Cotter's replacement would ask me to work a shift or two at the *Post,* but only a few months after my rabbi's death, those calls all but stopped.

Then, in September 1993, on a rain-slick night, McAlary lost control of his car on the East Side Drive and slid into the divider. The columnist had been at a Yankees game and was, no doubt, headed to Elaine's. At the stadium, he'd drunk more than a couple of beers. He beat long odds just to survive the crash but spent months and months recovering. There would be no more cartwheels in McAlary's life. I went to see him in a long-term rehabilitation hospital in Manhattan. Just as the elevator door opened on his floor, a nurse was walking him down the hallway. He held on to an aluminum stand with a tall pole on which was hung an intravenous bottle. He was skinny and bit embarrassed to be seen in his condition. A small, almost frightened smile came to his face.

Before the accident, when he was whole, I saw in McAlary everything I wanted to be. He once told me he'd been on the diving team; I don't know whether it was at Syracuse, where he went to college, or back in high school. But even with the pool a distant memory, he entered every day of his life with a jackknife off a springboard. He didn't stop long enough to have an inferiority complex. He didn't seem to care if people were looking at him. He certainly didn't care about the cursor on the computer screen. I spent my whole life wondering what others thought of me. Each day I awoke afraid of what would happen, like a child from a nightmare.

But more even than his courage, what I admired most about Mike was his heart. One night the cigarette store next to Elaine's was robbed. The criminal had pistol-whipped the Pakistani behind the counter, who couldn't have been more than nineteen and weighed no more than a hundred and twenty. The young clerk bled from his nose and mouth. As soon as we heard, McAlary and I hurried over, and when we arrived the young man was still shaken, his eyes wet with tears. McAlary hoisted him up onto the counter like he was a six-year-old who had just fallen off a swing. He wiped the young man's face with a handkerchief and comforted him with a soothing tone. The clerk buried his head in McAlary's chest and began to sob. McAlary was still holding him like that when the police came. That night I saw Mike McAlary in the hospital I wanted to lift him from under his arms onto a counter. I wanted to soothe the fright from his eyes.

By 1995, I'd been attending Fordham for six years, all the time working Elaine's bar at night. I'll admit, there was short period when I resigned myself to thinking I'd just be one of those bartenders with a college degree. Like actors, there are plenty of them in New York City; they're usually pretty good at bar trivia, and once in a while you see one get a shot on *Jeopardy!* But unlike the dreams on the junk pile from my early sobriety—becoming a stand-up comic or becoming an actor—the idea of becoming a writer had lodged itself, like my drinking, deep in my soul.

The roots of my desire to write began in acting class. It was then that I happened to mention to my father that I wrote some of my monologues and scenes. Soon after, he gave me his typewriter, the same Underwood that had sat on his desk at the Forty-first Precinct. It was heavy as a safe, but I hauled it up to my apartment, where I taught myself to type. First on that typewriter, and later on the word processor I'd bought for school, I began writing every morning. In the beginning it was just fifteen minutes or so, but as my writing wind strengthened, my morning sessions reached an hour or more. Morning writing became a dedicated routine. Even in the drowsy A.M.'s after long nights behind the bar, I'd put in my time in front of the computer. During my New Age phase, a friend in the program had given me a book by Julia Cameron called *The Artist's Way,* a program of exercises designed to help you find your creative voice. One of the exercises was called "morning pages," a free-association journaling you do, longhand, as soon as you awaken. I altered *The Artist's Way* a bit by using the computer instead of pen and paper.

I also started freelancing, selling feature stories and profiles to the *Daily News.* The old axiom for beginner writers is to "write what you know," and, working at Elaine's, I had great beginner material. One feature piece I wrote was about a Harley motorcycle gang that was mostly composed of dentists and voice-over guys who hung out at the restaurant. Two dozen Hogs were parked on the sidewalk in front of Elaine's when they'd hold their meetings in the back room. They were so upscale, they'd ride to meet the Beaujolais nouveau shipment at Kennedy Airport. Another piece I did was on Father Peter Colapietro, Elaine's resident priest.

Pete grew up in the Bronx, where his father owned a saloon. His first parish out of the seminary was St. Vito's in suburban Mamaroneck, New York. Pete thought it was the only St. Vito's in the country and would joke that Vito, a name that seemed more appropriate for a bookmaker than for a martyr, was the patron saint of broken legs.

In the summer, Father Pete would tend bar in a place in Hampton Bay. As long as I've known Pete, he's rented the same summer-share house. When I first began working at Elaine's, Pete was assigned to St. Joe's, just two blocks from the restaurant. He came in for a drink on a couple of occasions. One night Elaine asked him to be her date for a roast for Barbara Sinatra. It was a formal affair, Elaine explained, and Pete would be perfect in his priest outfit. From what I understand, Elaine and Pete were the hit of the dinner, and Pete made quite an impression on 'Ol Blue Eyes. After that, the good father was a staunch regular at Elaine's. He drank bourbon, Rebel Yell, and by the end of the night would tell off-color nun jokes using a napkin on his head as a whimple. Among other titles Pete held was chaplain of the Manhattan Restaurant Association. Unlike at most services at Catholic churches in Manhattan, when Pete was saying Mass at St. Joe's, you couldn't get a seat. Every bartender, saloonkeeper, bookmaker, and reprobate in the neighborhood would be looking to

Pete for salvation. He was a Damon Runyon character in robes. One night he was telling Elaine that the church building badly needed a paint job and a new roof. Elaine marched him right over to a table where a couple of perfume guys, one of them the president of Elizabeth Arden, I think, sat. "He needs a roof," she stated. "Why don't you get the company to pony up for something worthwhile?" The following week there were two very substantial checks from the perfume companies on Pete's desk.

Though Pete had his share of detractors, most of them tight-assed traditionalists, they were far outweighed by those who knew how much of an asset he was (and still is) to the Church. One of the enlightened ones was Cardinal O'Connor. Pete wasn't exactly on the cardinal's dinner party list, but one evening O'Connor invited Pete to attend the ordination of a new class of priests. During his speech, the cardinal pointed out Pete in the audience and said something to the effect of "If any of you are wondering how to be the best priest you can, I suggest you talk to Father Colapietro, because there is no better priest in the archdiocese." When Pope John Paul II visited New York City, Pete did the play-by-play for the local CBS Channel 2 news, and he was as good as the voice of the Dodgers, Vin Scully, in his prime.

Out of my morning routine, an idea for a novel started to form, an inspiration sparked by my love of Raymond Chandler. Soon my morning pages were given over to the detective story in my head. To be truthful, my creativity was not unbounded. The story I was writing was a roman à clef, with Jack Maple, John Miller, and Mike McAlary as supporting characters. My hero was Walter Moss, a lightly veiled version of Wally Millard, Elaine's resident retired NYPD first-grade detective. I had nearly three hundred pages written within six months. With equal anticipation and trepidation, I handed the manuscript to Josh, a regular customer who looked a bit like Tom Selleck, drank like the world was going to run out of Bacardi rum any moment, and had made a fortune publishing trashy romance novels. He sent "Dead of Winter," my book, to a number of editors in publishing houses around the city. One by one, the rejection letters piled up. Some of the letters were of the thanks-but-no-thanks form variety. Other had warm wishes, like "I know we'll rue the day, but we'll pass." One rejection was a handwritten hyperbole comparing me with Raymond Chandler. Right.

Here's one that an agent named Jay, who agreed to represent the book, received back from St. Martin's Press:

Dear Jay:

I've read Dead of Winter *and I had some other readers look at it as well. There are some really strong points to this mystery: he's terrific at describing Manhattan, giving the reader a real sense of the city and I thought some of his dialogue was excellent—funny, fast, colorful. I also like the opening premise of the plot, i.e., that an old Park Avenue dowager is murdered and there are any number of suspects.*

There are also some real problems: the narrative prose is rough and would need a lot of line work and, in terms of story, the plot begins to really lag after the wham bang opening. The consensus here was that this was an admirable first effort but that, given how competitive the mystery market is, it would have a tough time. McDonald should be encouraged, however, because he's got real talent.

All best,
Charles Spicer

Like a lot of alcoholics, I had a propensity for emotional highs and lows. But I wasn't about to kill myself over publishers passing on my book. I didn't just shrug the rejection off either, though. It hurt. But this is where my friendship with Elaine began to help me change the way I saw myself in the world, how I saw myself as a writer.

One night, I came in to work and found a cryptic message for me written by one of the waiters. I finally deciphered it to be a phone number for a *New York Times* editor. The *Times* asked me to write a short anecdote about a bar character of my choosing. The editor had heard about the bartender from Elaine's working his way through college and thought that would be a good backstory. All of the insecurities I'd felt while working for the *Post* came flooding back. I left work early, and well into the next morning I sat in front of my new computer feverishly writing. I had plenty of characters to write about and made a few false starts. Finally I chose to write about Jimmy the Hat.

A big, florid-faced Irishman, the Hat was out of proportion. He was as big as a parade balloon, with big sweaty hands that felt like calves' livers. He wore a porkpie hat that sat on top of his head like a bottle cap on a pumpkin. A used-car salesman, Jimmy regularly went on benders that, by way of Atlantic City, would find him parked at the end of Elaine's bar. There, one night, he engaged a pleasant-looking stranger, who spoke in a clipped English accent, in a discourse about the poor parking situation in New York City. Trying to disassociate himself politely, the Duke of York told Jimmy that he lived in Sunninghill Park. With a thoughtful shake of his big red head, Jimmy said he didn't know a lot about Queens.

The Hat offered plenty of material. I settled on this story:

One New Year's Eve, because of the phalanx of limousines in front of the restaurant, Jimmy parked his ten-year-old white Sedan de Ville Cadillac with the "For Sale" sign in the back window three wide out on Second Avenue. The

Hat had planned to only stop in for one. One drink, as it often did with Jimmy, led to another. As time passed, the limos separating Jimmy's car from the curb began to pull away, leaving the Caddy in the middle of the avenue like an island. Jimmy must not have noticed the distance his car was from the curb as he staggered to it and climbed into the back seat for a snooze. He was snoring peacefully when the city tow truck attached the hook to his car. As the de Ville was towed west, through Central Park, down the West Side Highway, and through the gates to the city pound on the Hudson River piers, Jimmy didn't even stir. God only knows what went through the big Irishman's mind the next afternoon, when he finally opened his eyes to see a seagull perched on the hood ornament of his Caddy, with the choppy water of the Hudson behind it.

Though only a few paragraphs, the story took most of the night to write. Early the next morning, I printed it out and ran it over (in those days before e-mail) to West Forty-third, the old *Times* building. That night, I sat bleary-eyed at work waiting for the editor to call. Finally he did. The piece wasn't what the *Times* was looking for, was all he had to say.

That night I wrote in my journal: "I am grammatically challenged, I've decided. I spent the formidable years of my education in bowling alleys and racetracks. I didn't go to college until I was 35. In the interim, anything I learned from high school sank deep into the dark recesses of my gray matter, corroded by ten years of gin abuse, and twenty years of barren conversations."

When Elaine found out about the *Times* turning me down, she scrunched up her face in one of her patented what-the-hell's-wrong-with-you expressions. "Who cares about the *Times?*" she said. "It's boring." She went on to lecture me that there were plenty of other places to publish stories, and that I should just keep writing and the opportunities would show up. My boss wasn't exactly Richard Simmons when it came to handing out encouragement. Being a cheerleader just isn't in Elaine's makeup. Looking back, I now see that the pass from the *Times* was important only in that it made me realize how supportive Elaine was of my writing.

Although I wouldn't dare tell anyone back then, I knew in the same way I knew how to make a scotch sour that all the college credits in the world wouldn't add up to what I was learning at Elaine's.

Chapter Seventeen

TRYING TO BE A WRITER while working at Elaine's is a little like the guy selling stadium hotdogs who talks about playing center field for the Yankees some day. The restaurant, however, did provide moments of inspiration after which I was absolutely sure of my intentions. One of them was the memorial for Terry Southern. I wrote in my journal that it was the best night I had ever spent in Elaine's. Gay Talese, George Plimpton, Kurt Vonnegut, Bruce Jay Friedman, and Rip Torn, all read passages from Southern's works: *Candy, Blue Movie, Dr. Strangelove.* "Tonight made me want to be a writer," I wrote in my journal when I got home.

But there was one aspect of Southern in particular to which I was drawn. In perhaps the hippest time this country has known, the sixties, Terry Southern wore the title of the "hippest" guy on the planet. He drugged with the Stones and Beatles, worked with Stanley Kubrick and Peter Sellers; he loved women and amphetamines and booze. He loved Elaine. The last time I saw Southern in the restaurant, I remarked to Elaine that he looked pretty good, considering. His longtime girlfriend overheard me and gave me a sad, sweet smile. There was a resignation to Southern. Perhaps he knew that each breath he drew might be his last. Cigarettes, and pot, and God knows what else he sucked into his lungs for decades had signed his last orders. But what I saw was a wounded hero from the front. He drank like every day was France in 1942. I longed for that life, a life I thought Mike McAlary lived, and Hunter Thompson lived, and Capote and all the others who struggled and wrestled with their talent all day and put the demons down each night with a shot of scotch or bourbon to the head. My dream of being a writer was healthy; the fantasy that I started to surround it with was anything but.

I'm only kidding myself, however, if I place the blame on any outside influences. The reason I began thinking of picking up a drink again had little to do with romanticizing writers or being a bartender or anything other than the fact that I am an alcoholic and to drink is my nature. I started to move away from the program, going to fewer and fewer meetings. Partly, my full schedule—writing, going to school and work—kept me from the church basements. But there was another part to my disassociation from the meetings that was much darker than a busy schedule. I thought I'd heard all there was to hear in meetings. Whereas the shared experience of other recovering alcoholics once illuminated me, I now found those stories repetitive and trite. And coincidentally, bar stories that once were the most boring things in the world to listen to sober, began to take on a compelling narrative. It was almost as though my two worlds—Elaine's and the program—switched identities.

In the late winter of 1995, Michael the waiter and I decided to go on vacation together. Originally, we planned to go to Miami, but Elaine talked us out of it. "Florida's for kids," she said. "Go to Europe." We took her advice and booked a trip to Paris. I worked the night before we left, and at the end of the shift Elaine called me over to table 4. She stuffed five hundred dollars in my hand, pulled me close, and kissed me on the lips. "Have some fun," she said, smiling.

At first, Paris was gray and unwelcoming. Our hotel on the Left Bank was the size of the walk-up in which I lived in Manhattan; our room was just a little bigger than an elevator. The manager of the hotel was aloof and inflexible when I asked if we could get larger accommodations. But Michael, who in spite of the way he butchered the language (he would say "Bon jour" to the manager each night and "Bon soir" each morning), somehow charmed the man into giving us a two-room suite.

On our second day there, I walked the streets by myself. I visited the famous Shakespeare & Company bookshop. A wizened reed of a man with a shock of George Plimpton–like white hair attended the shop. Proud of my recent bylines in the New York paper, I introduced myself as a journalist. "Really," he said with a British accent. "For whom do you write?" When I said the *New York Post,* he replied: "Don't worry. Your secret is safe with me." In a small shop, I'd purchased some chocolate, and I walked the Petit Pont to Notre-Dame, where I left the silver package at the feet of the statue of St. Thérèse the Little Flower. I wandered over to Les Deux Magots, where I envisioned Hemingway and F. Scott Fitzgerald raising glasses of red wine. By the time I was back at the hotel, I was in love with Paris.

Coinciding with the week we were there, Robert Altman was wrapping *Prêt-à-Porter,* a film about the French fashion business. Michael and I both had become friendly with Altman and, especially, his wife, Katherine. We met Katherine for lunch at little bistro called Café Zinc and had dinner with the Altmans at La Coupole, a Paris version of Elaine's. In both places, I found myself thinking how nice it would be to have some wine.

After four or five days in Paris, Michael got the idea for us to go to Amsterdam. We left from the Gare du Nord. Outside the window of the train, places like Brussels and Antwerp streamed by. Michael talked gibberish to a Belgium soldier who humored him for most of the trip. In Amsterdam I again walked a foreign city by myself. As in Paris, at first I wasn't impressed. With the canal boats and multicolored streetcars, I thought it was like a Disney version of a European city. I wandered into a café and was handed a menu on which different types of hashish and marijuana were listed. I pointed at one and was brought a pipe and some hash. Although I'd smoked marijuana in high school, I'd never considered myself a pothead. I knew the program thought otherwise; you can't be high and sober at the same time is a favorite refrain in the rooms. It's only some hash, a voice within me nudged.

It's funny, for years afterward I completely blocked the memory of that hash house in Amsterdam. Only now, as I look back, does some of that afternoon come back to my thoughts. After I smoked the bowl, I tentatively stepped out into the low winter light. All the street names, with their double vowels, looked the same. It took me an hour to find my hotel, which was only a couple of blocks away. Acutely paranoid, I stayed in my room until the high wore off. That night I went to the red-light district and up a flight of stairs into a bar over a brothel. I ordered a Beck's. I didn't drink it. I just held it in my hand for a moment and left before the prostitutes had a chance to proposition me.

The summer of 1995, I went to a meeting held in a sober beach house in Quogue on Long Island. I was staying at the house with a girl I was dating. Laura was a beautiful but somber brunette who once told me she was far fonder of animals than of people. We courted in coffee shops after meetings and parties thrown by program friends.

The beach house was called Penn-Craig, after the Welshman who built it in the 1870s. It had been owned for generations by a family named Swan, the last lord of the manor having been Bill Swan, an attorney. In its heyday, the grand twelve-bedroom house was a model of seaside royalty, its most distinguishing feature an eighty-foot porch. But the barrister Swan had let it fall into some disrepair—wood floors sagged and creaked, walls were cracked, and crown molding had bowed. Ultimately, the house became one of the few rentals in the solid gold Hampton enclave. The meeting was held in what was once the dining room. An oak table, extended by leaves, that could sit eighteen easily, was the centerpiece of the room, which was painted cranberry red with white trim. On a level just below the ceiling ran a plate rail, on which candles burned during the meetings. People who didn't arrive early enough to sit at the table flopped on French bistro chairs, church benches, or in the two window seats at the front of the room.

Most of the summer shares where taken by the younger set in the program. In their manner and expressions, I saw the passion for being sober that I'd once had: the quick laughter, the optimistic nods. But the light in their eyes was the biggest difference between them and me. Theirs shone with unshakable hope. That program light in my eyes had dimmed considerably, and the afternoon in Amsterdam had almost extinguished it completely.

Maybe it was that I'd spoken at meetings so much that I was able to fall into a well-worn routine. In front of that room, I talked about how my poor mom had suffered through my early drinking. How she had transformed her bureau into a kind of altar-shrine for me. She had a statue of St. Anthony, her favorite. From his outstretched arms hung rosary beads, worn to the nub by her novenas. There was my high school picture, eight by twelve, surrounded by prayer cards and other religious paraphernalia. I said the line that always got a laugh: that when I was drinking on clear nights, you could see the light from the candles she lit for me several counties away.

After the meeting, Laura and I walked to a swimming hole nearby. The water was illuminated by the full moon and had an almost neon blue color. Naked, we held each other in the waist-deep water and then made love on the sandy bank. The summer was nearly finished. There was the slightest of chills in the air.

The next day, Laura told me she was moving to Chicago. Her statement took me completely by surprise. I was furious at her for not giving me any warning. But something inside also felt released. She was my last connection to the program, the only reason I was still going to meetings. With her gone, my separation from the program would be complete.

Chapter Eighteen

I WAS JUST ABOUT TO GRADUATE Fordham when Elizabeth Stone urged me to apply to the master's in journalism program at Columbia. The only thing I knew about Columbia University was that they had a lousy football team. During one stretch, in the eighties, the Columbia Lions lost forty-four straight games. The university's marching band played the Mickey Mouse Club theme when the team ran onto the field. After they set a 1-AA record for the most consecutive losses, their coach told *The New York Times*: "I'm realistic; there's not a lot of talent here." Columbia, however, was about football as much as Elaine's was about the food.

I took Elizabeth's advice perhaps for the sole reason that I had no other immediate ideas. I didn't really think I was going to get in anyhow. For a couple of weeks, my life was like a blender on mix as I tried to assemble an application package. I asked two of Elaine's customers to write letters of recommendation. One was a federal agent named John O'Brien, the other was the writer Ed Klein, the ex-editor of the Sunday *Times Magazine* and

contributing editor to *Vanity Fair.* Though I wasn't overly hopeful about getting into Columbia, part of me was really excited
about the prospect. I would be the first in my family to go to an
Ivy League school, and in an Irish Catholic cop family, that's a
big deal. But if I didn't have a lot of faith in me, someone close
to me did. One night at the end of the bar while I was still waiting for word, one of the regular customers asked Elaine if she
thought I would be accepted into Columbia. "If Brian really
wants it, he'll get it," my boss said with a certainty that made me
wonder if maybe she was right.

But when the prescribed time for notification of acceptance
came and went, I let the idea drop onto my pile of junked dreams.
Then, just a few weeks before the term was to start, I received a
phone call from the journalism school's dean of admissions offer-
ing me a spot in their part-time program. They'd had a few last-
minute drop-offs, and I had been on the waiting list.

It was the late summer of 1995 when I first stepped onto the
university's grounds, a rectangle of buildings that takes up a half
dozen blocks in a neighborhood in southern Harlem called Morningside Heights. As I walked through the main gate from Broadway and 116th Street (Columbia has its own subway stop there), I
had my first view of the journalism school: its rear end, a rather
unimpressive angle that looks like an apartment building in the
Bronx. Around the front of the building, which faces the new student center, there is a bit more character—specifically, the statue
of Thomas Jefferson that sits on a brick and cement terrace and
faces away from the building toward a large oak tree in front of
Furnald Hall. From the terrace in front of the journalism building, I looked out on the neatly kept square of lawn. Students decades younger than me tossed Frisbees or lay flat on their stomachs
with chins propped on their palms, lost in Nietzsche or Schopen-
hauer, or so I imagined. Behind them loomed the Parthenon-like

Butler Library, with its engravings of Classical writers—Homer, Herodotus, Sophocles, Plato, Aristotle, Demosthenes, Cicero, and Virgil—over the entrance. I knew six out of the eight and made a mental note to look up Herodotus and Demosthenes. Only once before was any member of my family inside the confines of Columbia. As a rookie cop, my brother Frankie had stood guard at the front gate after the 1968 riots; there he was spat on and called every imaginable derogatory name by students and faculty alike.

Though I wasn't overwhelmed by the surroundings, I felt a tinge of ancestral discomfort, a sensation of being less than that was as old as peat fires, or went at least as far back as the first MacDonalds, who, sometime in the fifteenth century, when they hadn't yet lost the *a* in *Mac,* sailed the Irish Sea from Scotland. In what would become the Northern Ireland county of Monaghan, they would build a stone hut in the side of lush hill and not dare think of a higher station. Of course, station and edification are two different things. And the Irish have had a long scholarly history and no beef with continuing your education as long as you're taught by someone who can also consecrate a Host and, of course, you don't forget from whence you came. But Elaine's had alleviated much of my Irish ground-level view of the world. Though I hadn't gained a higher station in my years working behind Elaine's bar, station had for me lost its lofty place. At Elaine's the more importance you awarded yourself, the less importance you were afforded. Chutzpah aside, though, I was still as nervous as, well, a kid in a new school.

There were about fifteen of us in my section of the part-time program. The designation *part-time* is a bit misleading. A few years before, the journalism school had decided to tap a reservoir of prospective students by stretching out the ten-month master's program to two years. The idea was to attract people who worked for a living. There just aren't enough hours in the day for a full-timer to hold a job. But the part-time workload was still considerable, and often the classrooms were filled with bleary-eyed students and jumbo cups of coffee.

That first day the introductions began. Of course, everyone wanted to make an impression. Although there were a couple of Yalies in the class, Ivy League degrees were actually in the minority. Much later, I went through the "face book," which listed my classmates' undergraduate colleges, and I was very surprised at the proletarian schools represented: University of Scranton, Rutgers, and Brooklyn College, to name a few. But what I didn't overestimate was the careers most of my fellow students were segueing out of. There were a couple of lawyers, an Army captain, a few journalists, a professional musician, an English teacher, and a Wall Streeter or two.

Worried that the class would turn their noses up at my bartending, I felt a bit of relief when the guy before me started talking about his plumbing expertise. Bill Hughes was a carpenter and plumber, but one, I would come to find, with the heart of an Irish poet. When it came my turn, the collar on my shirt had somehow shrunk several sizes. When I mentioned what I did for a living, an uncomfortable silence enveloped the room. Someone cleared their throat. I shifted in my seat.

But Columbia J School professors don't go into their first classes without having done their own homework. Ari Goldman, my RW1 (Reporting and Writing, the basic course) teacher, had read my folder. "Brian works at the famous Elaine's," Ari said with a smile.

Several students nodded their heads, impressed. The others, who didn't have a clue what Elaine's was, didn't want to look uninformed and nodded along. Somebody asked if the class would get a discount at the bar, and everyone laughed. I didn't know whether I was being accepted or made fun of. Someone then asked, a bit patronizingly as I remember, if I'd seen any famous

writers recently. The afternoon before, in the back room, Annie
Leibovitz had done a photo shoot of Vietnam War correspondents
for *Vanity Fair.* In Leibovitz's lens were Peter Arnett, David Halberstam, Horst Faas, and a few other news icons of that era. "Well,
as a matter of fact . . . ," I began.

It might have been in that moment that I realized Columbia
held Elaine's in a higher regard than Elaine held Columbia. Not
that she thought it was a bad idea for me to be attending the
school. My enrollment actually worked in her favor by keeping
me at the restaurant for at least two more years. She also thought
my going to graduate school would help my self-esteem (she said
exactly that to me one night). But Elaine just didn't comprehend
what all the fuss was about. Although not right away, I eventually
found myself thinking along those same lines. It was not that Columbia didn't live up to my expectations. It did. It was just that I
started to hear a voice within, faint at first but unmistakably similar to Elaine's, that said to me I was a good as anybody else in the
school, and maybe even better than some.

Compared with my preconception of what a journalism professor looked like (the John Houseman crusty, no-nonsense dictator who with one raised hairy eyebrow could send shivers through
the most prepared student), Ari Goldman was cast against type.
Slight of build with a boyish face, Ari wore round, frameless
glasses and had a sweep of hair the color of rye bread. He looked
less like a professor and more like a grad student just back from a
summer at a kibbutz. The word most commonly used to describe
him was "sweet." Though he had the demeanor of a good coun-
selor at camp, Ari had fought in his share of journalism trenches
(there are at least four J school professors, Ari included, cringing at
my flagrant use of mixed metaphor–cliché). One was the Crown
Heights riot, which he'd covered for *The New York Times.* For a
few days in August 1991, that riot turned a section of Brooklyn

into a battleground between blacks and Hasidic Jews. But for most of the time, Ari was the *Times*'s spiritual voice, covering their religion beat. In 1985 the paper gave him a year off and paid for his study at Harvard Divinity School. From that experience came a book called *The Search for God at Harvard*.

Predictably, Ari was fair. But he also knew how to teach and imparted to his class that semester the basic tools to gather and write news. Each student was charged with finding a neighborhood from which he or she would report. Ari had only one stipulation: our locale couldn't contain a Starbucks. The no-Starbucks edict naturally excluded any namby-pamby location in Manhattan or Brooklyn Heights. No nail salons or sushi joints for us. Good old-fashioned, gritty, get-your-hands-dirty reporting. When we first heard Ari's proviso, I remember some in the classroom wearing rather uncomfortable expressions. One Wall Streeter's deficiency of courage showed in his bright red cheeks. But there was also plenty of nerve in the most unlikely candidates.

Erin was from a tiny town in Indiana. Young, tall, and with wheat-colored hair, she was smart in ways Columbia couldn't teach. She once told me that she was a terrible student all through high school, mostly as a result of not going to class and instead driving around with her boyfriend Hoss in his pickup and listening to country rock. But at some point in her senior year, Erin realized that she needed something dramatic to happen fast or she'd be riding in pickups for the foreseeable future. Then she read an article about noblesse oblige in major colleges. She set her sights on Sarah Lawrence, sat at the kitchen table, and wrote, in longhand, a letter annunciating every last unfortunate detail of her situation. You could have wrung the sheet of paper out and come up with half a cup of tears, she told me. In response, she received a letter telling her she'd been given a full ride to the lock-jawed, once all-girl college in Bronxville, New York.

It wasn't as though Sarah Lawrence got the short end in the deal. Once Hoss and his pickup were removed from the equation, Erin's academic ability was boundless. She also had talent as a dancer and studied ballet at college. She graduated close to the top of her class undergrad, was accepted to Columbia J School, and, for good measure, took a second master's, in anthropology, at Columbia.

Sometimes after class we'd meet on the steps and smoke cigarettes. I don't know how much I contributed to the short conversations we had. Each time I tried to talk to Erin, my mouth would lose its ability to form words. I felt like I'd eaten a pail of sand, pail and all. The crush developed further when she told me that she was a *Simpsons* fan, and that one of her favorite Homer moments was when he shaved his shoulders for a date with a younger woman. One of the few sentences I was able to articulate to Erin that first semester was that I too had shaved my shoulders—once or twice. I wanted to reel those words back as soon as I heard myself say them. But when Erin laughed, I felt warm.

Though we weren't in the same section, I tried my hardest to follow Erin's progress at school. When I heard what beat she was assigned—West Harlem, on 125th Street, from the Apollo Theater to the Cotton Club—I was sure she was going to head right back to Indiana. Nothing against Harlem, but you couldn't have blamed a towheaded Midwestern gal for thinking she could never fit in. But Erin had no problem with Harlem, and Harlem seemed to like her just fine.

I got my neighborhood by default—no one else wanted it. Red Hook, Brooklyn, was one of those parts of the city whose poverty and crime were partly by-products of the design and construction projects of Robert Moses, known as the Master Builder. But Moses's Brooklyn-Queens Expressway severed the one square waterfront mile on the Brooklyn docks that made up Red Hook from the rest of the world. I knew all about Robert Moses because, one, the J school strongly suggested that its incoming students read *The Power Broker: Robert Moses and the Fall of New York,* Robert Caro's dictionary-size biography, which I did, and, two, Caro was a regular customer at Elaine's.

I saw Robert Caro in the restaurant a half dozen times before I knew who he was and what he did. He certainly didn't look to me like a writer. With his short-cropped black hair and black-framed Buddy Holly glasses, he looked more like a sixties TV scientist hawking fluoridated toothpaste or an Elvis Costello impersonator than like one of America's foremost biographers. Unlike many of Elaine's famous stable of writers, he was also friendly—he made it a point to stop by the bar on his way in for a few words and a smile. At table 11 in the back alcove, where he normally sat, he was always surrounded by a large group of family and friends. Wine flowed at his table like it was the wedding at Cana, and laughter filled the back of the restaurant when he was there. Several times while I was reading *Power Broker,* I brought the book to work with passages marked and the intention of talking to him. I found out that he too had attended Columbia's J School. One night I did get a chance to talk to him a little about it, but I felt like I was imposing on his good time and didn't ask him about the book again.

Red Hook was once a brass knuckle of a place. Neighborhood lore has it that Al Capone received his legendary scar on the docks in Red Hook before the gangster moved on to Chicago. Though the scenes were actually shot in Hoboken, New Jersey, the Red Hook docks provided the inspiration and storyline for *On the Waterfront,* the movie in which Marlon Brando utters the famous line "I coulda been a contender."

But by the 1980s, most of the inhabitants had left Red Hook or retreated into the Red Hook Houses, a housing project built in the late 1930s. The population of Red Hook dropped from 26,000 plus in the days of the bustling docks to just over 8,500 in the depths of the crack cocaine devastation. Having consumed the neighborhood, and leaving in its wake abandoned lots strewn with the glass of cheap liquor, forties, and crack stems, the rapacious virus of drugs and crime burrowed through the red bricks of the projects, too. The crime in Red Hook got as bad as that of any neighborhood in New York City. In 1992, the Seventy-sixth Precinct, which encompasses Red Hook and the surrounding area, counted nearly five hundred robberies, over three hundred and fifty assaults, twenty-two rapes, and seven homicides, including the murder of a well-liked principal who was caught in a project's gun battle while he searched for a nine-year-old who'd left school that day crying after a fight.

But there was another Red Hook, one that survived the drug plague, and one that I would gleefully explore: a magical place by the sea. On a block that dead-ended on the harbor, there were abandoned red-brick warehouses that dated to the Civil War. Faded but multicolored "captains' houses," so tiny they looked like they were built by Hobbits, lined cobblestone streets. One of those cobblestone blocks seemed to lead right into New York Harbor. The skyline of Manhattan looked close enough to swim to yet a universe away. The Statue of Liberty was so near, it seemed as though she could hand you her torch.

By the late 1990s, Red Hook started to rebound a bit, attracting artists drawn by the cheap rents and space for studios. Following the artists came a wave of the edgy downtown crowd with tattoos and Halloween-black lips. Sometime later, a *Times* segment entitled "If You're Thinking of Living in . . ." featured Red Hook. The story mentioned a sign on Coffey Street that read: "Coming Soon, Starbucks Coffey." It was a joke, of course, referencing what the article described as Red Hook's "nascent gentrification." *Nascent* was being generous. I was in no danger of Ari disqualifying my neighborhood.

It was a warm, late-summer afternoon when I first wandered my beat. Maybe it was the ghosts of the longshoremen, long dead, or the lap of the harbor water on what was left of the piers, but I started to feel the echo of Red Hook deep within. Faintly famil- iar, the feeling was like the one I got as a kid from playing hooky, or drinking beer during recess, or being buried in that snowfield. Just being in Red Hook felt like getting away with something. The forlornness of it, its proximity to the sea, spoke directly to the dormant drunk in me. It was perhaps no surprise then that the first thing I reported and wrote about was a saloon, then Red Hook's only saloon, and a saloon with a story.

That first afternoon, I walked into John's just as the sun began to drop behind the Statue of Liberty and into Jersey. The barroom was small and dark, with three or four booths and a length of oak smooth and worn at the edges from innumerable elbows. Behind the bar were maybe a half dozen bottles of booze, some contem- porary brands, like Jack Daniel's and Cuervo Gold, some, like VAT 69 and Four Roses, from another time. The bar lights were also from another era and incongruous: one was from Pabst Blue Rib- bon, not even a New York beer, a giveaway from a distributor, no doubt. The joint was empty, but there was jazz coming from a tape player behind the bar.

"Like him?" a gaunt, gray, stringy-haired man who appeared from the kitchen with a sandwich on a plate asked me.

I shrugged.

"Getz," he said, pointing to the stereo with an upward point of his chin.

Before I learned that I was speaking with Sunny Balzano, the bar's proprietor, I found out that the recording was made while Stan Getz was in Europe when he was at the top of his craft. The history of the jazzman became a natural segue for Sunny to tell me his story. Without doing a thing, I found out a basic lesson in reporting. Just go to a bar and sit there. Jimmy Breslin made a pretty nice career out of doing just that. Sunny had been born in Red Hook in 1934, in the red-brick building attached to the saloon. His father and his uncle, John, for whom the bar was named, ran the place and performed other nebulous duties around the neighborhood. One of Sunny's earliest recollections was a murder. Someone shot the iceman and left the smoking gun wrapped in the *Brooklyn Eagle* in one of the booths. According to the *Times,* Sunny's uncle was arrested but released a few days later, when it was found out the murderer was a Sicilian who harbored an unknown vendetta against the victim.

When Sunny first showed an inclination and talent for drawing, his father lectured him that he had better start being serious about school or he'd never get a real job. His father's words were prophetic. Sunny's relationship with his dad, and his departure from the neighborhood, was like Getz's departure to Europe, at least according to Sunny. For twenty years Sunny knocked around the Village with the artist crowd and never once went back to the place of his birth. He also had no communication with his father. Although Sunny never found fame as an artist, he lived his life as he wanted to, not as his father wanted him to. Then, in 1987, after a marriage, the birth of a daughter, and a divorce, Sunny found out that his father was terminally ill. Like Getz coming back to New York, he said, he returned to Red Hook. There was softness in Sunny's voice as he remembered that time.

Though Sunny was again his father's son, he stayed his own man. He brought his art back to Red Hook with him. He bought a small row house to use for a studio. Although it was the low rent that attracted the artists to Red Hook, it was Sunny who led the revolution. Seven years after he buried his dad, his uncle died, and the bar was left to Sunny's charge. Legally, however, ownership was a tangled mess, with an expired liquor license and numerous summonses and violations, none of which seemed to bother my host in the least.

When Sunny finished telling me his story, he stepped behind the bar, punched the eject button on the player, and flipped the tape. Once again, Getz's soulful sax filled the room. For just a fleeting moment, I craved a beer—even a Pabst. Just to be able to sit there at the end of the world, listen to Sunny and Getz, and drink the heart out of the rest of the day. A horn sounded out on the harbor, the Staten Island Ferry. The sea sounds and the thought of ghosts gave the setting just enough mystery to get drunk in. Perhaps it was on that dead-end dock, as I dutifully wrote in my reporter's notebook, that I took my first step back toward a drinking life. Maybe that was the moment when my sobriety became a thing of my past.

Chapter Nineteen

THERE ARE TIMES when I think the most impressive part of my brain is its ability to forget. I have a friend in the program who has often pointed out that I have a large body of evidence that proves I can't safely pick up a drink. And yet the memory of the effect my drinking had on my life somehow became diminished.

Some of my classmates would gather each evening at a bar across Broadway called the West End. I went along. It was my kind of saloon, one with a past kept alive by barroom historians and wooden booths and tables carved with initials from across the decades. Jack Kerouac and Allen Ginsberg drank there. So did Mark Rudd and other sixties student protesters. As did Fidel Castro on a visit to New York.

With the image of the dictator and ghosts of the Beats at nearby tables, we would talk with fervency about politics, Whitewater, and O.J. We would champion our favorite writers. I'd always lead with Raymond Chandler. We would even, with adolescent writers' bluster, spray-paint graffiti on the literary pantheon: "Mailer needs an editor." "*Moby-Dick* is overrated." Though our ages and back-grounds were vastly different, our eyes all shone with the same brilliance of dream. The dream was intoxicating.

One night at the West End, Erin asked me why I didn't drink. I looked directly into her youthful blue eyes and, for the first time in fourteen years, didn't have an answer. Though I truly did have many reasons supporting why I shouldn't drink, not the least being that I was an admitted alcoholic, in that moment I was convinced that things had changed. I wasn't the wild kid who drank himself out of jobs and into blackouts. I wasn't the same person who drove into that family's station wagon. I was a college graduate and in the midst of obtaining a postgraduate degree. I had a steady job that I'd held for ten years. I was forty-two now. My body had chemically changed, I thought. Once in a meeting I heard a guy describe waking from a bender in a doorway on Broadway on Thanksgiving morning. The first sound he heard was trumpets playing "The March of the Wooden Soldiers." That experience was enough to scare him into the program, where he stayed sober for seven years. Then one fall afternoon he was at his dentist's, where he read a story in *Reader's Digest* about how all the body's cells regenerate in seven years. With all new cells, it occurred to him, there was a good chance he was no longer an alcoholic. He went to a nearby saloon that very afternoon and had a beer. Several weeks later, on Thanksgiving morning, he awoke in the same doorway he had seven years before with the sound of trumpets blaring in his ears. It was a funny story, I thought, but one that was not at all applicable to me. All those years staying away from the first drink had built in me a healthy respect for alcohol. This time it would be different.

I was energized, thrilled with the newness of my life. I liked the fact that I was at Columbia; I liked being around younger people who were enthusiastic about their futures. God, I really felt like a kid again. The cinders of my addictive personality had begun to glow.

It was in between my first and second semesters at the Morningside campus that I booked the trip to Dublin. In the wet Irish chill of my first evening there, I walked the cobblestone streets of Leopold Bloom. I stayed in a hotel just off St. Stephen's Green. I was lucky to have accommodations. Every room was booked. The lobby was filled with people wearing robin's egg blue and yellow jerseys, hats, and scarves. That week, the All-Ireland hurling finals were being held, and the hotel was awash in the colors of County Clare. I eyed the crowded barroom as I carried my bags to the elevator. The laughter from within was inviting. In the lift, a Clare rooter, dressed in a blue-and-yellow jersey, sat on a barstool holding a pint of black Guinness, his eyes just as dark as his drink but twinkling with mischief. Once I was in my room, I sat on the edge of a mattress that sank like sponge cake under my weight. There was no wrestling match with my conscience. It had been a long time coming. I had made up my mind in the West End weeks before, when my blue-eyed classmate asked why I wasn't drinking. I wasn't going to deny myself anymore.

Back downstairs, I pushed open the swinging cut glass and wood doors. The room was thick with drink and brogue. I caught the busy barman's eye and ordered a pint. Those unfamiliar words seemed to suck all the air from the room. In that vacuum, I was acutely aware of what was transpiring. I watched the bartender pour half the pint, then let it sit on the drainboard. Guinness is not just slopped into a glass. Its preparation takes expertise and time. Enough time to change my mind. The program flashed through my thoughts. But the remembrance of its cautionary tales didn't stop me. Much of my resolve to drink again came from thinking I was different now, but some of it came out of a need to throw caution to the wind. I wanted to live my life without having to wonder how much I'd missed.

Though it had been fourteen years since my last, the lifting of the Guinness to my lips brought no immediate consequence. There was no clap of thunder or flash of lightning. In fact, it was somewhat anticlimactic. Of course it was.

Chapter Twenty

E LAINE COULD BARELY WALK. What each night had been a grand entrance, with flowing cape and determined visage, had deteriorated, along with the ligaments and cartilage in her knees, to the Burma death march. All those years carrying all that weight had worn away all that was bendable. She had trouble managing the one small step from the sidewalk, and a simple trip to the ladies' meant stopping several times to hold on to a chairback or tabletop, as if she were in a trapeze act. I'd see her grimace as she slid off her barstool and the knee would begin to buckle like a Russian weightlifter's, but I never heard her say a word in complaint. There were times I wondered how she managed to get into the shower, how she pulled on her stockings. Still, once she was inside the restaurant, sitting at her table or on the barstool doing the checks, she looked the same as she had all the years I'd known her. Only a few of the regulars knew the pain she was in.

Someone—I think it was Josh, the onetime romance novel publisher—bought her a cane. Obviously expensive, it was ornate with a wonderful brass handle. When he handed it to her, Elaine scrunched up her face. In that moment I remembered one busy night when a very well-dressed man walked in holding his hat and an umbrella. Elaine was doing the checks and was swamped with dupes. The man cleared his throat several times to get her attention. When she finally looked up, he said, in a refined accent, "Madam, there doesn't seem to be a coatroom." Elaine told him that there were hooks on the wall behind the tables and to hang his coat on one of them. She went back to writing, and again he cleared his throat. "But what of my hat?" he said, a bit louder. Elaine tapped the eraser end of her pencil on the stack of checks. "There are plenty of hooks," she said in a measured tone. She again began to write. "And what am I supposed to do with this?" the man said, holding up his umbrella, his voice at a high, indignant pitch. Elaine placed her pencil on the bar. She looked not at the man but at me. She raised her eyebrows ever so slightly. Of all the retorts Elaine had delivered over the years, the one she didn't make to the man with the umbrella was maybe the funniest. She couldn't believe that someone would leave themselves that wide open.

Probably because Josh hemorrhaged money in the joint, she held back with him, too. "Very nice," she said evenly as he handed her the cane. She had one of the waiters put it in the liquor cabinet, from which it departed to parts unknown. Elaine never touched it again.

Soon, however, her condition degraded to the point where she was almost immobile. Carlo would wait anxiously by the front door for her to arrive each night. When the taxi door opened, he'd rush out to support her heavy carriage. One night it had snowed, and the Second Avenue plow had left a small mound in front of the restaurant. Elaine had to wait for Carlo to shovel a path. Through the front window, I could see the embarrassment in her expression.

Finally she gave in and made the arrangements for knee replacement surgery. As hospitals go, Doctors was one of a kind.

Built with blocks of stone in the year of the great stock market crash, the hospital looked like a staid apartment building on Park Avenue. It had once featured suites with oak furniture and was originally used as a sanitarium and dry-out place for the rich and famous. Among the notables who were admitted "for exhaustion," as the society columnists would then put it, were Eugene O'Neill, James Thurber, Eddie Cantor, and Clare Boothe Luce. Marilyn Monroe convalesced in the hospital when she miscarried during her marriage to Arthur Miller. Just a year before Elaine checked in, Michael Jackson stayed there for a couple of days to have an irregular heartbeat monitored. Elaine chose it because it was only a couple of blocks from the restaurant.

She took a private room from which she could see East End Avenue, Gracie Mansion, and the East River. Her surgeon, the same guy who operated on the Knicks center Patrick Ewing, had said that she needed both knees replaced. Elaine told him to do them at the same time.

All in all, she was in the hospital for no more than a week. It was important, she was told, to start flexing the new knees as soon as possible. Michael the waiter and I went to visit her several times during her stay. For the first couple of days after the operation, Elaine was in a rather amiable mood. Of course, she was, by her own estimation, "schnockered to the eyeballs" with a Demerol drip. But when she went home, and off the hospital drugs, the pain she endured had to have been excruciating.

While the boss was convalescing, Diane, the manager, Michael, and myself decided to give the joint a badly needed paint job as a surprise for her. From the walls and the shelf above the tables, we pulled down the book jackets and mementos that had accumulated over the thirty-plus years Elaine's had been in business. It was an amazing array. There were photos, most taken in the restaurant, that were intimate frozen moments of famous lives: One was of Sinatra sitting at a back table. In it, the crooner looks middle-aged and full-faced, his thin transplanted hair pulled across his head. Sinatra rarely came into the restaurant, partly, one could imagine, because Mario Puzo was a steady customer. According to an interview Puzo gave, Sinatra walked into Elaine's one night just after *The Godfather* had been released. Puzo, who was having dinner, knew that Sinatra was not happy with the author's lightly veiled caricature of him in the book. That night Elaine tried to act the peacemaker and asked Sinatra if he wanted to sit with the author. Sinatra emphatically said no, had a drink at the bar, and left. Elaine and Sinatra, however, remained friends and had good friends in common, including Danny Lavezzo, who owned P.J. Clarke's. And my boss continued to be on Sinatra's short list when the singer hosted a New York party or fund-raiser.

When I took down the Jackie Gleason photo, I experienced some residual emotional pain, the cause of which I will get into later. Other photos that came down included Barbra Streisand, Elaine with Malcolm Forbes, and one of Elaine with Jackie Onassis. I remembered one night when Forbes parked his Harley on the sidewalk in front of the place when he came in for dinner. When Caroline and John Jr. were still children, Jackie O would drop them off in the early evening and the waiters would feed them and babysit until Momma Onassis came back later that night. There was a Dondi sketch by its creator, Irwin Hasen. I was there the night he drew it. There were two caricatures of Elaine, penciled on the backs of menus, one by the cartoonist Mel Lazarus, the other by Tony Bennett, who did the sketch while sitting at the bar. Some of the memorabilia we took down had been there long before I started working in the restaurant. There was a poster for a Supremes concert announcing a ticket price of $3.50. There was a gift from Rod Steiger: a black-and-white photograph of Toots Shor's softball team, which included players such as

Jonathan Winters, Ernie Kovacs, and Phil Silvers, along with Steiger, Sinatra, and Gleason. There was also a lot of junk, including a placard for a play called *Lawrence of Latavia* and a book jacket for a novel called *Murder at Elaine's*. We had several big cardboard boxes, destined for the basement, for the stuff we wanted to get rid of. Personally, I didn't care what stayed or got tossed. Michael, whose background was theater, made most of the decisions, and he did so with the cold hand of a casting director.

A firestorm ensued when we put the book jackets that had made Michael's cut back up on the freshly painted walls. A book by Jimmy Breslin ended up, somewhat callously, in the liquor cabinet (Breslin gave up a big drinking habit long ago), and George Plimpton was displeased with the new placement of a *Paris Review* cover, not far from the entrance to the bathrooms. (Sometime after the paint job, Plimpton came in with a bust, actually just a sculpted head, of himself. To mollify his hurt feelings, Elaine allowed it to be mounted in a back alcove of the restaurant.)

Elaine's recuperation was nearly miraculous. I would imagine recovery from knee surgery is arduous under any circumstance. But having both knees operated on, and having those knees carry the weight that hers did, seems to me to stretch the limits of human capability. I remember a day or two after the operation when I visited her. Elaine was sitting on the side of the bed, testing how much weight her legs would hold. She was up and walking with a walker that afternoon. She had a physical therapist in her apartment every day for the following couple of weeks. Elaine's housekeeper told Diane that the rigors the therapist was putting Elaine through were torturous. But when I spoke to my boss on the phone and asked her how it was going with the therapist, she just said, "He's cute."

She was back in the restaurant as soon as she could get herself showered and dressed. At first, she had to use one of those crutches with the arm support. But soon she had me stash it behind the bar and was gimping around on her own. In no time, she was better, more mobile, than I could remember. I thought back to my early days at the restaurant, in those days when she willed the place busy again. Throughout my years in saloons, I've known my share of tough guys. All my life I've been surrounded by New York City cops. I don't think any of them had the will and the constitution for pain that my lady boss possessed.

When Elaine walked into the restaurant and saw the paint job, she was overcome with joy—well, at least she smiled and nodded her head in appreciation, which is as close to *overcome* as Elaine gets. It was the best gift we could've given her. She also didn't give a second thought to the placement of the books on the wall. I always wondered what the writers would think if they knew how little she cared about things like that. I remember one night Carl Bernstein lovingly handing his new work, a book about John Paul II called *His Holiness,* to her with great excitement. Elaine took the book, shrugged as she glanced at it, then handed it over her shoulder to an uncaring waiter, leaving its display future in doubt.

The honor of the wall, however, was not lost on me. Just for a moment, as I helped Michael and Diane hang the book covers, I allowed myself to wonder how it felt to have a book there.

Chapter Twenty-one

WHEN YOU FIRST MEET Judith Crist, you're not afraid. Diminutive, with a rugose kisser and a pair of liquid hazel eyes, she makes you think of scotch sours, matinees, and doilies. That is until the first time she leaves claw marks on your weekly written submissions. Like razor cuts, her tight, red script slices the triple space she demands of her students. But her written observations were just flesh wounds compared with the open-heart surgery she performed with her remarks in class. After one such session, I excused myself, went out behind the Thomas Jefferson statue, and threw air punches while I fought back tears. Think I'm being a bit of a sissy? Billy Wilder, the legendary director, once said this about Mrs. Crist: "Inviting her to review a movie was like inviting the Boston Strangler to give you a neck massage."

In the waning hours of a golden age of New York City newspapers, Judith Crist was the girl with a curl and a typewriter from which sparks flew. She held the powerful position of film critic for the *Herald Tribune,* a bastion of writing that at one time or another held the services of Mark Twain, Grantland Rice, Henry

James, Heywood Broun, John Lardner, Robert Benchley, Red Smith, Walter Kerr, Tom Wolfe, and Jimmy Breslin. Judith Crist's boss was the zillionaire, war hero, and playboy Jock Whitney, who ran the paper with a heart as big as his bank account.

A few weeks after Crist had become the *Herald Trib*'s movie critic, she reviewed a picture that starred Henry Fonda called *Spencer's Mountain*. The syrupy movie was the inspiration for the popular television show *The Waltons*. Her review was a pan and began with the facetious line that Radio City Music Hall was running a "dirty movie" for Easter. The producers, Warner Bros., weren't happy. They immediately sent word to the paper that Crist was barred from all of their future screenings. Then Radio City Music Hall, which had nearly six thousand seats, was the largest indoor theater in the world, and bought ad space in the *Herald Trib* three hundred and sixty-five days a years. When the Music Hall withdrew its advertising, Crist got a call from her boss. "Don't worry about a thing," Jock Whitney assured her. That same week the *Herald Tribune* ran an editorial defending their movie reviewer.

In the early 1960s, following the demise of the *Herald Trib,* Crist became perhaps the best-known film critic in the country when she took a job at NBC's *Today* show. She worked with a young reporter named Barbara Walters. Having made a name for herself at the paper, and now a part of the ever-growing influence of morning TV, Crist, by her own admission, began to acquire an inflated ego. One chance meeting brought her back to size. On vacation with her husband and son at a resort hotel in Puerto Rico, Crist saw a woman on the beach who looked vaguely familiar. Trying to impress, she introduced herself as Judith Crist "from the *Today* show." Whatever reaction Crist expected, she didn't receive it. When she pressed with a "Don't we know each other?" the wife of the future vice president gave her a pained smile. "I'm Happy Rockefeller," she said. "And I don't think so."

My association with Judith Crist was dramatic from the start. I'd begun smoking cigars, having given in to the Cuban cigar hysteria that gripped New York City in the nineties. I really didn't have much of a choice: I was smoking them without lighting up anyhow. In those days, before Mayor Bloomberg's no smoking laws, working Elaine's bar was like being a backroom politician. On any given night, the oak would be elbow to elbow, French cuff to French cuff, with smoking Cohibas. You literally had trouble seeing the person on the stool next to you. Anyway, since I lived in a studio apartment with little ventilation, I did a great deal of cigar smoking two blocks away, in the small, leafy park that surrounds Gracie Mansion, the mayor's house.

To get into Crist's class, you had to submit a five-hundred-word essay for her approval. So one warm evening, dressed in Bermuda shorts and a polo shirt, I grabbed a notebook, a pencil, and a La Gloria Cubana (a kind of Cuban knockoff), and headed to the park to smoke and ruminate on ideas. I wasn't on the bench two minutes, hadn't even lit up yet, when I heard the rustle in the bushes behind me. The next thing I knew, the barrel of a very large pistol was pressed to the side of my head. The gunman was flanked by four of his pals, all dressed in knee-length T-shirts, baggy shorts, and sneakers. Apparently, the young gunman had seen enough gangster movies to emulate a voice that was steady and forceful for a kid his age holding a gun on a full-grown man. He told me not to turn around, a senseless attempt to keep his identity cloaked. From the corner of my eye, I'd already captured a pretty damning description of him: no older than fourteen, red basketball shirt on which was a white number eleven. I stood to reach in my pocket. In doing so, I towered a foot over him. I pulled a crumpled ten from my shorts.

"That's it?" he asked.

I shrugged.

As the kids scampered back into the bushes like squirrels, I looked over at Gracie Mansion, no more than fifty yards away. At the foot of the driveway entrance is a small booth in which at least one cop is always posted. The cop hadn't noticed the mugging and was quite surprised when I told him. I'd be lying if I said the irony of having just been mugged within a sand wedge of the law-and-order mayor Rudy Giuliani's house was lost on me. In fact, I distinctly remember thinking that the incident would make a terrific "Page Six" item and provide a good laugh at the bar at Elaine's. I didn't call it in—I didn't want to get the cop in trouble. Instead, I gave him a description of my muggers and he put it out over the radio. Within fifteen minutes, the suspects had been apprehended.

I went down to the Nineteenth Precinct to view a lineup that was about as fair as a three-card monte game. The young man still wore his number eleven jersey (though it had been turned inside out) and was about twenty years younger than the guys standing with him. When I mentioned the inequity of the procedure, the arresting officer, a female detective, shrugged her shoulders. "It's not a perfect system," she said in an even tone that had long since lost any judgment. A week or so later, I testified in front of a grand jury.

I thought I had my essay for Crist. I wrote about how conflicted I was. The gun turned out to be a pellet gun, not that I could've told the difference, and not that a pellet gun shot point-blank into my temple wouldn't have done damage. But as much as I espouse my NYPD upbringing and values, I was and am as big a lefty as any Ivy Leaguer. My brother the cop jokingly calls me a "bomb thrower." That part of me wanted Number Eleven to have a future; I didn't want him to go to jail. But I also felt violated and truly angry. What's the old saying? A Republican is a Democrat who's been mugged.

In the end, I didn't submit the mugging piece to Crist because I was too embarrassed to. The thought of me getting stuck up in my Bermuda shorts by a fourteen-year-old still makes me cringe. Instead, I ended up writing a sappy piece about the ornamental pear tree that grows in front of Elaine's. I wrote how I identified with the tree rooted in the sidewalk, and that each spring the brilliant white blossoms gave me hope or some such crap. I don't know why Crist let me into her class. She certainly wasn't impressed with the fact that I worked at Elaine's. In fact, it turned out my teacher wasn't fond of Elaine at all.

The acrimony between the two women apparently dated all the way back to the days when Crist was on the *Today* show. Eleanor Perry, the screenwriter of, among other movies, *Diary of Mad Housewife,* had invited my teacher to Elaine's. There the two friends apparently lingered over their predinner cocktails longer than Elaine would have liked; according to Crist, she stopped by the table several times to ask if they were ready to order. What made Elaine even angrier was the fact that she was hamstrung to say anything more to the women when several regular customers, most of them newspapermen, including David Halberstam, joined Crist's table. Instead my boss just glowered at the table from the end of the bar. When Crist asked Perry what Elaine's problem was, the screenwriter replied, "Elaine doesn't like women cluttering up the place."

There was a well-worn story, one that happened before my time at the restaurant, that featured the lady friend of Norman Mailer. Aroused perhaps by her association with the famous writer, the young woman began to order the waiters around. According to the tale, Elaine marched over to the table, pointed at Mailer, and said, "From him I have to take this, but I don't have to take it from a half a hooker like you." Mailer left in a huff, towing his girlfriend behind. The following day a several-page, handwritten diatribe from the famous author was delivered to the restaurant. Elaine read the first couple of lines, then took a Magic Marker, scrawled "Boring, Boring, Boring" on it, and sent the letter back. I forget how long it was said that Mailer stayed away from the joint, but I do know he came back (in my career at Elaine's, I mixed many a bourbon and orange juice for him) and did so contritely.

It wasn't that Elaine hated women, it wasn't about jealousy or anything like that. When it came right down to it, what my boss didn't like was people who didn't spend money, and sometimes women fell into that category.

In another setting, Crist and Elaine might have been friends—they were similar in many ways: Both grew up in working-class, Jewish, New York City families. Both went to public schools in the Bronx. Both were intelligent, outspoken women. They even shared a Woody Allen affinity (Crist revered Woody's work, critic and director were good friends, and for years Woody would screen his new movies at Crist's film festival in Westchester). But in Elaine's it was their similarities that snipped the possibility of even a cordial relationship. As usual, Elaine's bluntness in overprotecting her business was rude, and Crist wasn't exactly a girl who gave you the benefit of the doubt—or let bygones be bygones. Back in class, my association with Elaine only brought a teacher I wasn't impressing anyhow disturbing memories.

In my first class with Crist, I mentioned that I worked in Elaine's and received a smirk, very much like the ones my boss handed out, in return. Oblivious to the warning signal, for one of our first assignments, a descriptive exercise, I chose to write about a picture that hung over the wine cabinet on Elaine's wall, a picture that reminded me of my favorite moment in Elaine's.

I almost didn't recognize him on the evening he walked into the restaurant. Liver and colon cancer would kill him less than six months later. His clothing hung from a skeleton frame, yet, with his pencil-thin mustache, there was some of his jaunty confidence left. Giovanni the waiter showed the Gleasons to a table across from the bar. But before sitting, Mrs. Gleason, an elegant woman but one who wore the taut expression of someone who hadn't smiled a lot lately, marched right over to me.

"Under no circumstance," she began with a rigid smile, "do you give my husband anything, *anything!* alcoholic to drink." She turned on her heel and joined Jackie, who sheepishly ordered a club soda. Just after Giovanni set the drinks down, Mrs. Gleason made her way to the powder room. As she disappeared around the corner, Jackie got up like a shot and was at the bar holding his club soda. "Pally," he began in that unmistakable growl, "throw a little vodka in this, she'll never know." For a moment I was torn between the cautionary words of Mrs. Gleason and the twinkle in her husband's eyes.

The grainy black-and-white *Jackie Gleason Show,* the one that had the Joe the Bartender skit with Frank Fontaine as Crazy Guggenheim—"Hiya, Joe. Hiya, Mr. Donahee, hee hee hee . . ."—was a vivid part of my childhood. When I was a kid, on Christmas Eve, my brother Tommy and I would perform that skit on the second landing of the staircase in my home, with me playing Crazy (my brother has officially disowned me now that I have disclosed this fact). We did it for at least two or three years and brought the house down each time. And I couldn't count the nights I watched reruns of *The Honeymooners* from my couch, either broke or still too hungover to get myself up. Even in the worst of my physical or emotional pain, Jackie Gleason or Art Carney would deliver a line or a look that would make me laugh.

That evening Jackie had only the one, and a soft pour at that. And, given the stage of his condition, it's doubtful the drink made any difference. I watched him pick and push at his meal. Once or twice, he looked up and caught me looking. When he did, he smiled and winked. After dinner, he came back up to the bar, but this time in full view of his wife. He asked Elaine if she would mind. My boss's face brightened. As she slid off the stool, she gallantly waved him by. Behind the bar with me, he grabbed an old rag, started to wipe the mahogany, and then began to sing: "She's only a bird in a gilded cage."

For my class assignment, I meticulously described the lines in the photo of Jackie Gleason's face, the flap of his jowls, his lips ever so slightly curved into a half smirk/half smile, the "Clark Gable mustache," as I wrote. But I didn't stop there; I described the frame of the picture, cheap black balsa wood, the smudged glass, and the black-paneled wall on which the photo was crookedly hung. After several rewrites, I printed the piece out, sat back, and read it with the satisfaction only an unseasoned writer can understand.

A lot happened in the few days between when I dropped off my Gleason piece to Crist and her class in which it would be critiqued. I had a small skin cancer lesion (a product of the knockoff Cubans, no doubt) sliced off my lip. Though the procedure was fairly simple, the bandage I wore covered half my mouth and chin. I looked like Claude Rains. On the way to Crist's class, still wrapped in gauze and bandage, I stopped with my pal Bill Hughes at a saloon near Columbia. The O. J. Simpson trial verdict was to be read on television at ten in the morning L.A. time, one o'clock in the afternoon in New York. In retrospect, the event should have given me pause. I was studying journalism in a time when *The National Enquirer* outreported, outwrote, and beat *The New York Times* to just about every single scoop in perhaps the biggest national story of that decade. Some 150 million Americans tuned in to see the verdict, five times the number of people who saw the

bombing of Baghdad during the first Gulf War on CNN, or three
times the number of TVs tuned to the last $M \star A \star S \star H$ episode,
which, at that time, was the highest rated event in television history.

The bar was like St. Patrick's Day without the green plastic hats
and drunks. Most of the crowd was Columbia students and faculty between classes. "We the jury . . . ," came the words. The reaction was audibly emotional. There were gasps and cries of "no,"
and "holy shit." It was as if O.J. himself had kneed the wind out
of white America.

But my reaction to the verdict was tempered by the worry I
had invested in my Gleason piece. That night in my journal, the
O.J. verdict received one line; Crist's reaction to my description
of the Jackie Gleason photograph filled the rest of the page.

I remember my writing teacher asking me if I owned a dictionary. When I disclosed that I in fact did, she asked if I had ever
opened it. One of my lines was something like "Gleason has the
sleepy eyes of someone who's just woke up," which garnered this
reaction: "Woke up? Puleeease." She ended her critique by just
pursing her lips and shaking her head.

After class, I wandered outside, sat on the wall by Thomas Jefferson, and stuck a Marlboro Light into my bandaged mouth.
Crist's critique was just the last in a series of emotional setbacks.
For weeks I'd been lamenting in my journal my drinking in
Dublin. Under a thin layer of bravado, those hundreds of cautionary tales I'd heard in church basements began seeping back
into my thoughts. To quell my anxiety, I went to a friend who
played amateur pharmacologist. I began taking her leftover
Prozac and some kind of antianxiety meds. Still, I'd awaken often in the middle of the night with heart-pounding apprehension. In several entries in my journal, I wondered if I was going

to make it. It wasn't that I was suicidal; I just thought my heart would explode.

Adding to my anxiety was the thought that I'd made a huge mistake by going to Columbia. In my journal, I wrote that it would probably be best if I quit school after the semester. I was too old; I was getting myself too far into debt. Besides, I reasoned, I didn't have it that bad. Elaine's would take care of me. I saw the evidence of Elaine's long-term care every night. Carlo and Elvino, two of her old guard of waiters, were gray and weathered. Even Tommy, who never seemed to age a day, had begun to look leathery. I certainly wouldn't have to worry about the restaurant closing. Elaine was, as Tommy always said, going to outlive us all.

Maybe it was the notion of getting old at Elaine's that kept me going. Or maybe I just couldn't bear the thought of telling Elaine that I was going to quit. How could I tell my boss I was going to leave school after watching her, night upon night, hobble into the restaurant on balky knees that could barely hold her weight? Or seen the times when her asthma constricted her airways so badly her whole chest would heave with each simple breath? How could I tell her that I couldn't take Judith Crist's criticism after watching all the barbs and arrows she'd taken over the years from gossip columnists who piled on as her business slipped, or just the drunken jerks who would pass derisive comments about her weight? One night, a woman with blond hair, dressed like a Connecticut soccer mom in slacks and a fleece sweatshirt, was at the bar drunk and causing a ruckus. Elaine walked over and told her to calm down. The woman cocked her head and let go with a stream of obscenities that ended with the words "fat pig!" Elaine shook her head slowly at the inadequacy of the remark. "Oh, that's original," she said. No, I wasn't about to quit school, if only to keep from having to tell Elaine that I had.

Each week I went through the same anguish over my assignment for Crist, each week found me in front of my computer working on a lousy thousand words for hours and hours, and each week she slaughtered me in class. I wrote about the New York Public Library on Forty-second. I even sat on Patience or Fortitude (I don't know which is which), one of the huge lion sculptures that guard the steps, trying, through osmosis, to embody those characteristics. For one of Crist's assignments, I wrote about *The New York Observer,* the salmon-colored broadsheet with snooty gossip and a real estate section that would make a Saudi prince tear up. While working one night at Elaine's, I walked around the dining room with a reporter's notebook and collected quotes about the *Observer* from the writer Sid Zion, *The Nation's* editor, Victor Navasky, and Jerry Nachman, who then ran the newsroom at Channel 2 and was later the editor of the *Post.* Crist wasn't impressed.

But, without me realizing it at first, something was changing within. Although they still stung, Crist's bites seemed to heal more quickly. In hindsight, I see that it might have been her plan all along to toughen up my writer's skin, although, like the old story of the scorpion and the frog, I think it was just her nature to sting. But the more she stung, the less it hurt. After going through yet another hash session with my teacher, I wrote in my journal that I wasn't going to let her or any of the other "saddle-shoe assholes" at Columbia get me down. "That's it for the old biddy," I wrote.

Then one week Crist assigned a first-person piece. I didn't give writing about Elaine's a single thought. In fact, I debated very little over my subject matter. My mom's health had been deteriorating, and I'd spent some time with my parents in the house in which I was raised. Memories of my childhood had been playing like movie trailers in my thoughts. As I sat alone in the living room one day, my memory brought me back to when my father still worked as a police detective in the Bronx. I knew from very early on that growing up with a cop for a dad some- how separated my family and me from the rest of the universe. That day at my parents' house, I clearly remembered the mo- ment I first made that realization. For Crist, I wrote about that memory:

One Saturday, when I was eight or nine, and my parents were out shopping at the Finast supermarket, I took it from my father's closet. I was surprised how heavy it was. The leather of the holster felt smooth and hard. It slipped out easily into my hand. The steel, snub-nosed barrel and cylinder were cool against my palm. Currents of power and fright surged through me. But the fear I felt was not of the gun itself, but the scolding I was sure to take if my father ever caught me. My curiosity, however, demanded to be satisfied.

I had watched his ritual a thousand times. At night, when he came home from work and stood in front of the hallway closet, my imagination saw a Wild West gunslinger. I can still hear the slap his belt made as he whipped it off, his left hand at his side holding the holster. I watched him—through the screen door as I stood on the stoop or peering over my comic book as I sat in the living room—while he snapped open the cylinder and let the bullets drop into his hand. I watched as he locked the bullets in a metal box, then wrapped the belt and holster together and placed them deep on the top shelf of his closet and shut the door.

I held the gun only a minute or two, aiming it at an imaginary bad guy, as I watched my reflection in the living room mirror, all the time listening for his car to pull into the driveway. I remember how the .38-caliber Police Special fit perfectly in my small hand.

I wouldn't go as far as to say that Judy—it was Judy now, not Crist—gushed over my first-person story, but her critique certainly sounded a lot different than the assessments of my work that had preceded it. She told me that I should keep working on the piece, that it had a potential to go places. Judy knew what she was talking about.

Chapter Twenty-two

I SAT BY MYSELF AT THE BAR in the West End as the two paths of my life entwined into one rope that I would grab with both hands and use to swing myself off a cliff. Somewhere during the second or third Coors Light, the anxiety I'd written about in my journal disappeared. By Coors Light number four, I began to think that my drinking alcohol again was actually a healthy thing, that it was adding needed spontaneity to my life. By Coors Light number five, I'd begun to romanticize the writers I'd seen drink at Elaine's: There was Jim Harrison at table 2, plump as a Mexican cook, one beefy paw cupped around a V.O. on the rocks, his crooked eye looking at me, or by me, I couldn't tell; Gay Talese at 3, dapper and trim, like his standing-up Beefeater martini; Hunter S., alone at 8, drinking 151 rum shots with White Russian chasers; Mailer at table 5, an angry fist around a bourbon and orange juice, his hair yanked and twisted as though he had combed it with a blender. There was Vonnegut at 7, a billow of smoke around him, his nicotine-stained fingers pinching the stem of a wineglass; there was Dan Jenkins, with Elaine, at 4, drinking scotch—"Dewar's"—with water and backing it up with a cup of coffee. There was Winston Groom at 6, his slurry southern drawl curled by the straight Jack Daniel's in front of him. And around the room it went.

As if the Elaine's writers weren't proof enough of liquor as a muse, I began to conjure the long, illustrious history of drunken quills who by chance or some intrinsic attraction I began to read gluttonously: F. Scott's *Gatsby* over and over again; every word of Hammett and Chandler. At the thought of Chandler, I raised my beer glass. "The moments went by on tiptoe, with fingers pressed to their lips." Somewhere in my Chandler obsession, I'd read of his drunken suicide attempt. In his lake cabin in California, soon after his wife had died, he went into his shower with a loaded pistol and tried to shoot himself but missed—twice.

I ordered another Coors Light and looked around the barroom, imagining the moment at the dawn of the Beats. I remember once telling my friend Bill Hughes that I wanted to end up like Kerouac. "Yeah," he said with a smirk. "Wearing diapers and living with your mother." Fuck it, I thought. He had a good run and died for the cause.

My theme for the night was set. I would drink to drunken dead writers.

"Fookin' Jameson's," I said with an Irish wink to the barman. "To 'The Short Happy Life of Francis Macomber,'" I whispered as I raised the tiny glass to my lips. And down the whiskey went. Poor Ernest. Impotent in phallus and phrase, hemorrhoids like pineapples, a liver like a catcher's mitt. I would've toed the trigger myself. How about Dylan Thomas? I asked myself. As I motioned for a refill of the Jameson's, I thought about Rodney Dangerfield's rendition of "Do Not Go Gently" in *Back to School*. I'd read where D.T. drank eighteen shots of Irish whiskey at the White

Horse and collapsed in his room at the Hotel Chelsea. An exaggerator. Down the Jameson's went.

I had a moment of liquid silence for Capote. I know people from the program who were in two of the dry-out places he'd spent time: Silver Hill in Connecticut and the Smithers Center at St. Luke's–Roosevelt Hospital. Capote was once prescribed Antabuse, a medication that causes intolerance to alcohol. If you drink on Antabuse, you'd projectile puke all the way to Jersey. I took it once, early on in my first sobriety.

Down the gullet went another Irish whiskey.

I moved on to Fitzgerald and O'Neill. I tried to remember Jamie Tyrone's speech about the whore Fat Violet, in *Long Day's Journey into Night,* but couldn't recall a line.

Damn, I knew every pause, I mumbled to myself with proper melancholia.

I forget at which point during this revelry I became totally warehoused. I staggered to Broadway and fell into the back of a cab. It was my first true drunk in fifteen years, and, honestly, it felt wonderful. I might not be able to write like them, I thought. But I can go drink for drink with any of those bastards.

That evening at the West End bar was both good and bad. I was becoming the person I genuinely wanted to be, a writer, but in that journey was growing back into my alcoholism. I was gaining my dreams and losing them at the same time. There was something both sick and poetic in that mind-set. I really believed that I couldn't have one without the other: I'd ultimately have to lose myself to fulfill my vision.

In October 1996, I celebrated my tenth anniversary at Elaine's by sitting in the back room having a shell steak and a half bottle of California Cabernet. Elaine had known plenty of drunks. For every writer who had his or her moment of fame, she saw ten go down in flames. Still, as I remember, she didn't gasp when I told her I was having a glass of wine, "just wine," as I qualified it (I also conveniently left out that I was drinking a sixty-dollar bottle of wine). "Why not?" she said, slowly twirling her hand as if she were signaling me to get on with my life. "You're a grown-up now."

But Elaine had never seen me in a blackout or with my head ripped open from a car accident; she didn't see me sick for days with hangovers, she never saw me with the shakes. She had no idea how bad I could be. I remember once, years before, coming into one of the bars I worked at with a horrible hangover and a case of the shakes as bad as I ever had. As my luck would have it, the first customer ordered a vodka martini straight up. I was able to negotiate, barely, assembling the mixture of booze and ice in the shaker. Two-handed, I was even able to pour it into the martini glass. Then the horrible thought dawned on me that I had to pick up the glass and place it in front of the customer. When I did, the vodka flew all over the bar, the customer, and the customer sitting next to him.

But I kept telling myself that this time would be different. And I thought I had evidence to support my theory. The program says that when you "go out," the euphemism for a relapse, your misery picks up right where it left off. But early on in the second act of my drinking, that wasn't the case. Yes, the hangovers were just as bad, but my life was in order and headed in a positive direction. In the months after I picked up a drink again, the program's premise seemed even more inaccurate. In fact, considering how my life was about to change for the better, the program's guidelines seemed just wrong. It was almost as though the glass of Opus 1 in my hand had some kind of miraculous power. This time it would be different, I thought. And for a while it was.

Chapter Twenty-three

UNDOUBTEDLY, one of the most erudite men ever to carry an agent's identification badge, John O'Brien, had at one time in his career crashed through doors to execute gun warrants on gang members and large-weight drug dealers. But O'Brien's facility with words was an even bigger asset to the Bureau of Alcohol, Tobacco, and Firearms. Though his heart stayed on the street, he soon found himself in the public information office. And, though he was good at what he did, his timing wasn't the greatest. One of his first assignments as a press officer for the agency was to try to make some sense out of the ATF's raid on the Branch Davidian ranch in Waco where seventy-four people died. I remember seeing one press conference on the network news. John was articulate and composed in front of a bank of microphones. He had a master's from Columbia University in Irish literature. He was an agent on the streets for many years. Handling reporters' questions didn't make him sweat.

John was a fairly regular customer. One night he came in with an agent who had once worked for him on a warrant team. Lori was tall and blond, and seemed too pretty and shy to me to be a cop. "Don't let her fool you," John said. "She's been first through more doorways than I have."

He wasn't exaggerating.

In what was called a joint task force, Lori worked with several undercover city police officers charged with taking guns off the streets in some of the toughest sections of the Bronx and Manhattan. Lori and I became friendly and even went, once, to a movie together. Riding in a car with her nearly frightened me to death. She drove the company Crown Victoria like we were in a scene from *The French Connection*. She carried her nine-millimeter in her purse.

Unlike some of the cops who hung out at Elaine's, telling war stories in the hope of hooking into a book or movie deal Lori rarely talked about her work—at least to me. But she did know I was going to journalism school, and about my master's project, the J school's version of a thesis, for which I was struggling for an idea. Almost as an afterthought, one night she mentioned a big case she'd worked. Though I had to wrestle the details from her, I managed to find out that the guy she'd arrested was about to go to trial in federal court in downtown Manhattan.

About the same time, two of the editors, and some of the reporters, for "The City" section in *The New York Times* began to hang out in the joint. At first, Elaine wasn't thrilled with the group, mostly because they rarely ordered anything to eat but also because she had had a few bad experiences with the paper. One night a *Times* editor had talked Elaine into doing a column for the paper called "The Soapbox." Elaine told the editor to go ahead and write it for her. When the piece came out, my boss thought it made her sound "inarticulate." Elaine rarely read the *Times*—she really did think the paper boring. But for a short time, she got into the habit of reading the *Times*'s obituaries, the "scratch sheet," as she called it. One day the phone rang in my apartment. "Come over, quick," Elaine huffed. "You gotta read this." I remember the obit clearly. It was about a Spanish bon vivant who'd spent his days on the Costa del Sol and his nights passing bad checks and fleecing rich widows. "He's like some of my best customers," Elaine said with a giggle.

But even her infatuation with the scratch sheet was brief. I sent a fan letter to the obit writer and invited him to stop by. He came into the restaurant not too long after, got sloppy on martinis, and wasn't half as fun as his writing. Elaine didn't go near his table. When he came over and tried to kiss her, Elaine quickly bowed her head, and the writer ended up with a face full of hair. Maybe she stopped reading obits because one afternoon the *Times* called to update hers.

I wouldn't go so far as to say that Elaine grew fond of "The City" crew, but she seemed to like Joan Nassivera and Dave Smith, who ran the section. I became friendly with Joan first; she was well aware of my journalism school quest and several nights suggested that I "pitch" a story idea to her. For the most part, "The City," a weekly section that came out on Sundays, ran neighborhood pieces and features. Unlike the rest of the *Times,* freelancers wrote a good deal of this section. But after the Jimmy the Hat story disappointment, I wasn't all that confident in my ideas. Newspaper people have an expression, "fresh eyes," meaning that someone new to a story, event, or place will see things that others who are more familiar with it will miss. I hadn't had fresh eyes in Elaine's for a long time. If an orangutan came in and ordered a banana daiquiri, I wouldn't have given it a second thought (I would've told him, however, that we don't make those drinks at Elaine's). One night, Dave Smith stopped by the bar by himself. As he surveyed the room, he marveled at the opportunity. "There have to be twenty stories here right now," he said as he looked over the assortment of cops and criminals seated at the tables.

I wasn't totally unconscious when it came to the newsworthiness that surrounded me at Elaine's. One evening a woman with a blond, braided ponytail, transparent skin, and the arms of an old junkie sat at the end of the bar. It was a fairly obvious that she hadn't always been a woman. And just from an aesthetic standpoint, one had to wonder if her decision to change teams, as it were, was the soundest. She looked like the Bowery Boy Huntz Hall in drag. Anyway, she told me she had just signed a book contract to write about her relationship in jail with Nicky Barnes.

Leroy "Nicky" Barnes was maybe the most famous drug gangster in the history of New York City. An associate of the mobster "Crazy" Joe Gallo, whom he met in jail, Barnes was in the sixties and seventies perhaps the biggest heroin dealer in Harlem. He was certainly the most flamboyant. According to a *Times* article, at the time of his final arrest, in 1977, Barnes owned three hundred suits, one hundred pairs of shoes, and fifty leather coats. His fleet of cars included a Mercedes-Benz, a Citroën Maserati, and several Thunderbirds, Lincoln Continentals, and Cadillacs. It was Barnes who inspired the Hollywood character Super Fly, with his look of exaggerated collars, full-length leather coats, and hats with feathers.

I never heard what happened to Barnes's supposed cell mate, whether she ever wrote the book (Amazon.com doesn't list it) or whether there was any truth at all in what she told me. But I don't doubt that she could have had a book deal if she wanted. I'd worked publishing parties at Elaine's for books with a lot dumber ideas than one featuring jail sex with a gangster.

Though Lori's case had none of the salacious aspects of Nicky Barnes's cell mate's, it certainly had all the gangster components. And when I saw Dave Smith about it, be liked it right off.

"Go down to the court. I'll buy some of that story," he said to me.

Much like Nicky Barnes, Jose Reyes was a self-made drug lord who had a penchant for fancy cars and clothing. He didn't, however, cut the same sartorial figure as Barnes. For one thing, Reyes was in a wheelchair.

Born in Puerto Rico in 1970, Reyes moved to the Washington Heights section of upper Manhattan with his mother in 1975. By the time he was a teenager, his adopted neighborhood was inundated with cocaine and heroin. Just over the George Washington Bridge from New Jersey, Washington Heights in the 1980s was a veritable drive-through window for suburban cokeheads and junkies. By the time he was fifteen, Reyes was already a lookout for a local dealer. They called him Feolito, "Little Ugly," because of his stocky build and pit bull features. In only four years' time, Feolito became El Feo, his street name now the Ugly One in deference to his position as the major dealer on 167th Street in the block on which he grew up. By the time he was twenty-two, he was paralyzed from the waist down by a bullet lodged in his spine. But the attempt on his life only strengthened his determination. His operation grew from one street outlet to over twenty distribution locations in Manhattan and the Bronx. He had vans customized to access his wheelchair and lived for a good part of his run in a fancy hotel in suburban Rockland County. At his zenith, El Feo was making over a million dollars a week. And he was vicious.

Accused of having a part in seventeen murders, Reyes kept a hit man named Francisco Medina on a ten-thousand-dollar-a-week retainer. A Dominican who went by the street name Freddy Krueger, Medina was your worst nightmare if Reyes targeted you for removal. One of Medina's more memorable hits occurred midday, in bumper-to-bumper traffic, on a bridge from Manhattan to the Bronx. Armed with a Ruger nine-millimeter and an AK47, he climbed over the car behind him, stood on that car's trunk, and riddled the gypsy cab in which his victim sat with over thirty rounds. He then calmly walked back to his car, pulled a U-turn, took a hit off a bottle of Rémy Martin that he always had with him, and drove away.

With the exception of the accused, the judge, the jury, and the lawyers, the courtroom was empty. Day after day I found a seat in the vacant third or fourth row, took out my reporter's notebook, and dutifully scribbled away. Every now and then, Reyes would turn to look at me. For the first few times he did, and in spite of the fact that he was bound to a wheelchair, I felt a shiver down my spine. But more than once he smiled at me. When he did, his face changed from that of an accused killer to that of a kid on a playground.

Though the story the prosecution assembled was chilling, much of Reyes's personality was downright charming and surprising in its depth. Though he hadn't finished high school, he could recite chapter and verse from *The Art of War,* by Sun Tzu, *The Prince* by Niccolò Machiavelli, *The Prophet* by Kahlil Gibran, and *The Annals* by Tacitus. He also knew by heart whole scenes of dialogue from *The Godfather* and *Goodfellas.* His best friend was a groundskeeper and garbage man at Columbia-Presbyterian, the huge hospital in Washington Heights. Jimmy, the friend, had no connection whatsoever to Reyes's drug business and, as far as I knew, didn't so much as smoke a joint. But Jimmy and Reyes spent many nights together in one or the other's apartment, eating Chinese takeout and watching movies, while outside their doors Reyes's operation churned.

The first story I submitted for the *Times* concerned the testimony of one of Reyes's closest business associates, Raul Vargas. In his late twenties, athletically built, and handsome, Vargas gave testimony that was part spellbinding—hits performed on motorcycle, hundred-mile-an-hour car chases through Manhattan—part fascinating—a fleet of tricked-out automobiles with secret gun compartments, license plates that slid out of view, and strobe lights that blinded cops and victims—and fully chilling—his voice a steady monotone, devoid of emotion as he described the murders. Not once did he look at Reyes. When I walked from the courtroom that afternoon, I knew I had a pretty good story.

Joan Nassivera called me the following Wednesday and told me they were going to run the piece. It was only five hundred or so words, but I didn't care. It was *The New York Times*. I waited at a neighborhood newsstand, like Kerouac, that Saturday evening for the first edition of the Sunday *Times* to come out. Maybe the Kerouac analogy is little extreme. Gilbert Millstein's review of *On the Road* propelled the Beat writer to literary superstardom. Still, I got goose bumps when I saw my byline.

A few nights later, Joan arrived at Elaine's with the lithograph plate of the story, a tradition, she said, for all new writers with the section. I forget who it was, but later that week someone came in with the story framed. My boss had one of the waiters hang it right under George Plimpton's *Paris Review* poster.

Chapter Twenty-four

FOR THE FIRST TIME in a lot of years, my social circle was outside of the program, some of it as far from the program as you could get. I liked Bill Hughes from the first uncomfortable moment we shared during the introductions in Ari's class. We became tighter still as the luck of the draw placed us in most of the same classes. Equal parts wild man and poet, Bill was like the bad kid your parents warned you about, the one you couldn't stay away from. He had an ex-girlfriend who would periodically mail him a pair of her panties. Several times a year, he and a couple of his Brooklyn buddies would rent a cabin in rural Pennsylvania, where they would drink Jack Daniel's, ride motorbikes, and shoot shotguns. Often he'd come to morning classes with a thermos of Bloody Marys. He was also, in my opinion, the best writer in the school.

The big assignment in Ari's class was an investigative piece of our choosing. Bill and I teamed up to report and write about the resurgence of the mob's influence in Broadway unions. Most of our sourcing came from theater people who hung out in Elaine's. We decided that I would write the lead and first few pages, and

Bill would write the body of the story. With just a couple of days to deadline, my pal hadn't even started. I called his apartment the evening before the morning the assignment was due. He said he was going to pull an all-nighter in the computer lab at school and "knock the piece out." I might have had confidence in him had he not been slurring his promise. I hung up the phone convinced that we were destined for an F. The next morning, as I turned the corner to the entrance to the J school, I saw a body lying under the tree in front of the Thomas Jefferson statue. On closer inspection, I realized it was Bill, sound asleep. What was more, he had a stack of paper on his chest—the investigative piece, which would draw copious praise from Ari.

Though I was ten years older than Bill, I looked up to him, and envied him. The way I saw it, there was a part of me long buried under the meetings and constrictive principles of the program. I wanted to bust out like Bill. I wanted to ride motorbikes and have ex-girlfriends mail me their panties. I wanted to drink like it was my Irish birthright. I'm not saying Bill was a bad influence . . . Well, I guess I am. But I liked the way he looked at the world, the way he grabbed it by the soft skin. Anyhow, it wasn't as if he was dragging me to bars with him every night. He didn't have to drag me. My love affair with saloons, which had dried up in my sobriety, sprang back to life when I began to drink again.

Between going to classes, doing assignments, running around the city reporting, and working Elaine's each night, there wasn't a whole lot of time for me to get in trouble—at first. On a couple occasions, when Bill would suggest a beer after class, or when I'd get together with Erin, I'd have a couple of drinks. One night, after a couple of glasses of wine with Erin, I wrote in my journal that the idea of me being an alcoholic now seemed absurd. All those years, all those meetings—literally thousands of meetings—for what? I wasn't ruing wasted time, rather I was excited that my time was finally served, sentence executed; now it was time to get on with my life.

A few nights before Christmas, Erin and I went shopping in SoHo. I spent five hundred on a leather coat in a small boutique trying to impress her. I hadn't expected to spend that much, but after Erin said she liked the way the coat looked on me, I would have bought it at twice that price. When I came to know Erin a little better, I realized that spending money didn't impress her at all.

While taking the double master's major at Columbia, she worked as a waitress in a place called Boxers in the West Village. I knew the joint well; at least I knew what it used to be. Before Boxers, it was a notorious Village hangout. Jimmy Days was one of the Manhattan nightspots I'd frequent back when I was taking buses into the city to do my partying. On several occasions, I drank at that Village saloon until the sun came up. One of the regular bartenders made me look like a teetotaler. One night, he was chained to a support beam behind the bar so he wouldn't wander off. On another night, just as he served me a drink, he collapsed drunk on the floor like someone had shot him. The other bartender didn't bother to pick him up, just stepped over him and continued serving the customers.

The new owners had gussied the place up a bit. And instead of the hard-drinking local crowd I remembered, Erin served mainly twenty-somethings from New Jersey who drove their Lexus SUVs into the Village to see the queens and trannies, most of whom had moved out twenty years before. Rue the boy, however, who gave Erin a hard time. Once, she told me, she turned around and slapped a spoiled Jersey brat who had pinched her on the butt. One young jerk got a lapful of onion soup, à la Elaine in Portofino, croutons and all.

With the leather jacket in a garment bag, Erin and I walked around SoHo. She wore a full-length shearling coat, unbuttoned, with her hands in her pockets. Tall and thin, Erin reminded me of Darci Kistler, Balanchine's last diva, whom I'd see having a salad and a Perrier all by herself in Elaine's. Erin studied ballet, and her posture was both athletic and elegant. Her favorite shoes were beat-up old cowboy boots. I liked that look on her, but, at times, the boots seemed incongruous on feet positioned as if she were about to do a plié. Erin once told me that those very boots were on her feet when she kicked out the windshield of Hoss's pickup after arguing with him about something or other.

We stopped at Fanelli's, an old-time bar and grill on Prince Street that was there when SoHo was called "Hell's Hundred Acres." It had the best hangover-curing Bloody Marys in the city, Erin said. We drank wine and made fun of the students in our classes. Erin had a giggle that came from deep in her throat. Her cigarette habit further cured the sound. She lived in the maid's chamber in a small building near Columbia. In the mornings she'd sit in the windowsill overlooking a back garden, drink coffee out of a cereal-bowl-size cup, and smoke cigarettes. She liked calling me "darling" and "baby." Once she left a message on my answering machine that sounded like a young Lauren Bacall wrapped in a silk sheet. I left the message there for a year. At the bar at Fanelli's, Erin spoke of home: Hoss, her sister, and father. I can't remember the details exactly, but I think her father had one of those gloomy drink-and-smoke-too-much stories. I do remember her saying that he was sick, maybe lung cancer. And I do remember that Erin's eyes welled when she talked of him. I opened my arms, and she pressed herself into me. I could feel her tears on my neck.

That week, before Christmas, we saw each other several times. One afternoon she took me Christmas shopping at Bendel's on Fifth Avenue. She went there every Christmas she was in New York, she said, because of their annual sale on cashmere sweaters.

Walking from the store, arms filled with packages, we almost
bumped into Marcia Clark, the O. J. Simpson prosecutor. Clark
had taken more grief than Hillary Clinton over her hairstyles and
was that day coiffed in a kind of Shirley Temple look.

That night, Erin, along with a girlfriend from Sarah Lawrence
named Cara, came into Elaine's and set the regular women chasers
into a spin. The heart of Elaine's resident cardiologist, Dr. Joe,
skipped a few beats at the sight of Erin. But she came into Elaine's
to see me, and it was me who she'd end up talking to the whole
time she was there.

Over the next week or so, I saw Erin almost every night. We
went to the movies and had drinks afterward. A few nights later,
she met me at a basement bar on Houston Street. It was a slipper
of a place, and Erin knew everyone there. We drank a few martinis, and I made a sloppy pass.

She told me she had a boyfriend, Brazilian I think, whom
she'd met while re-creating Che Guevara's travels. Erin was in
love with South America, especially the stars in the night sky and
the pregnant Brazilian women who, unabashed, would sun
themselves on the beach. She was also in love with the Brazilian
boy. I pretended to be happy for her, but silently I pined. It was
not as if Erin had led me on. And she did care for me, that I
knew. But aside from writing about her in my journal, most of
my feelings for Erin were contained in a running dialogue in my
own head. For a drunk who had just again turned the gas on
over the pilot light of his addiction, nothing could have provided a better reason to drink. It was poor me: I fall in love and
she's in love with someone else. In the program there's an expression: "Poor me, poor me. Pour me a drink, would ya?" Already in my second go-around with booze, I was looking for
excuses to drink.

Though the whirlwind of school had helped keep my mind

off it, there was emptiness in my life. There were plenty of nights after Erin told me about her boyfriend that I watched myself in a bar mirror lift glass after glass, drinking to forget the emptiness. Drinking that way always worked like a charm. Invariably, I would get myself to the point where I forgot what I was drinking to forget.

Chapter Twenty-five

THROUGHOUT MY TIME at Columbia, the restaurant stayed busy. Elaine's was constantly in the columns, with celebrity sightings, book parties, and movie launches. For me, the two major components of my life complemented each other. At school, Elaine's indeed carried cachet. My job was a wonderful conversation starter at the university's wine and cheese parties, a circuit on which I became a habitué. At work, my pursuit of a master's degree at an Ivy League school brought the cashier position a bit of dignity. Regulars took an interest in my schooling, and the boss was quick to tell customers of my latest scholastic triumph.

That first Christmas Eve while I was at Columbia the joint was packed, and the night went late. Elaine wanted to make sure to be open for Father Pete, who would come in after saying midnight Mass. One Christmas Eve, a customer named Frankie Gio and I snuck over to St. Joe's for the first half of Father Pete's service. Frankie was an ex-fighter and the first bouncer in a legendary New York discotheque called the Peppermint Lounge. It was there that Chubby Checker's Twist became the dance craze of the early sixties. More recently, Frankie was an actor. His claim to fame was his portrayal of the gangster Arty Clay in *King of New York*. (In one scene Frankie's character urinates on Christopher Walken's henchman.)

By the time we got to St. Joe's that night, the pews were shoulder to shoulder. We arrived about two minutes before Mass started, and, almost immediately, Frankie, who had more than a couple of vodkas in him, fell sound asleep standing up. He was snoring like a horse. The procession began, and when Father Pete walked by, he poked Frankie in the stomach, and Frankie let out this roar. The whole congregation turned to look, and Pete had all he could do to keep from busting out laughing. Back in the restaurant, I told Elaine the story, and she let out a deep chuckle.

Christmas wasn't an easy time for Elaine. It was one of the two days the restaurant was closed, the other being New Year's Day. Elaine never knew what to do with herself on those holidays. Anyone close to her, a very short list, had some type of family get-together. Katherine and Robert Altman were always in California with their children, Bobby Zarem was encamped in Savannah. Elaine's friend the socialite Ann Downey was usually in Palm Beach.

Except for her older sister, Edith, who lived right down the block from Elaine's and worked for a while as the bookkeeper for the restaurant, Elaine's ties with her family were practically nonexistent, at least by what I saw. Though I believe her brother lived, or had lived at one time, in one of the suburbs, Westchester or Long Island, I don't think I ever met him. Once in a while, Elaine would mention him or her nephew, but it was never in a particularly endearing way. As I remember, she visited him once on Christmas Day, and when I asked how it went, she shrugged and then didn't say a thing. Elaine's relationship with her sister bordered on contentious. Edith was far from a pest. Once a week or so she'd come in early, usually before Elaine arrived, for dinner with a girlfriend. Yet Elaine would always smirk when she saw her sister's dinner check left unpaid in the rack behind the bar. Ten years older than Elaine, Edith would each morning climb the long staircase to the cramped, stuffy office over the restaurant and spend a couple of hours going over the accounts. But I don't remember Elaine ever being nice to her. I do remember hearing Elaine's real-estate agent talking about how Elaine bought her sister her apartment.

For Elaine, even her penthouse apartment, one that had been featured in a photo spread in *Architectural Digest,* was a jail cell when she knew she wouldn't be leaving it to go to work. The first time I was in the apartment Elaine was in Deauville (she attended the film festival there every year). Her alarm went off, and the security company called the restaurant. My brother Frankie, who was then a detective in the Bronx, was having dinner with his wife in Elaine's that night. Together we went over to check. It turned out to be nothing, an electrical malfunction or perhaps the wind. The apartment had a wraparound terrace of I don't know how many hundreds of square feet. It was a warm night, and the lights from the brownstones below twinkled as a mirror image of the faded stars above the city. It was a beautiful spot. But Elaine's deck showed no sign of her, or anyone else for that matter, ever having been out there. There was a bare cement floor and a couple of deck chairs without cushions. My first thought was, Gee, what a waste. But then it occurred to me that the emptiness that surround Elaine's apartment was rather sad.

Elaine did manage to have steady company in the apartment. At first, Forence was hired to clean. But there wasn't a whole lot of cleaning to do. My boss almost never had guests and never cooked at home. But Forence (like Florence but without the *l,* as I remember) would dutifully come over a few afternoons a week. It was during these sessions that Elaine and Forence became friends, a mismatched pair if there ever was one. Forence lived, I think, in the middle of Harlem. A devout Christian, she would sing gospel while she dusted. From what I gathered, Forence wasn't all that impressed with the celebrity gossip that radiated from her boss's restaurant. All that mattered to her was that Elaine was generous, funny, and easy to work for. What started as a three-times-a-week cleaning job became more and more like a three-times-a-week visit. Forence began putting the stove to use, cooking meat loaves and fried chicken. In time, though, Forence started cooking low-fat for Elaine—maybe the only low-fat soul food on the planet.

I'm not sure how this occurred, and it didn't happen all at once, but at some point Forence moved in. Elaine had an extra bedroom and plenty of space, and she didn't see why her friend had to live all by herself way up in Harlem when Elaine was by herself in a pent-house on the East Side. On Sunday afternoons, Forence would en-tertain her church-lady friends. Elaine once told me she tried to get out of the apartment during these get-togethers but sometimes would get stuck. On those occasions, Elaine would wander out of her bedroom, still half asleep from working the night before, pull out a chair, drink some coffee, have a piece of cake, and listen intently to the Harlem church gossip being shared at the kitchen table—far dif-ferent from George Plimpton's witty banter. On Christmas, though, Forence, too, had family to be with. Holiday time would find her traveling to see them, which left Elaine all alone.

In the past I would have left the restaurant early on Christmas Eve. I always felt a bit like Bob Cratchit working that night. But that first Christmas I was at Columbia I stayed late and ended up sit-ting with Elaine and a few of the regulars until closing. I'd had a few glasses of wine and felt a warm flush in my cheeks. The restau-rant was decorated with strings of white lights and snow-colored branches. On Elaine's urging, I again told the story of Frankie Gio at midnight Mass, and the laughter filled the restaurant, now empty save for our table. That night was the happiest I'd been at Elaine's. I didn't want it to end. But I always felt that way when I drank.

On December 26, having fulfilled familial duties on Christmas Day, I stopped at a liquor store on Third Avenue and bought two very expensive California Cabernets. I went home, alone, opened the first, a bottle of Dominus, and put on a CD of the Rat Pack. Dean Martin had died the day before, and I raised a glass as he sang "On an Evening in Roma."

The next thing I knew, it was the following morning and I had a hangover that paralyzed me with its pain. Rumpled in a pile on the floor at the foot of my bed was my tuxedo. I had no idea why. On the living room floor, there were two empty bottles of wine. There were also the two bottles of Dominus empty in the garbage.

In my first go-around of drinking, when I would awake—or come to—from a blackout drunk, I would engage in a kind of emotional self-mutilation. I couldn't help trying to piece the fragmented memories of the night before together, no matter how agonizing even a partially assembled picture would be. But sometimes it was better that I didn't remember things.

Once, I awoke with an unforgiving hangover and vaporous memories of the night before. That day I somehow summoned the resilience and went on a deep-sea fishing trip—not the best of ideas considering my physical condition. A cop from my town named Bobby happened to be on the boat. I greeted him with a big hello, and Bobby looked back at me like I was Elvis Presley. I spent the whole trip below and in the head, heaving with every pitch of the hull. Bobby didn't say a word to me. Perhaps a week later, he came into Chuck's, where I was then working, and ordered a Coke. "You don't remember a thing, do you?" he said, his grave tone puncturing any illusion of a social visit.

In a slow, measured monologue, he recounted for me what had happened that night before the fishing trip. I'd been drinking in a bar in a town called Woodcliff Lake, in northern New Jersey. I didn't remember being there. On the road home, a cop from that municipality attempted to pull me over. Apparently, I made the brilliant decision to try to outrun him. By the time I'd reached the New York State line, and my hometown of Pearl River, I had cops from three New Jersey towns chasing me. Bobby happened to be working that night and heard the chase on his radio. I guess, in my booze-addled brain, I believed if I could get across the state line into Rockland County, I'd be okay. I slid to a stop as soon as I passed the "Gov. Nelson A. Rockefeller Welcomes You" sign. Bobby, who knew my older brother well, had all he could do to keep the Jersey cops from beating me unrecognizable. With our current drunken driving awareness, this could never happen today. But Bobby was able to talk them out of arresting me. At the bar, the shame I felt was excruciating. I tried to mumble some kind of apology. "Save it," Bobby said, pushing the Coke away and rising from the barstool. "And get yourself some help."

In the program, I'd heard the worst blackout stories imaginable. One was of a suburban drunk who was out all night and had driven home in the early morning. He was awakened by the scream of his wife an hour later. From the kitchen window she saw a bicycle wedged under the carriage of his car. The man had struck and dragged the bike and its child rider halfway down the block on which he lived. Another blackout horror story was of the cop who found out what he had done the previous night when the prison guard handed him the *New York Post*. The story was on the front page. He'd shot and killed his girlfriend during a drunken argument.

If there was any innocence to the second act of my drinking, its curtain had come down with my tuxedo blackout. In my journal, I wrote of being worried that I'd gone into Elaine's dressed that way. I called my friend Michael, and he assured me I hadn't. This time I'd gotten lucky. I even managed to see the humor in staggering to the liquor store dressed like Dean Martin for the other two bottles of wine. But I had had too many life-threatening experiences with blackouts to laugh for long.

I still managed to go out to bars several more times between Christmas and New Year's. One night I went alone to SoHo and came home half-drunk and sad. Without Erin or Bill with me, I felt completely out of place drinking in bars. I was paranoid, worried that people were watching me, as if they knew that I was on a slip from the program. New Year's Eve came and went without incident, except that Elaine was given advertising space on the Times Square ticker. She asked me for a suggestion. I offered: "Every night is New Year's Eve at Elaine's." I wasn't given credit, and rightfully so, since I'd amended an old Toots Shor line. Still, my writing had a live audience of one million plus.

I don't know whether the ticker had anything to do with it, but that New Year's Eve was the biggest night as far as receipts go that Elaine's had ever had. As usual, the night was a pain in the ass. Not because anybody got any more drunk or any more stupid than then usually did. The night just seemed to last forever. At two or three in the morning, there's always the late shot of people, like Jimmy the Hat, who've been to other places and parties and knew that Elaine stays open very late. It was not the most amiable of crowds. By the time I walked in the door of my apartment, it was after six. But it was more than just the late hour that had me tired.

When I was honest with myself, I knew I was an alcoholic; I knew that when I started drinking, I pretty much gave my power over to booze—I couldn't stop, or didn't want to for fear of withdrawal and hangover. But I thought I could manage my drinking life. I thought I could keep a lid on the insanity and the consequences to a minimum. That was my biggest mistake. The scariest part of my picking up a drink again was how patient that addiction was. And the vigilance I expended to guard against it was exhausting.

Chapter Twenty-six

AT THE END OF THE SECOND SEMESTER, just before the holidays, I'd applied for a class called Book Seminar taught by a professor named Sam Freedman. The idea was to finish a nonfiction book proposal by the end of the semester. Long-form journalism was appealing to me. As in my dream at the Pennsylvania rehab, I imagined myself sitting in some beach cottage poring over sheaves of the notes I'd accumulated in my ten years of research.

The class was limited to sixteen students, and to be accepted you had to come up with a commercially viable idea for a book proposal that could be reported and researched in or around New York City. About the same time, a friend of my father's named Jack Kelly was having an eightieth birthday celebration in Queens. My father asked if I would chauffeur him and a few of his friends, including Mario Biaggi, once the most decorated police officer in the history of New York City, and later a congressman from the Bronx. I agreed readily, but I had an ulterior motive.

The affair was like an octogenarian police smoker. There

were a hundred people attending, half of whom had been police officers. The war stories ricocheted around the room. Though the drinks might have been lighter, the laughter was as deep and rich as if they had just come in from a particularly amusing late tour. Canvassing the room, I talked to at least six old cops who said they were from three-generation police families; one said four generations. I'd gone to the party in the hope of coming up with an idea for Freedman's class and left assured I had one. I was going to write about families with generations of police officers.

Professor Freedman loved my idea—with one caveat: that I use my family's experience to tell the story. Sure, I said. After all, it was only for school.

Sam Freedman found the inspiration for his course from, among other places, the Iowa Writers' Workshop, the two-year fiction-writing course that launched a whole bookstore of literary careers. For years the director of the Writers' Workshop was an Elaine's pioneer. Frank Conroy's *Stop-Time* is considered a standard in the memoir genre. It was published in 1967 to rapturous reviews when Conroy was thirty-one. Like other early Elaine's inhabitants, writers including Philip Roth, Joan Didion, and the *Paris Review* staff, Conroy was young and brash, and thought he could change the world with words. Elaine's was the headquarters of this new world order. The book launch party for *Stop-Time* was at Elaine's—the first book party held in the restaurant, I think. In hindsight, I'd wish I'd tried to talk to Conroy more than I did. Our interaction was limited to a few short over-the-bar conversations. I always thought of him as forlorn. He would hang out at a table in the back, sometimes all by himself, as if he were trying to conjure the Elaine's of circa 1967 and the literary summit on which he once stood. Once in a while he'd sit at the piano and struggle with a jazz tune he could never seem to get just right.

In its first incarnation, Freedman's course was called Reading, Writing and Thinking. In 1991, Freedman had a student named Leah Hager Cohen, who wrote for the class about her experiences as a hearing person growing up in a deaf community. Cohen's father ran the Lexington School for the Deaf, first in Manhattan, then in Queens. Freedman coaxed Cohen to write a book proposal for the idea, then coached her through the process. Within six months after she finished the proposal, with the help of Freedman's contacts, Cohen had literary representation and then a book contract. *Train Go Sorry,* an American Sign Language euphemism for "missed the point" was the title of her book (the full title was *Train Go Sorry: Inside a Deaf World*). When it was published, it garnered the cover of the *Sunday New York Times Book Review.*

Emboldened by Cohen's success, Freedman developed the Book Seminar. He warned us, in our first session, that the semester wasn't going to be easy. To punctuate his statement, he showed a short film of first a sprint race, then a marathon. "Your other classes are depicted in the first part of the film, my class in the latter," he said. Himself marathoner thin, with dark Old Testament features, Freedman gave off a first impression that was neither warm nor fuzzy. We met just once a week, on Fridays. But it was an eight-hour class with one twenty-minute break to grab some coffee or a sandwich. The door to the classroom was closed at nine-A.M. sharp. Ostensibly, if you were two minutes late, you had wait until the break to get in. But I don't remember anyone being late. We wrote weekly twenty-five-hundred-word assignments, which we were required to, as one of my classmates aptly put it, "report the shit out of." The workload was enormous. But nobody uttered a word of complaint—I mean after the initial requisite grousing. There is no room for complaint when it's obvious that the teacher is working much harder than you. Each week Freedman handed back to us meticulous and thorough line edits on our assignments. He once told me he edited thirty thousand words a week for his class. What was more, the edits were insightful and prodding. Though his shoves were not always gentle, they forced me to report more deeply, to write more clearly, and to remember, as Elaine had once said, to just tell the story.

Along with the heavy lifting came the required reading. We read a book a week for ten weeks, both fiction and nonfiction, then had the author of the work come to class. The common thread was a compelling narrative. Early on, we read Richard Price's *Clockers,* the story, in part, of a conflicted teenage drug dealer with stomach ulcers. When I was reading the book, I asked Elaine if Price was ever in the restaurant. She nodded, then held one arm close to her side, indicating that his arm was withered. Out of all the questions we peppered Price with the morning he was in our classroom, the one I wanted to ask I didn't. I wondered how he typed. I had written some questions for him in pencil on the inside cover of the book. The one I got to ask was how did he get the dialogue so realistic. He had spent a couple of years, he said, in neighborhoods and with real cops in Jersey City, which he calls Dempsey in the book, and his own childhood in the Bronx helped his ear.

We read Verlyn Klinkenborg's *The Last Fine Time,* still one of my favorite books, set in a bar in Buffalo, which starts with the line "Snow begins as a rumor in Buffalo, New York." The memorable comment Klinkenborg made in class was that his copy is so "clean" that line edits are rarely necessary. I almost quit writing right then. We read *The Tortilla Curtain,* T. Coraghessan Boyle's hilarious commentary on the convergence of the lives of an illegal immigrant and a homeowner from a gated community in Southern California. But one of the highlights for me was the week *Angela's Ashes* was assigned and Frank McCourt came to class. He was demure in our intimate setting despite his monumental literary success.

I had a vivid recollection of McCourt coming into Elaine's one quiet night. His trench coat was drawn tight to his body. His white hair was swept up and away from his impish face. The bar was empty, and he stood all by himself right in the middle. Elaine was at the end doing the checks. She looked up at him, and he held his wineglass in a toast. She nodded back, but I'm not sure she knew who he was. I believe he was still teaching at Stuyvesant at the time, but maybe not. McCourt's brother Malachy was once one of Elaine's steady customers. Tommy and Brian told me that Malachy could light the place up with his stories and antics, but that was before he had given up the drink. It was obvious that Frank McCourt was not the character or imbiber that his younger brother was said to be. He held the wineglass as if it were a flower. When I asked him how his evening was going, he smiled and said fine, but that was all he said.

If I have the timing correct, I believe his visit that night was just before *Angela's Ashes* was published, just before half the literate world began reading his book. Perhaps he was out congratulating himself on finishing the manuscript and imagining his book jacket hanging on Elaine's wall, or maybe he was imagining himself as one of her literary lions, sort of doing what I did on Woody Allen's table after hours. In class, when I asked McCourt about that night, he said he only vaguely remembered it.

A few weeks later our class read *Common Ground: A Turbulent Decade in the Lives of Three American Families,* by J. Anthony Lukas. The book, about forced busing throughout the seventies in Boston, won the 1986 Pulitzer Prize. Perhaps my recollection of Lukas as reserved and spiritless is colored by the event that occurred the following year. Just two months after Lukas talked to that vintage of Freedman's class, he committed suicide. In a laudatory look at the writer and his literary career for *Salon* magazine, Freedman remembered that Lukas had given his class a hint of the bleakness that can permeate a writer's life. Lukas's wife had caught him alone, sitting in the dark, drinking Jack Daniel's, "as is my wont," he said.

Perhaps it was not his words to our class, or even the ones on the pages of his book, that had the most effect on me but the echo of them in the emptiness he felt—a sound with which I identified. In the program they call that vacancy a "God-sized hole in your soul." I'm not sure about that phrase, my belief in a higher power changes with mood and circumstance. But I do know there isn't enough booze to quiet my echo; in fact, it only got louder with each drink I took. I remember once when I was only eighteen or nineteen, drunk and despondent over what I now can't recall, and sitting in the playroom of my parents' house holding a bottle of Bayer aspirin. My mom walked in before I swallowed them. Undoubtedly, I was only looking for attention. But there were of plenty of drunken nights and hungover mornings that, had a painless means, like pills, been available, I have no doubt I would have ended my life. By definition, an alcoholic is in a continuing state of suicide. The only question is how long the booze takes to complete the deed. Although I didn't realize it that day in class, it was not his Pulitzer Prize–winning work but the cautionary tale of Lukas's hopelessness that affected me the most.

Each week Freedman would also parade in front of our class editors from the publishers and agents who represented some of the biggest names in the business. In the second half of the semester, we started working on our proposals. Most of my submissions came back covered with enthusiastic remarks. It was all fine and good, but I never believed that a story about my family would go any further than school. Just that Freedman was interested in my family was, to me, remarkable enough.

I found writing the essays easy. A lot of what I wrote about came from tales I'd heard my whole life—war stories of the New York City Police Department told by my father, by my mother about her father, and by my brother. I'd heard them at the kitchen table. I'd heard them in the living room and on the back patio. I'd heard each of them so many times I knew the inflections and pauses.

At the beginning of the semester, I'd asked my father to put together some of his remembrances of the department. A month or so later, I received a manila envelope on which my address was written in his unmistakable strong, looping script. Inside were twenty-five or so handwritten pages of remarkably vivid and well-constructed memories. My father's ability to assemble such a body of work didn't come as that much of a surprise. That envelope, and a few more that followed, were only the last in a long line of clues to his true identity. A voracious reader, my father spoke more like a college professor—more like a writer—than like a cop. Though he went no further academically than high school, I don't think he's ever gone an entire day without reading a portion of a book. For fourteen years he had sat in front of his typewriter that sat on his desk in the Forty-first Precinct. Literally hundreds of murders, rapes, and robberies were accounted for on those keys. How much, I wonder, of my father's cop stoicism found escape as he slammed the carriage return lever thousands and thousands of times? Sometimes I pretended his fingers were guiding mine as I sat in front of that same typewriter. "It's in us, Brian," he says in my daydream. "Don't let them tell you that you can't write."

After numerous drafts, and the incorporation of profuse comments and suggestions by Freedman, the final proposal for my book was eighty-eight pages long. Most of my father's and brother's stories were second-sourced; all of them were researched for accuracy and historical backdrop. Then there was my grandfather's era, at the turn of the last century, and the painstaking archival research it entailed. I don't mean to crow, but it was the hardest I'd ever worked on anything in my life. And it showed.

Chapter Twenty-seven

B Y THE BEGINNING of my second year at Columbia, my job at Elaine's began to have a major effect on my burgeoning writing career. One night at the restaurant I was talking to Dave Smith about the progress of my master's project. He asked if he could see a draft. I handed one to him over the bar a few nights later. A couple of weeks passed before I saw Dave again. I assumed he'd read my story, didn't like it, and was too embarrassed to come into Elaine's to tell me. Then, maybe three weeks after I'd given it to him, he came in with Joan Nassivera and sat at table 6. He called me over. "We've put it on the schedule," he said. "We're going to do it as a section cover."

In the whole scheme of things, my front-page story in the *Times*'s "The City" section wasn't exactly Mailer's "The Steps of the Pentagon" in *Harper's*. First of all, the section doesn't go national with the rest of the paper. In fact, it doesn't even make it as far as the suburbs. But in my universe, which then included Columbia University's J school and Elaine's restaurant, it was to be a major coup. It also brought Elaine's book-jacket-adorned wall a step closer.

But there was work to do. The reality was, a master's project draft is a long way from *Times* newsprint. What I thought was a nearly finished product, one that needed just a tweak here and there, was, in Dave Smith's mind, only a start.

For an entire week before the piece was to run, Dave ran me like a bicycle messenger. I was on the phone, or up to Washington Heights, to check and recheck sources. Joined at the hip, we sat next to each other in front of computer terminals. During that period, the *Times* newsroom was undergoing renovations. The temporary location of the section, with a half dozen or more computer stations squeezed one on top of the other, seemed awfully claustrophobic. Down the hall was the smoking room. No bigger than a kitchen, it had walls yellow from nicotine and smelled like the inside of an ashtray. That week I spent a lot of time in that room. Once or twice, I thought about Sam Freedman and a profile he did on David Mamet for, I think, *Rolling Stone.* In the piece is a quote from Mamet that Freedman was especially proud of extracting. It was the playwright's take on Chicago writers and went in part: "You don't have guys sitting around in cafés with cigarettes trembling—'Oh, my God. I'm a writer, but I can't write.' Well, in Chicago, the answer is, 'Go home, you sissy, if you're a writer, write.'"

As the deadline drew close, and I was still a long way from finishing, Dave jumped in and rewrote a good chunk of the story. On the Thursday night before they put the section to bed, Dave drove me from the *Times* building to Elaine's. He asked me not to tell anyone that he'd had such a large hand in the rewriting. I don't know if he was protecting me or himself, but it is a promise I've kept until now.

What first had seemed like an opportunity with no downside

was now a cause of conflicted emotions. Part of me felt like a fraud, the same way I had felt when the *Post* editor ran my byline on the Cardinal O'Connor story. I began to tell myself that the only reason Dave had considered my story was that I worked in Elaine's. He probably just gave me the shot so Elaine would think better of him—and give him a good table. It was that kind of thought process that often led me to a bottle and large swallows of booze. It is my experience that an alcoholic sees the negative in situations for exactly that reason: an excuse to drink. My negative thoughts might have continued to corkscrew had not Saturday rolled around and the Sunday *Times* begun to hit the newsstands. I almost floated off the sidewalk when I opened to the section. The layout was striking; the headline read: "The Rise and Fall of El Feo." There was a photograph of Jose Reyes wearing a birthday hat, taken at a party for an associate's son. The text ran in two columns beneath the photo, and the jump was a full page and a half, a five-thousand-word story under my byline in the Sunday *New York Times*.

Though at first I would allow myself only to scan the article, afraid that my fledgling writer's ego wouldn't be able to take all of Dave Smith's rewrites, after a quick look, an amazing thing happened. I began to own my part of the piece. After all, it was my idea and my reporting. Sure, Dave had rewritten chunks of it, but that's an editor's job. And enough of my writing had survived his edits that I recognized my voice. Late in the afternoon, Sam Freedman called to congratulate me. As it happened, his book *The Inheritance* had been featured on the front page of *The New York Times Book Review*. His voice no longer sounded like that of my teacher; rather it had the intonation of a buddy, a pal, and a comrade in arms. We were in this together now, it said. We were writers.

That night in the restaurant several people congratulated me, including Robert Altman, who said that he liked the piece, "even the part that was too long." It was right about this point when Elaine's literary magic started to rub gently against me. Sitting with her was Chris Calhoun, an agent from Sterling Lord Literistic, Inc., one of the best-known literary agencies in the world. Calhoun had read the story, and when Elaine told him that I had written it, he came up to the bar and talked to me for twenty minutes or so. He handed me his card and told me to call him the next day. There was something prophetic in the fact that I was about to call Sterling Lord's agency. Years before, when I'd worked in the restaurant on Madison Avenue, Mr. Lord had been a steady customer. Several times a week he would come in and sit at the bar for a late lunch. Affable and humble, he never gave an indication of his lofty literary position. As well as representing a dozen writers whose names even I knew back then, Mr. Lord had been Jack Kerouac's agent. Although we rarely talked about books, one afternoon I told him that I had an idea for one. "Really?" he said, surprised at my boldness. "It's about my life as a bartender," I said. "I'm going call it 'Behind Bars.'" Mr. Lord chuckled. "You write it, I'll sell it," he promised. I did call Calhoun the next day, but his enthusiasm was tempered a bit compared with the night before. Still, he wouldn't be the only literary agent who had read my story.

On Monday morning I went to my Journalism and the Law class. It was held in a huge room with amphitheater seating, the kind you see in the movies and television shows when they want to depict the Ivy League. There were a couple of hundred students seated when I arrived. As I walked up the stairs, several students offered their congratulations. My friend Bill Hughes was in the top row. As I climbed into the seat next to him, he handed me a flask of bloodies.

Sometime that week, or perhaps the week after, an agent who was a fairly regular customer of Elaine's invited me to her office to talk about the story. Jane Dystel has a metabolism like the

Energizer Bunny. Tiny and blond, she makes up for her diminutive stature with the focus of a NASCAR driver and a booming
voice that manages to contain a giggle in the same breath. Dystel
is a legendary name in publishing. Jane's father, Oscar Dystel,
practically invented the paperback. In 1954, Oscar took over as
president of a struggling publishing company called Bantam and
turned it into the largest paperback publisher in the United States.

I sat in the cramped waiting room of Jane's office in the top
floor of a building on Union Square. I should have been nervous,
but I wasn't. Instead, I found myself looking at the book jackets
that hung on her walls, lost in a daydream. Like I had many times
at Elaine's, I imagined a book with my name emblazoned across
the cover: "by Brian McDonald." I knew I would never become
blasé if that happened. I would be humble, I thought. But never
blasé.

The fantasy was shattered with Jane's hello. She brought me to
her office and offered me a chair in front of a huge desk that was
piled with books and manuscripts. Though friendly enough, Jane
came right to the point. There's not a lot of money to be made in
true crime, she said. Plus, the competition is fierce. For a first-time
author, the odds are the longest. In that moment, I remember
thinking: Why the heck did she ask me to come here, anyway? I'd
been under the naive assumption that publishers who had read the
New York Times piece were just waiting to throw me a couple of
hundred thousand to write the book. With my delusions of
grandeur successfully deflated, Jane switched to the good agent
part of her good agent–bad agent act. She said she would work
with me to develop a book proposal on El Feo. It was the word
proposal on which the tenor and substance of the conversation
dramatically changed.

In retrospect, I don't know why I didn't immediately think of
telling Jane about the book proposal I'd been working on for the

prior six months in Freedman's class. When I finally mentioned it, I did so in such an offhanded way that she almost missed the point, train go sorry. But when the words registered, her eyes blinked wide open.

"You have a proposal about your police family? Written?" she asked, saying the words like she was holding each up for measuring.

Well, yes, I said. I'd written it in a class at Columbia Journalism . . .

The working title for the book proposal was "My Father's Gun," referencing the anecdote I'd written in Judy Crist's class, which served as the prologue. It was a catchy title, one that did what good titles are supposed to do: pique your interest. It was also loaded with connotation, and Freudian innuendo, most of which played out not nearly as loudly to others as it sounded to me. When Sam Freedman had suggested that I write about my own family, my father, I'd thought, Yeah, when doughnuts are good for you. Even though my relationship with my father had been repaired in a miraculous fashion thanks to my years in the program, the thought of excavating his life, spending hours and days interviewing him, felt like the prospect of pulling apart a just-sewn wound to see what the stitches were made of. And that anxiety didn't even include how I would feel about writing about my brother and other family members.

The only way I was able to jump those hurdles in school was by reasoning that the material would be read only by the class. When I signed with Jane to represent the proposal for "My Father's Gun," I had to readjust my parameters. Now my family secrets would be read by an agent, people who worked for her, then editors at publishing houses. It was still a fairly controlled group. I mean, what was the chance of an editor from, say, Random House running into my father at ShopRite in Pearl River? But as more people were given access to my story, my anxiety increased. To allow strangers into my home, to open the doors and windows, to air our dirty laundry, in the oft-used phrase, maybe was not a mortal sin, but it was as venial as one could get. In a Freudian sense, my title might have been provocative. But it was also a danger sign. For me it said: "You're going to be sorry." The more I thought about having a book published, the more I realized how steep the emotional cost would be. If my dream was realized, it would come at the expense of my family's privacy.

Perhaps the biggest reason I was twisting what was easily the most wonderful and exciting opportunity in my life was that all of these voices of worry were taking place within the confines of my skull. The actual people involved, my family, hadn't weighed in because I hadn't told them I was speaking with agents.

For over a decade I had advisers who were privy to the inner workings of my mind: Frank, program people, and therapists. When I reintroduced alcohol into my life, those guiding lights were extinguished. So, alone in the dark recesses of my own brain, I figured the quick and easy answer to quiet the inner chorus of doom and gloom was to have a drink. It gave me a place to hide from the guilt I was beginning to feel about my proposed book. Even the couple of blackouts I experienced, and the horrible hangovers that had come back in full horror, seemed worth the price.

Chapter Twenty-eight

IN THE BEGINNING of November, I asked Erin out to dinner at the Rainbow Room. Charlie Baum, who, along with his legendary restaurateur father, Joe Baum, ran the restaurant atop Rockefeller Center, was a regular at Elaine's. A nice table, with a view of the New York City universe, was assured. I don't know whether Erin got cold feet or a call from her South American boyfriend, but she dropped off the radar screen for a couple of days and didn't answer any of my phone messages. The night of the supposed date came and went, and I didn't hear from her. Then one night, completely unannounced, she wandered into Elaine's. The blown-off date was not mentioned, and as soon as I looked into her sparkling eyes, I quickly forgot about it.

Instead of the Rainbow Room, the following afternoon we met for chili-bacon cheeseburgers at the All Star Café on West Seventy-second Street. We drank mugs of beer, smoked cigarettes, and laughed with the regular assortment who crammed the bar. Erin knew most of them. The All Star was a stopping off place for her, a spot to blow off steam or study journalism law. One of the barflies was a retired detective named Glenn, who had worked in my father's old precinct. I knew him from Fordham, where he took one class a semester. Glenn had been going to Fordham for four or five years when I was a freshman, and he was still in his sophomore year when I graduated. When I asked him about his slow pace, he answered: "What's the rush?"

Later that night, Erin and I went to Vince & Eddie's, a West Side restaurant and lounge with a fireplace. Erin wore leather pants and had her short hair pulled back in an abbreviated ponytail. We sat close to the fire. She reached into her bag and took out a copy of Hemingway's short stories. As she handed me the gift, she kissed me on the cheek.

I'd had stories published in the *Times,* I was talking to literary agents about representation, I was breezing through graduate school, among my close friends I counted my boss, who was maybe the most famous restaurateur in the world. I was sitting in front of a fireplace nuzzling perhaps the best-looking girl I've ever been with. And I was drinking a beer. What the hell was I thinking all those years in the program? I had a lot of time to make up for, a lot of things I wanted to accomplish. Unlike Glenn, I was in a rush. I didn't realize it then, but as fast as I was moving, my addiction, like a few of the racehorses I'd bet against in my lifetime, had me measured.

The following week, on a whim, I booked a flight to Miami. I stayed in one of those Art Deco rooming houses in South Beach. Elaine had told me to stop by Michael Caine's new restaurant on Lincoln Road. There I drank a half bottle of overpriced California Cabernet. Later that same night, I was in a club on Washington Avenue. In the men's room, I ran into a local guy I knew from a previous trip. He was dosing his nose with water. He smiled and asked if I wanted some. I took the folded dollar bill into the stall and poured a line on the paper towel dispenser. My first go-around with drinking, I was mostly what they call in the program "garden variety drunk." There were only a few coke episodes.

From that same guy I bought a gram, and I went back to my room. I did a couple of lines and made my way to the beach. I sat at an outdoor bar in a place called the Clevelander and ordered one of those birdbath frozen margaritas. The pretty young Asian girl behind the bar happily complied when I asked her to "float" a shot of Cuervo Gold tequila on top. This technique, I told her, counteracted the head freeze you can get from drinking frozen margaritas too fast. She smiled and floated away.

A warm breeze blew in off the ocean. The palms hanging above gently rustled. The cocaine and Cuervo raced to my cerebral cortex. There they pulled off all their clothing and started to make love like cheaters. Miles out into the ocean, a streak of lightning split the vast darkness. Another streak followed, and then another. Each flash illuminated the backdrop of purple-black thunderclouds. As I watched the electric show move out to sea, the drugs and booze brought me to a very welcoming place. A party was starting inside my head, and I was being waved inside. The combination of dry and wet goods was perfect. All at once I was smart enough, good looking enough, and funny enough. God, I was funny enough. I was overwhelmed with the moment. This was the best I'd ever felt—by far.

Chapter Twenty-nine

ALTHOUGH I DON'T REMEMBER the exact number of publishers, Jane Dystel had received considerable interest in the proposal for "My Father's Gun." I'd like to say that my writing sample dazzled them, that there were whispers of another F. Scott at lunches at Michael's. More likely it was that the whole package was easy to like: a generational story of New York City cops, with a strong historical backdrop, told by a Sam Freedman–trained researcher-reporter. But it was the backstory that made the proposal almost irresistible for editors: the writer was a bartender at Elaine's.

It was in the middle of November 1996 when Jane called to tell me she had accepted a floor bid of a hundred grand from an editor named Rosemary Ahern at Dutton. My agent was confident that the proposal had enough serious interest to warrant an auction. The auction, which I believe involved three publishers, pushed the advance considerably higher. To be clear, they weren't talking about never-having-to-work-again money. But it was more than I'd ever seen wrapped in one rubber band before. It was certainly enough for me to leave Elaine's.

After my boss found out about my advance, she sat me down at a table in the back room, a place where she went with the same regularity as she visited the kitchen, and told me not to leave. She'd seen it happen countless times over the years to countless writers with quicksilver advance money. "Put it in the bank," she said. "You went to school during the day, you can write during the day." I remember her words clearly. But I kept thinking about what Tommy the bartender would say when people asked him how long he'd worked at Elaine's. "Over twenty years," he'd growl. "But I'm coming up for parole."

I knew Elaine couldn't understand how I felt. Her restaurant was her whole world, her reason to live; outside of it nothing really existed for her. By Elaine's measurement, if I was to leave her employ, I might as well move to Mars. But I had gooseflesh over the prospect of not working in a restaurant anymore. I knew her advice was sound. But in my mind, a secure future came in a distant second to a life in the present that I would be proud to talk about. I wanted to be at a cocktail party and have someone ask me what I did for a living. I wanted to say I was writing a book. I'd gladly talk about my time at Elaine's, but only in anamnesis, anecdotes remembered fondly, the way alumnae remember the homecoming games. To stay at Elaine's would have been to betray myself, my dreams. My book was the miracle for which I had prayed.

Though she didn't say as much, I knew that part of the reason Elaine wanted me to stay was simply that she didn't want me to leave. She didn't want me to follow Elio, Pepe, and even the pompous Englishman out her front door. Once again, she'd let her guard down to a man, only to have him bolt. I tried to explain that I wasn't moving away from her. I was going from one side of the bar to the other. I was going to be like the scores of other grown men before me—writers mostly, but others, too—who looked to her for grounding and consistency in lives that were missing those components. It was her common sense that cut through all my mishegaas, as she would say. I told her that I, and all the others—the writers, the actors, the tough guys—before me, could rely on her being in the restaurant every night giving comfort. "Have something to eat," she'd say, her fleshy hand smooth and warm against the side of my face.

At the back table, I couldn't bring myself to tell her that I was leaving. And my reticence gave her hope that I would stay. She put her hands on the table and pushed herself to her feet. "I know what I'm talking about," she said softly. "Don't be stupid." On the page, those words seem condescending. But they were said with as much love as Elaine ever showed me.

Just after the proposal sold, Sam Freedman called a columnist for the *Daily News* named Jim Dwyer. The following Sunday, on page 2, complete with a picture of me with the hip, hundred-dollar haircut I got in South Beach, a full-page story ran of the sale of my proposal. Later, the *New York Post, New York Newsday,* and the *Times* would also chronicle the Elaine's bartender who took "the Write Turn."

Anecdotally, I knew how episodic notoriety could be. At Elaine's I saw my share of shooting stars. Maybe my favorite was Morton Downey, Jr., the chain-smoking talk-show host who really was a nice guy but whose celebrity disappeared so quick someone should have said "abracadabra." But I'm susceptible to things that make me feel good no matter how fleeting they are or how horrible they make me feel afterward. And I liked the way the spotlight felt. Don't get me wrong. It wasn't as if the whole world knew that I had received a book deal. Far from it. But all of Elaine's knew. Supposedly, I was doing the checks the night the column came out, but it was more like I was receiving my public. The highlight of the night had to be Walter Cronkite, who walked into the restaurant and announced: "I want to shake the hand of the famous bartender."

As I look back on that night, I can't remember if Elaine said anything to me about the story in the *Daily News*. I'm sure the subject came up at the tables. I know Jane, my agent, later told me that Elaine was aglow in her pride for me. Jane even said that Elaine's opinion of her as an agent increased markedly. Up until the sale of my proposal, Jane was under the impression that Elaine thought of her only as Oscar Dystel's daughter.

Usually around eleven, or when there was no one of interest to keep her busy, Elaine would amble up to the bar and offer to take over writing the checks and give me a dinner break. As I remember, that Sunday night was busy, with plenty to keep Elaine entertained. It was almost midnight when she did come up to the bar. She had already asked me to stay working at the restaurant, and I hadn't responded. Perhaps she'd kept away from me that night because she was afraid of what I would say. A feeling of expectation permeated our space. It seemed she was giving me my chance. As the moments ticked by in silence, she knew my answer. For a fast moment, I didn't want things to change. Everything would be different if I stayed. After all, I wasn't just a bartender anymore. I had a book contract. I was writing a book! But just as quickly as that thought came, it evaporated. I had waited so long to walk away from the bar. I had no choice. I stood from the barstool and slid past her. I could feel the silk of her dress, could smell the fragrant Chanel. Slowly I walked through the kitchen and downstairs to the wine cabinet. I took out a half bottle of Cabernet. In the back room, I drank my dinner alone.

I remained working at the restaurant until the spring. Throughout that time, Elaine was bittersweet. On the one hand, she was really proud and happy for me. The Jewish mother in her was kvelling. She didn't care at all that I spent more time sitting at tables with customers over those weeks than doing the checks. I felt like I was on a victory lap. One night Elaine called me over to sit with her and Dick Wolf, the producer of the *Law & Order* TV shows (as I write this I realize that I had no idea of the extraordinary access I took for granted at Elaine's). Since televisions had antennas, Elaine has been putting writers together with movie and TV producers. But now she was playing the dealmaker for me. Wolf knew, I think from Elaine but maybe from Dwyer's story, about the sale of my proposal. But he said he wasn't really interested in my three-generations-of-cops story. "I had the same idea ten years ago," he said.

So what? I thought, swept up in my single headline. There are a hundred Dick Wolfs out there.

In February 1997, Judith Crist hosted her annual we-survived-the-holidays party, held in her commodious Riverside Drive apartment. I remembered thinking, as I was handed a glass of white wine by the bow-tied, tuxedo-vested bartender, that I had somehow walked into a *New Yorker* cartoon. There were ancient men wearing tuxedo jackets that might have fit them twenty years ago. There were women who smoked cigarettes with holders. Everyone looked vaguely familiar, as though I'd seen him or her on *The Joe Franklin Show.* Judy's son, Steven, who then was the editor of the *Daily Racing Form,* the Thoroughbred past performance sheet that he would later publish, was at the grand piano in the living room. An old dame, perhaps a soprano before the thousands of cartons of Merits she'd smoked, began to warble a tune from her youth—Bunny Berigan's "I Can't Get Started," I think. In the mix were also Judy's students from classes that spanned the teacher's forty years at the J school.

The best part of the party for me, however, came at the very end.

I was proud of the way I drank that night, pacing myself, just enough lubrication to loosen the inhibitions but not enough to say something that would reveal my true identity as alcoholic and addict in relapse. Part of the night, I was taken hostage by an ancient stage actress whose name I now forget, who told me stories from long ago using only first names of those involved. She might as well have been talking about the roster of the Bosnian Olympic volleyball team. Several of my J school classmates were there. My pal Bill Hughes, wearing a sloppy grin and sipping a gin and tonic with the side of his mouth, stood in one corner.

By around two in the morning, most of the crowd was either in taxis or already in bed. A half hour later, the party had winnowed down to just four. There was Judy, Bill, a French woman who had taken Judy's class the year before and was writing, as I remember, for the international *Herald Tribune* (the *New York Times* organ, not the paper for which Judy worked), and myself. The four of us smoked cigarettes and drank as we listened to Judy tell stories of her newspaper days, her time on the *Today* show, but mostly about her husband, Bill, who had died six or seven years prior. Her eyes, liquid any time, were especially fluid when she talked of her late husband. It was while listening to Judy's stories that I experienced an epiphany:

The moment is literally couched in the elegant, old New York surroundings of Judy's apartment. The soundtrack is Judy's smoky voice, Bill's and the French woman's laughter. I stand in the foreground of the memory, my expression slack from drink, but the clarity of my thoughts is remarkable. It wasn't how I drank in the past that was the problem, I realized then, but where and with whom I drank. This very night, I thought, is the beginning of my new life. So, on an early spring evening in 1997, when Elaine asked me to go with her to George Plimpton's town house for a party he was hosting, I thought it would be a good test of my new theory.

I don't recall the occasion for Plimpton's party. It might have been a book *The Paris Review* was launching. I do remember being very excited about going. As much as I, and the rest of Elaine's staff, made fun of Mr. Plimpton's penuriousness, his parties, we all knew, were legendary.

According to a story in the *Times* by Warren St. John, Plimpton's town house, tucked in a cul-de-sac at the very east end of Seventy-second Street, was originally a tenement and had been converted to flats in the 1930s by Carmel Snow, the *Harper's Bazaar* editor. Snow refurbished the tenement for housing for friends down on their luck during the Depression. In the late 1950s, soon after Plimpton returned from Paris, where he founded his magazine with Peter Matthiessen and Harold L. Humes, he moved into a rent-controlled one-bedroom apartment at the address. In the 1970s, the building went co-op. He then was able to acquire and join four apartments, with the first floor turned into the office for *The Paris Review*.

Over the next thirty years or so, Plimpton hosted hundreds of parties for every literary event imaginable. An egalitarian, the towering, white-haired writer was famous for welcoming crashers. So along with those of the Mailers, the Southerns, and the Taleses of the world, Plimpton's parties would have healthy doses of young dreamers who saw sneaking into the bustling town house as a rite of passage to becoming a writer.

I remember frantically throwing clothing over my shoulder with my head stuck in my closet looking for an appropriate writer's outfit. You would think, after all my years behind Elaine's bar, I would have known how a writer dressed. I actually did know, but that information didn't help, because it spanned the whole apparel spectrum, from Tom Wolfe's cream-colored ensemble to the

Post's cop beat reporter's uniform of blue blazer and jeans. I saw Peter Maas once wearing a stadium coat and woolen scarf, which I thought looked writerly. I also one night saw Robin Cook, the medical thriller author, wearing a bomber jacket that I thought looked like he was trying too hard to appear tough. I didn't own a bomber jacket or a stadium coat. And I didn't have anything remotely close to Wolfe's attire, but I did have a blue blazer. I wore it, with a button-down shirt and khaki pants.

The party was three flights up. On the first landing, the door to *The Paris Review* office was ajar. Inside, desks were piled with manuscripts. Above one desk was a chair nailed to the ceiling. It was a lion tamer's chair, fairly well chewed, from one of Plimpton's famous literary stunts. There was also a bicycle in the room, the same one from which I'd seen the writer dismount in front of Elaine's on numerous occasions.

Elaine had difficulty climbing the stairs. By the second-floor landing, she had to rest her new knees. She let herself into Plimpton's apartment and sat in a wing chair. She looked right at home. On the walls above her were posters by some of her artist customers, Larry Rivers and Helen Frankenthaler among them. I remembered one night in the restaurant when Frankenthaler had said that the copper-colored shirt I was wearing "was just perfect on me." I wore that shirt until it almost fell off. In Plimpton's apartment, I waited for a bit, but then Elaine told me to go ahead. I had to turn a shoulder to navigate past several pretty interns and a couple of floppy-haired guys, aspiring authors no doubt, smoking cigarettes on the staircase.

Through the doorway, I could see that the party was crowded. The chatter was a din. A pool table in the middle of the room, covered with a tablecloth, served as the buffet table, though the fare was rather pedestrian: some cubes of cheddar cheese and a few Ritz crackers on which sat smears of tuna salad. Across the room, however, was a bar lined with an army of booze and wine bottles ready to march. Mr. Plimpton's priorities were firmly in place. I once read how Plimpton had orchestrated a fund-raising campaign selling prints of works donated by his famous artist pals. Andy Warhol had enlarged and signed a bill made out to *The Paris Review* from Regency Wine & Liquors for a bottle of vodka and two bottles of Blair House scotch.

It's funny, thinking back, how out of place I felt in that room. Sure, it was chockablock with famous writers. Jay McInerney was there. One night at Elaine's I recall seeing him and his beautiful then-wife, Helen Bransford, and thinking that he was the literary prince of New York City, the heir apparent to a throne occupied by several kings, Plimpton among them. At the party, I had a quick fantasy of what it would be like if it were I, not Jay, who'd received the call that afternoon. "Brian, it's George, George Plimpton. A few of us, Norman and Gay and some of the others, we're getting together tonight at my place. I was hoping you and Erin would come. You can expect the usual: fabulous people, good scotch, and few laughs at the expense of those less talented. It would be so much more wonderful with you along." In one corner of the room stood a sour-looking Peter Maas; in another corner was Lewis Lapham, trench coat thrown Sinatra-style over his shoulder.

I don't know why I was so fixated on the faces I'd seen hundreds of times. Maybe it was that I was without the three-foot width of oak in front of me that always served as a divider and equalizer. Without it, I felt less than those surrounding me. What's more, I didn't have Elaine to hide behind. As usual, when she finally did make it up the stairs, she did one turn around the room, gave me a little wave, and then headed back down (as hard on the knees as coming up, I'd imagine) and back to the safety of the joint. The moment she left, I made my way to the bar.

I didn't engage in a whole lot of conversation, even after having a few red wines. I did speak with one young, pretty *Paris Review* staffer. I had her complete attention when I told her I worked as a bartender at Elaine's, but she seemed to lose her enthusiasm toward me when I told her about my book. She gave me a pert "Good luck with that" and disappeared into the crowd. Soon I was standing in a corner by myself, self-conscious in both the surroundings and the fact that I was an admitted alcoholic who was drinking again. I drank the wine in a gulp, and my discomfort subsided, but for only a few moments. I had to get out. I looked around for someone to say good-bye to. Finding no one, I just made my way out and hailed a taxi on York Avenue. I ended up in a place on Eighty-ninth Street, all alone at the bar, drinking myself into semioblivion on Cosmopolitans and bursting to tell someone where I had just been, but the only other person in the bar was the bartender, and he was watching the Rangers on TV.

Chapter Thirty

IN MAY 1997, after graduating from the journalism school, I worked my last official shift at Elaine's. For whatever cosmic reason, my career at Elaine's was bookended by the appearance of Ben Gazzara, who was in that night for dinner. But other than that weird symmetry, the night was rather anticlimactic. I think Michael and a few of the other waiters brought out to the bar a piece of cake into which they had stuck a candle. I remember Elaine mumbling something to the effect of "Don't forget where we are." I assured her that Elaine's was still an integral part of my life, and that I only lived down the block. She shrugged as if to say she'd heard those words before. But in my head it was all planned out. I would do what no one before me had done; I would make the improbable transition from Elaine's employee to Elaine's friend and customer. I would be just like the writers I had for eleven years watched walk through her front door.

The first lesson I learned about writing a book is that you spend an awful lot of time alone, and an awful lot of time in your own head. I remember a reporter interviewing Elaine for a piece on her restaurant. My boss was asked her secret about getting along with writers. She wagged a finger above her forehead and said, "You have to know that they're all up here." As the book-writing process swallowed me, I realized exactly what Elaine had meant. It's not only your writing voice, the narrator of your story, or the characters you're writing about who rent space in your thoughts, though they're a big part of it. It's also the filibuster held by the inner critic and a whole Greek chorus that echoes each negative evaluation. The cross talk of narrator and character, combined with the who do you think you are, Hemingway? voice, causes quite a traffic jam in the cerebral cortex. Add some rpms of ego, broadside that with a truckload of further low self-esteem, throw in a couple of cocktails, and it's no wonder Elaine uses the international frontal lobotomy sign when she gives her interpretation of a writer's mind-set.

I spent days on end virtually alone in my thoughts. Some of the solitude was enjoyable. Part of "My Father's Gun" entailed research into my grandfather's era in the New York City Police Department—the rich and virile 1890s and early 1900s. The time I spent digging for Grandfather's life in the main branch of the public library was wondrous. The library still operated with the antiquated systems used when it was first opened, in 1911. Pulleys and dumbwaiters hoisted books from the basement shelves. Miles and miles of pneumatic tubes whisked your requests. The seventy-five miles of shelves held a million books.

One day during my research, the threat of a hurricane virtually shut Manhattan down. I called the library that morning to ask if they would be open. Yes, came the reply, as long we can keep the staff here. I hurried to the subway and took a nearly empty 6 train to Grand Central Station. There was only a trickle of taxis on Fifth Avenue. I bounded up the steps past Patience and Fortitude.

Inside, I felt like Indiana Jones exploring an ancient temple. Except for the skeleton staff, there might have been a total of five people in the vast building. For much of that day, I was seated in the reading room. With row upon row of oak tables holding green-shaded reading lights, the room is nearly two blocks long. As the skies cleared, it became magically dissected with shafts of sunlight that coursed through the towering windows.

Months later, when I was well into the writing, I spent a few weeks on the very eastern tip of Long Island. Montauk in the middle of winter is both beautiful and solemn. At night alone in a room on the beach, I was lulled to sleep by the sound of the surf—that and the few Corona beers I allowed myself each night. At first light, I'd walk the desolate beach, searching the horizon for ships and inspiration.

Soon after the Montauk trip, back in the city, I went one night with my friend Bill to a symposium at the Museum of the City of New York. I was happy to get out, to see other humans. For a long stretch, the only interaction I had had was with the Chinese take-out delivery guy. Plus, the night out would give me a chance to hear Pete Hamill, who was giving a talk on his favorite subject: Brooklyn. Afterward, Bill and I milled around in front of the building, hoping we'd get to chat with the writer. We did. And the three of us, Bill, Pete Hamill, and myself, walked fifteen blocks or so down Fifth Avenue toward the subway.

Back in the 1960s and early '70s, in the heyday of his drinking life, you could count on Pete being at a back table at Elaine's. During my era in the joint, however, he was no longer a regular customer. A couple of times a year, like a guilt-ridden son, he'd stop by to fulfill his filial duties. When I told him I had worked at Elaine's, he seemed more wistful than interested. Even when I informed him that I was the bartender at his wedding, and that I'd been to his mother's wake, having chauffeured Elaine out to the

Brooklyn funeral home, and that I'd spent some time in the news-room with him at the *Post,* my words seemed to stream by him like the taxis down Fifth Avenue. He spent most of the walk "all up there," as Elaine would say.

Pete Hamill had always been a writing hero of mine. Long before I'd started to read my way through Elaine's wall, I'd read his columns. Though falling far short, I tried to emulate his tough-guy prose. When *A Drinking Life* came out, a number of people I knew in the program chastised it as egotistical and self-congratulatory. In the book, Pete writes about giving up drinking without the help of AA or any other program. I defended his version of sobriety and dared any of them to find a better story of the saloon culture. The prospect of having a private chat with him on Fifth Avenue was exhilarating—like being a kid and getting to have a catch with Mickey Mantle. It's not fair to characterize a man on the basis of one half-hour walk. But for me it turned out to be a disappointing moment, as Pete seemed self-absorbed, and not very happy.

Bill had to rush home to his girlfriend, and I went back to my apartment. There I poured myself a Jack Daniel's, took down my copy of *A Drinking Life,* and began again to read it until the words went fuzzy with sour mash.

During those first months after I'd left the restaurant, I couldn't stay away from Elaine that long. Mostly in the afternoon, when I couldn't stand the computer screen one more second, I would wander over to the joint. Sometimes, on the way over I'd stop by E.A.T., Eli Zabar's remarkably overpriced restaurant and take-out place on Madison Avenue. Then I'd walk into Elaine's holding a paper bag filled with delicacies in each hand. Diane or I would set the naked, rutted, and chipped tabletop with a fresh cloth and napkins. In the kitchen, I'd pour the borscht out into soup bowls and arrange the halved sandwiches on a platter so we could have lunch together.

But soon my relationship with Elaine started to change, and the lunch ritual began to seem forced. My boss had always viewed the world in a delineated fashion: either you worked for her or you didn't. I remember once Elaine hiring back a waiter whom she had employed for years but who had left for another restaurant. She mentioned him often while he was gone, and always in a nostalgic way—he was the star of several of her stock funny stories. One day he came into the restaurant looking for his old job back. Elaine hired him but fired him a few weeks later. "I knew it was mistake," she told me. "It's never the same the second time." I often thought that I drifted away from Elaine during this time. But in looking back, I see she was moving just as quickly away from me.

As the winter of 1998 melted into spring, my anxiety over the book was palpable. I had strata of it. A first-time author, I doubted just about every line, even every word, I wrote. I'd signed a contract that gave me one year to report, write, and deliver the manuscript, and the deadline, with a few months' extension, was fast approaching. If I'd had all the time in the world, I would have been under pressure. With the big clock ticking, I was an absolute mess.

And my deadline anxiety was only the shark's fin. The idea of anybody being able to read the penetralia of my family deeply frightened me. Some of my paranoia was overblown—an implosive combination of ego and low self-esteem. But I was writing from inside a family of cops, and that culture is unique in its level of guardedness. Maybe I did make more of the Blue Wall than actually exists. But in my guilt-ridden delusion, I was committing the worst of sins: being a rat. I'd find some relief from anxiety with a couple of drinks, but most times I wouldn't stop at just a couple. The next day I would awaken with the same apprehension over the book, but it would be amplified by the remorse I felt in my hungover state.

I tried to keep my drinking controlled while I was writing the book, and I did manage to stay fairly disciplined. But my Chandleresque white-knuckle abstentions would last for only so long, a couple of weeks tops. Book anxiety, or some other false pretense, would demand to be medicated.

These shore-leave nights I marked with Xs in my journals. The entries for the days after the X-outs would be written in a contrite, embarrassed tone. "I feel really guilty," I wrote in one. "And, I wonder if any of last night will come back to haunt me." A few of the entries even had promises to go back to the program. And I did go back: to one or two meetings during that year. But I stood in the back of the room and felt like an interloper. I talked to no one and left before the meetings were over.

I'd successfully distanced myself from my program friends. Frank and several others would call now and again, but I don't think any of them wondered whether I was "out," the program lingo for drinking again. Lives go on. It wasn't that they didn't care for me; it was just that the last thing they expected was for me to be drinking again after fourteen years of sobriety.

When I'd run into someone from the program, which I would occasionally on the street or in the market, I'd feel a wave of melancholia. I'd see the light of the program in their eyes and know deep within that I'd made the biggest mistake of my life. Manhattan is a big island, though. And as my circle of life orbited farther away from the program, I would run into my old friends with less frequency. I also have what the program calls a "built-in forgetter." It's easy for me to not recall what alcohol does to me. I had a friend in the program who used to say: "If tomorrow I awoke like I did every day when I was drinking, I'd call 911 because I'd be sure I was dying." I suffered that same degree of hangover, a horrible death's-door sickness that sometimes would last for days. But give me a week's distance from that hangover, maybe even less, and I'll start saying I wasn't that bad. For every foxhole prayer of "Oh, God, please, I'll never drink again if you get me out of this . . . ," within a couple of days I'd be in negotiations: "I didn't really mean *never* . . ."

Chapter Thirty-one

ON APRIL 13, 1998, just about a year after I left Elaine's, I printed out over three hundred and fifty pages of an admittedly rough first draft of my book. I wanted to celebrate, but I couldn't think of anyone to call. Several times I picked up the phone to call Erin but then hung up, afraid she'd be too busy or, worse, with her boyfriend. I knew she was working for the UN internal magazine and spending a lot of time in places like Uzbekistan and Afghanistan. One night when we did get together for a few beers, she giggled as she told me she often had to wear an Islamic burka in the places she traveled, but she did so wearing nothing underneath. But that night I didn't want to pretend to be happy for her and her boyfriend. I wanted to drink without distraction.

Alone then, I ambled down First Avenue to perhaps the only unfriendly Irish bar in New York City and proceeded to get warehoused on straight Jameson's and Coors Light. Soaked in a blissful combination of a sense of accomplishment and self-pity, I fantasized about South Beach. For the prior couple of months, I'd used South Beach as a motivation to finish the book. The sultry sexuality, the

unending flow of tequila, and the easy access to cocaine called to
me. I wanted to experience again that feeling I'd had at the Clevelander bar. If you pressed me, I would have told you I wanted the
book to be finished more than I wanted the book to be good.
Though I'd only completed the first draft, I felt the reins come off
a bit, and I liked the freedom of that feeling. Around midnight, I
stumbled home, picking up two six-packs of Coors Light on the
way. I then watched *Frasier, Seinfeld,* and *Frasier* again, the late-night
rerun lineup on Channel 11, until I blacked out. The next morning
I awoke on the couch with someone trying to pry the top of my
head off with a crowbar—or so it felt.

It took almost another year and a month from that first draft for
the book to be published. For much of that time I was rewriting.
Rosemary, my editor, was of a breed that has all but disappeared in
publishing: an editor who actually edited. Reminiscent of those
of Judy Crist, though not nearly as caustic, the marks on my manuscript were voluminous. One section, a series of pages on which
I thought I'd dripped the very lifeblood from my veins, came back
with a single diagonal red line running from the top left-hand
corners to the bottom right.

Rosemary didn't coddle me, nor was she interested in being my
friend during the editing process. I remember once I called her at
home about something or another and received a frosty response.
She had told me to use her home number only for very important
matters. But as each submission was returned (parts came back
three times), the manuscript gained definition, even, in places,
muscle. Soon the revisions became fun. With Rosemary onboard,
I didn't feel so alone in my writing. There was also a sense of
completion. It seemed forever ago that I had been in Jane's office
to sign the contract. She had said, in an offhanded way, "Now all
you have to do is deliver." As my rewrites gained momentum, I
was positive that I *would* deliver.

Chapter Thirty-two

I'D WORKED DOZENS of them. They were mostly for celebrity memoirs by people like Regis Philbin or Michael Caine. Some of the parties launched more substantive books, like Willie Morris's *New York Days*. Most of them drew the same ensemble, Bobby Zarem's go-to list: Barbara Walters, Walter and Betsy Cronkite, Valerie Perrine, and Kirk and Anne Douglas to name a few. But the bulk of the attendees at book parties were anonymous midlevel publishing people who rarely saw the light of day and who drank, when it was on someone else's dime, like pirates. For the employees, book parties were the biggest of pains. Held in the early evening, they usually came at the expense of regular business, from which the tips were considerably better. In fact, tips at book parties were nonexistent unless you did the old prime-the-pump trick, an open-bar technique I first learned from Joe back in my days at the English pub. When the open bar begins looking like a feeding frenzy, you find the one person in the crowd holding a dollar bill. No matter how far back he is, that's the one you serve. The idea gets passed around pretty quickly that you'll wait forever for a drink if you don't tip.

It took me a while to realize my place as the celebrant and not the server. For a few moments, the evening bordered on surreal, like being at my own wedding but without a bride. You have to admit, though, going from behind Elaine's bar to having a book party of my own at Elaine's was a pretty neat trick.

As far as celebrities go, my book party was a nonevent. Elaine Koster, who then ran Dutton Publishing, wasn't impressed at all. On being introduced to me, she looked out over the two hundred or so guests and said, "I hope this party is worth it." The only one of Bobby Zarem's stable who came was Keith Hernandez, the ex–Mets first baseman, and that was just by coincidence. He happened to be walking by the restaurant and wondered what the ruckus was about. The only one of Elaine's writers who showed up was Peter Maas, who had read the galleys of my book and written a wonderfully supportive blurb for the back cover.

The lack of celebrities mattered little to me. My eleven-plus years at Elaine's had given me my fill of them. My dad sat with his cronies, Mario Biaggi and Jack Kelly, at a back table like it was Toots Shor's and they were still running detective squads. Halfway through the party, they were joined by Sonny Grasso, the cop who, along with my sponsor, Frank, had broken the French Connection case. And the guns didn't stop there. The place was "crawling with cops," as the *Times* said in a piece about the party. My brother Frankie and his pals who had worked undercover and in anticrime were huddled at another table. John O'Brien and Lori represented the Feds, and there was even a suit or two from the Southern District of the U.S. Attorney's Office. Along with the generations of cops, there were generations of Elaine's workers. Tommy, Brian, and

Frank all came. I didn't see how Elaine welcomed them, but if history is any guide, my guess is she wasn't swept up in the nostalgia.

Elizabeth Stone, my teacher from Fordham, was there, as was Judy Crist, who, still holding a grudge against Elaine, whispered, "I'm only here because of you." Sam Freedman came, making good on a promise that he would not set foot in Elaine's until I had a book contract. Although Freedman acknowledged the established writers who were habitués of Elaine's, he also thought the place was filled with "wannabes." In one corner, unimpressed by the assembly, Bill Hughes sipped a gin and tonic with the side of his mouth (I never asked him why he didn't drink straight on). Erin could stay only a short while. She kissed me, hugged me, and then hurried from the restaurant. Jocelyn, another J school classmate, came. Like Erin, Jocelyn was a tall, willowy blonde on whom I had a crush and around whom I felt like an Irish setter puppy. She had landed her dream job, as an editor with *Gourmet* magazine. But she had also landed a husband.

A few months later, Jocelyn would give me an assignment to profile Elaine. In the role of editor, my just ex-classmate was every bit the professional. She sent back the first draft I'd dropped off saying that it was far too promotional. Elaine let me have it when I told her. "They don't want a blow job, give them the dirt," she said. In the revised version, I wrote several anecdotes that I'd left out of the first draft, including the time when Elaine found out her ex-husband had died and told me to open a bottle of Cristal and pour glasses all around. When the issue came out, I got a call from Diane, the day manager of the restaurant. She was indignant, saying that I had been mean-spirited toward Elaine. I felt as though I'd stepped on a mousetrap. But that all was months ahead. At the book party, Diane was thrilled for me and, at one point, reminded me not forget about Elaine.

Shimmering in crimson silk, the fragrance of Chanel No. 5 surrounding her, protecting her, Elaine sat on the same barstool on which she'd sat countless nights when I worked with her. For most of the party, her arms were folded tight against her chest, her uneasiness, no doubt, stemming from the fact that she knew practically no one in her restaurant. With no checks to write, as it was all prepaid by Dutton, she felt out of place in her own place.

A few times I'd stopped by the restaurant in the weeks leading up to the party. It was obvious that Elaine had begun to move away from me. She would initiate little conversation and respond to my words with a clipped sentence or a shrug. By her own estimation, Elaine has separation anxiety that most times culminates in total detachment. On an emotional level, she kills you off. I'd seen her do this many times with customers and employees alike. I always said, You could fill Yankee Stadium with ex-customers of Elaine's. Though, at times, I thought I could be the exception, when I was honest with myself, I knew I was going to end up with a seat in the upper deck. The expression Elaine wore throughout the night of my party, however, had little to do with my leaving. She looked, and perhaps only I see her this way in hindsight, like she knew what was going to happen to me.

As my book party began to wane, Elaine took a new stack of dinner checks, snapped off the rubber band, and riffled through them. She leaned toward the backbar and jabbed a new number 2 pencil into the sharpener. The waiters began to set the tables with new cloths and silverware. Carlo slid knives and forks into place like he was working the arrow on a Ouija board. Maple, Dr. Joe, and some of the other regulars wandered in. They sat at table 4, now cleared of all vestiges of my book party and me. But above them, on the wall behind the shelf, right between the fake Oscar and the Second Avenue streetcar sign, just to the left of Jim Harrison's *Wolf,* and to the right of Peter Maas's *Serpico,* hung the jacket of my book.

Chapter Thirty-three

I n the wake of the book's release, there are moments of fantasy come true: a book tour, complete with four-star hotels and limousines, book readings and TV interviews. I have a dinner at Daniel with a movie producer at which I swirl Cabernet in a balloon glass. There is another trip to South Beach. But the money, the little of it, goes with amazing alacrity, as if I'm throwing the hundred-dollar bills out the hotel window. In reality, what I'm doing is calling my coke dealer daily. He drives a yellow cab and is at my apartment literally minutes after I hang up. On several occasions I wait with him at an ATM for midnight to pass and my withdrawal limit to reset. In no time I'm broke and need a job. The thought of crawling back to Elaine's comes to me often. All of a sudden, it feels as if I've stepped out of an airplane.

The week before New Year's Eve 1999, Elaine calls and asks me to work the big night. I walk in around nine o'clock, having been up for two days smoking cocaine. The restaurant's ceiling is covered with balloons with tails of ribbon. I'm writing the checks, and the numbers begin to dance. In the middle of the shift, I start to crash. Customers I haven't seen in months come up to congratulate me on the book, only to turn away quickly when they see the condition I'm in. Jack Maple is one of them. He looks right into my coke-fiend soul with his cop eyes. He shakes his head and walks away. Elaine doesn't say a word to me the whole evening, doesn't even come up to the bar. At midnight, Elvino and Carlo walk through the restaurant with spitting sparklers popping the balloons. For me, the noise is like gunfire, and I flinch with every burst. The whole staff lines up to kiss Elaine. I stand in my station, too paranoid to let her see me.

Only one more time would I walk into the restaurant, months after the publicity of the book had died, long after my book tour was over, and when the number of books sold was far less than expected. I staggered into the joint and plopped my drunken self down at her table. As soon as I sat, Elaine got up in a huff. "Go back to the program," she barked.

Taking her advice sober was one thing; active in my addictions was a different story. It would take me five years to listen to her, and by that time it was almost too late.

Somehow, I manage to sell another proposal and write another book—this one about an American Indian baseball player. There is no romance in being a drunken writer. I'm months late delivering the manuscript. I've written it under the duress of being months behind on my rent. But my landlord has to wait in line, for my addiction gets paid first when the advance check comes. The book sells in microscopic numbers. With no choice, I have to go back behind the bar. Not at Elaine's, though, but on the West Side, for my old roommate Randy, who, along with a partner named Terry, had bought a saloon. Months before, I'd sold the rights to my *My Father's Gun* to The History Channel. It seems everywhere I look there are advertisements for the documentary, in magazines like *GQ* and *Esquire,* on billboards throughout the city, and, especially, at bus stops. And yet I'm rummaging for bus fare behind my couch. The History Channel sends me on a press junket with a week in Pasadena, of which I remember only drunken, out-of-focus snapshots. I'm tending bar the night the show airs. I have it on the television in the joint—for a little while at least. Then someone yells to put on ESPN.

My drinking progresses to the point where I can't even hold the bar job. Half the time I don't show up for work. When I do, I treat my shift like a cocktail party. I make it my mission to get the customers just as loaded as I do. I'm drunk behind the bar on the second Monday night in September 2001. In hindsight, it seems like I had a premonition, but in that moment it was just a mission to drink, then drug, with the ferocity of someone who thinks *his* world is going to end. The shattered memory of that night, spent in and out of a blackout, still humiliates me. I pass out at about eight o'clock on the morning of September 11. I awaken—rather, I come to—about five o'clock the next evening. I finally pick up the phone, which has been ringing all day. The attack on the World Trade Center is only five miles from my apartment, yet I'm among the last people on the planet to know it has happened.

Afterward, I begin a spiral into a maudlin, self-centered, drunken mess. Nearly three thousand dead in the collapse of the towers, and it is my life that makes me cry. I drink bottles of the most inexpensive vodka, something called Svedka, and I drink it warm, in a glass with filmy tap water. Soon I'm out of vodka, money, and options. Alone in my apartment, so drunk I don't know whether it's night or day, I hear a knock at my door. Called by my neighbor, two New York City police officers, a man and a woman, stand there. The apartment is a shambles; my glass coffee table is in shards. My feet bleed from stepping barefoot on glass crack stems. My thumbs are blistered from torch lighters. There is enough paraphernalia lying about for them to arrest me easily. Instead, the lady officer asks me if I think of hurting myself. I mumble some kind of affirmative response. Minutes later I'm handcuffed and lying on a gurney in the back of an EMS truck on my way to Metropolitan Hospital, where I spend twenty-four torturous hours strapped to a bed detoxing. And yet my drinking and drugging continues for two more excruciatingly long years.

As the nightmare continues, I stay as far from Elaine's as I can, at times going blocks out of my way so as not to walk by the joint. Partly I'm embarrassed, at my condition, at how I screwed up the opportunity I was given, but mostly I don't want to bump into her and see the disappointment masked by contempt in her eyes. Her eyes haunt me every day anyhow. Elaine's black-framed glasses look down on me from the Jamie Wyeth poster that hangs on my living room wall, the one I refuse to take down no matter how guilty it makes me feel, the one with her tiny script that reads: "To baby Brian, love, Elaine."

There are stretches, weeks, when I don't drink or drug. I can't, I barely have enough money to eat. When I do have cash, it all goes to one thing. The purchase of drugs awakens the underground network that crawls up through my floorboards. My apartment is host to a steady stream of drug dealers, drug users, and all types of prostitutes. Cocaine eliminates all moral constraints. After a run, I'm awakened one morning—I think it was morning—by the slam of my front door. I am toxic from days of drugs and booze. It hurts to move. When I look into the living room, which I can see from my bed, a guy I barely knew whom I was getting high with is no longer sleeping on the couch, where I last saw him.

For some reason, my eyes are drawn to my golf bag, which has been moved from the corner of the room in which it has stood for years. In the bottom, inside pocket of the bag I'd hidden the watch Elaine gave me—the last thing I owned of any worth and of such emotional value to me it had survived even the most overwhelming urges to sell it for drugs. I don't even have to search the bag—I know the watch is gone. I can hear the guy walking down the stairs of my building, but I can't move because of the pain. It hurts too much even to cry. That night I find myself leaning over the railing on the promenade on the East River contemplating how long I would stay alive in the water before it pulled me under. It is not the first or last time I'm at that place and with those thoughts. As the river, black and silent, slides by, I see no way out.

Chapter Thirty-four

FEW THINGS are more unlikely than an addict honestly asking for help, and no moment is more spiritually powerful. I hadn't spoken to Laura in almost seven years, since the night she told me she was moving to Chicago. Then one day, several years back, I met her in front of my apartment building. A few weeks before, she'd come back to New York City and moved into a place a couple of blocks from mine. Laura was happy to see me. Her eyes were clear and bright. In a disarming, truly interested way program people have, she asked me how I'd been. I don't think she quite expected my response. Over a slice of pizza at a window table at a nearby restaurant, I told her I had been drinking and drugging for a number of years and that I didn't think my life could get any worse. My words came out in a rush, as if the truth was waiting there, behind my teeth, for the opportunity to escape. I told her I was scared.

Laura suggested I call a woman with whom I had gotten sober the first time, one of a gang that sang Beatles songs with me on the way to a meeting in Bedford-Stuyvesant. Though I was embarrassed and humiliated, I made the call. Ellen couldn't have been more gracious or understanding. She gently suggested I try meetings again. Just the sound of her voice evoked warm and happy memories. It made me long for that comfort I had once so readily embraced. Very early the next morning, after a fitful night's sleep, I stood across the street from St. Monica's Church on Seventy-ninth Street. In the basement of the church was a 7:15 A.M. meeting. When I saw someone I knew duck down the stairs, I almost lost my nerve. But I had the gift of desperation. I took a deep breath and walked toward my only real chance.

Though grace ushered me through the door of sobriety, staying sober again was far from easy. There were plenty of times I wanted out of the program and out of my life. For days, months on end I wanted to get high or drunk. There were many days when I awakened disappointed to be alive.

Ironically, I couldn't seem to make a living. I briefly tried to go behind a bar again but found I didn't trust myself around booze. For a while, I worked for a demolition-construction company. One August night they had me stripping paint off old radiator covers with a gelatinlike chemical that stung like wasps even through the galvanized gloves I wore. For a short while, I was a part-time teacher. I did some stringing work for the *Times*. I borrowed money from family and the few friends I had left. Still, I was in housing court every other month. At one point, I fell four months behind on my rent. I'd exhausted just about every possible loophole to keep my apartment.

I remember sitting in a meeting around this time, my head hung, telling the group that I felt absolutely devoid of hope. A younger guy, a street kid who was called "Bronx" Jimmy, came over to me after the meeting and said I could borrow his hope. Then he advised me to show up at housing court, be honest, and say a prayer. I wasn't so sure of the prayer part. Though I wanted to believe in God, the years of cocaine and alcohol had erased the evidence of Him in my life—or so I thought.

There was a line to see a clerk at housing court. The woman in front of me apparently didn't notice the sign that warned you to stay behind the yellow stripe painted on the floor until you were called. I thought the clerk was going to climb through the window as the woman approached. He was screaming at her like a maniac. Though I felt bad for the lady, I was more concerned with the fact that I was next. When it came my turn, I didn't dare step over the line. The clerk finally called me to the window, then asked my name. "McDonald," I replied.

"What do you own, a farm?" he asked.

"I'm getting evicted from it," I said.

The clerk laughed, and I felt like someone had lifted a bag of cement off my shoulder. Still smiling, the clerk made a call and found out that a judge would be in the courtroom soon. He quickly put my papers in order. "Get 'em to sign it," the clerk said. "And I'll get you the extension."

The judge walked into the courtroom in street clothing. He looked at me strangely. "Did you write that book about the family of cops?" he asked.

Out of all the good things to happen from *My Father's Gun*, this moment might have been the best. The judge signed the extension while he was talking about The History Channel documentary on my book. With the paper signed, I ran from the courtroom like a guilty defendant out of a mistrial. Later that afternoon, I shared my experience in a meeting, and everyone laughed, including myself. It was the first time I'd laughed in quite a while, and marked the day that the miracle of sobriety again began to happen in my life. I realized then that my first time in the program I'd had it all wrong. Sobriety doesn't promise you'll get rich or famous, it doesn't even guarantee you'll be happy. All it promises is hope.

For a while I thought my drinking and drugging had ruined any chance of a future writing career. I wrote two proposals in early sobriety, projects that took months of research and writing, and neither sold. In the wake of those disappointments, with my financial struggle, my thoughts went right to the most negative projection. Publishers aren't interested in my ideas anymore, I believed. They're not impressed by the past performance of my books.

Working construction, teaching, then stringing for the *Times* limited my time in front of the computer, but I still adhered to a writing schedule of an hour or so each morning. A remarkable thing happened during that routine. I started to find satisfaction in the work. It didn't even matter how good the words looked on the page. For me, the hardest part about writing had always been shutting out the outside world. It was always: What would my teacher, my editor, my reader think? Somewhere along the line in those lonely writing sessions, I found that the payoff comes just in coaxing those words from my thoughts, pushing them through my heart and out the tips of my fingers on the keyboard. Like sobriety, writing is its own reward. I didn't silence all of the internal critics; those voices are part of being a writer. And there is certainly a want for success within me. But I was able to quiet the need and critic enough to hear a voice, one that came out of my not-too-distant past.

I'd spoken to Elaine exactly once since the millennium New Year's Eve, a remarkable fact given that I still live only two blocks from her restaurant. As with my avoiding meetings, much of what kept me away was pride. I was ashamed of how our friendship had ended, especially the last shift I'd worked for her. On the urging of my new sponsor, one afternoon I put on a jacket and tie, and walked the same route I had thousands of times to work.

In the afternoon, Elaine's is somehow smaller than at night, when fame balloons its size. I like that time of day in the restaurant, the way the sun courses through the front window and the shadow from the lettering "Elaine's" is superimposed on the Spanish tile floor. I like when Carlo snaps open the folded tablecloths and spreads them lovingly over the four-tops. Some of my fondest memories of Elaine too are from the afternoons, when, cocooned by her restaurant home and restaurant family, she was at her least guarded.

As I walked in, she was standing near the pay phones at the end of the bar. I had heard that she'd had some health problems, asthma, I think. But aside from a few more streaks of gray, she looked just as she does in my mind's eye: her face smooth, her hair full. She greeted me with a small "Oh," as if my presence surprised her only a little. I'd rehearsed what I was going to say on my way to the restaurant, but the look in her eyes disarmed me. Those eyes had always seemed to possess the unlikely combination of shyness and defiance. I cleared my throat and managed to say I was sorry for the way I'd acted that New Year's, and I told her that I was going back to meetings. Then I waited in an uncomfortable silence for her response.

With scores of years in the saloon business, there hasn't been a lot that Elaine has missed. She's dealt with hundreds of drunks, scores of writers, and dozens of both. I myself had witnessed, on at least two occasions, contrite recovered alcoholics holding metaphorical hats in hand and asking for her forgiveness. She's a hard one in those situations; usually you get but one chance with Elaine.

Finally, and with a small shrug, she said she was glad I was back on the right track, her words coming in a kind of huff. Though part of me wanted Elaine to forgive me, to welcome me back, in my heart I knew that wouldn't happen—all of Elaine's relationships are framed by her front window, and I had moved out of those confines years before.

As I left the restaurant and crossed Second Avenue, I turned for a look. A couple of months before, the city had removed the tree I had written about for Judith Crist's class. I'm not sure of the reason. Perhaps it had been split in a storm or maybe the roots had started to burst through the sidewalk. I remembered one early evening, years before, when a lawyer, a fellow who has one of those firms that advertise on late-night TV with an "800" number, parked his candy apple–red Rolls-Royce convertible, top down, under the branches of the ornamental pear. In the spring, the tree would bloom in huge flowers that appeared and then fell quickly in a blizzard of white. They did that evening that the Rolls was parked underneath, hurried along by fat drops of rain from a sudden thunderstorm. The soft leather of the car was soaked and covered in wet blossoms. When the storm subsided, the lawyer stood on the sidewalk and screamed at the tree. Just then Tommy was walking into the restaurant to go to work. "Why don't you sue it?" my bartending partner said to him. In the ornamental pear's place, the city had planted a London plain tree, standard urban issue. No more than a sapling, it is about the size that the pear tree was when I first started at Elaine's.

The program promises that we will not regret the past, nor wish to shut the door on it. I don't know whether I've reached that point yet. There are still dark corners of my drinking and drugging that are painful for me to explore. But there is one door to my past that stays open, and that thought amuses me. For most of the eleven years that I worked behind the bar at Elaine's I wanted to be anywhere else. But now, as my time away increases, my memories of Elaine and her restaurant become more gilded, like the birdcage Jackie Gleason sang about. With my writing, I've learned that it's in the process, the journey, where joy and fulfillment exists. But that lesson can be applied to just about anything in life, and it can also be realized in hindsight.

I might be the luckiest guy in the world. The odds against an alcoholic getting sober once are long enough, and one day at a time, I've beat them twice. I'm also lucky to have worked for Elaine Kaufman. Maybe I could have become a writer while working in any restaurant, for any boss. Maybe. But then I wouldn't have lived nearly as good a backstory, or heard Elaine's words urging me to just tell it.

With nearly forty-five years and counting in business, my lady boss's restaurant now marches inexorably toward its last call. When those sad words are finally uttered, though hopefully not too soon, generations of writers, from the dusty dead to lucky ex-bartenders, will shed a tear. Imitators, no doubt, will come and go. But I doubt they'll measure up to the joint on Second Avenue, or the lady who runs it. For a saloon with a saloonkeeper like Elaine really only comes along once in a lifetime.